POLITICS OF OPPORTUNISM

POLITICS OF OPPORTUNISM

REGIONAL PARTIES, COALITIONS, CENTRE-STATE RELATIONS IN INDIA

RNP SINGH

Vitasta
LET KNOWLEDGE SPREAD

Vivekananda
International
Foundation

Published by
Renu Kaul Verma
Vitasta Publishing Pvt Ltd
2/15, Ansari Road, Daryaganj
New Delhi – 110 002
info@vitastapublishing.com

Co-published by Vivekananda International Foundation

ISBN 978-93-86473-52-3

First Edition 2019
MRP ₹750

Cover and layout by Vitasta Publishing Pvt Ltd
Printed by Chaman Enterprises

Contents

Acknowledgements

I gratefully acknowledge continuous support, encouragement and all care extended by Dr Arvind Gupta, (Former Deputy National Security Advisor), Director, Vivekananda International Foundation, for completion of the book.

I owe a special debt to Shri Ajit Doval KC, former Director, Vivekananda International Foundation and National Security Advisor, for his continuous support to my academic quest and for his kind gesture to spare valuable time from his busy schedule to release my earlier book, *Sardar Patel: Unifier of Modern India,* on 4 September 2018.

I am grateful to Shri CD Sahay, Distinguished Fellow, Vivekananda International Foundation, for taking pains to go through a few chapters of this manuscript and providing valuable inputs.

I am deeply grateful to Lt General RK Sawhney, PVSM, AVSM (Former Deputy Chief of Army Staff & Former DGMI), Centre Head & Senior Fellow, Vivekananda International Foundation for providing continuous moral support to carry on my writing.

I owe a profound debt of gratitude to Shri Chetnya Kasyap, a philanthrophist and currently Deputy Chairman of the Planning Commission, Madhya Pradesh, for his unabated support to my academic pursuit.

I am grateful to Prof Ashok Pankaj, Director, Council for Social Development (CSD), who spared his valuable time to go through the manuscript and make some suggestions.

My grateful thanks to Smt Anuttama Ganguly, Joint Secretary, Vivekananda International Foundation, for her sustained support to complete my undertaken projects.

I wish to express my deep appreciation and thanks to my younger brother SNP Singh for his incessant support to my academic quest.

My sincere thanks to Shri Sanjay Kumar, Librarian, Vivekananda International Foundation, for providing source material for the book.

I would be failing in my responsibility if I don't express my thanks to Shri Kamal Singh, Executive Assistant, Vivekananda International Foundation, for extending his helping hand in completion of this book.

Lastly, I doubt if I would have been able to complete the work I undertook, without the institutional facilities offered by Vivekananda International Foundation. More than institutional facilities which are excellent, however, is the helpful attitude of every member of the VIF.

Thanks are due to PIB, the government's Press Information

Bureau for providing some rare photographs of coalition governments and Director, Photo Division, Mr Ashish Maitra.

Thanks are due to the publishers, Vitasta Publishing and their support staff for all their hard work.

Foreword

With vast experience as a senior police officer and rich background in various fields of intelligence services, RNP Singh already has several prestigious titles to his credit. The present work, provocatively titled 'Politics of Opportunism' seeks to analyse the concepts and the working of what he calls 'Regional Parties, Coalitions and Centre-State Relations' in India.

The business of politics is pursuit of power – ideally for public service and to resolve people's problems but, in reality, more often for securing maximum benefits for one's self, family, caste, community or other narrow identity group interests. Political parties, in particular in India, are built on the bases of such loyalties and are actually mere transmission belts to power. Whatever be the motive, if 'opportunistic' means 'taking advantage of immediate opportunities', all politics has got to be opportunistic and excellence in the art of political management consists in converting every challenge into an opportunity.

The Constitution that the founding fathers gave us did not

contain any mention of political parties. The Tenth Schedule added by the 52nd Amendment in 1985 for the first time included a mention of political parties in the Constitution and that too, for the limited purpose of considering disqualification of a member on grounds of defection. While recognising that parties are an essential concomitant of elections in representative parliamentary polity, the National Commission to Review the Working of the Constitution (NCRWC) noted that the quintessential precondition for the success of the Westminster model is a system of two major parties based on ideological and programmatic orientation.

The overriding passion of our Constitution makers was to build a united nation and an integrated society. They hoped that a healthy, ideologically-oriented party system would soon evolve and contribute to societal integration, nation building and strengthening the edifice of democracy. Unfortunately, that did not happen. The Commission added that the 'source of many of our troubles during the post-independence period has been our failure to evolve a healthy party system ....' The 'transformation from one-party dominant system to a complex of multi-party system in which strong trends of fragmentation, factionalism and regionalism coupled with the desire to form alliances for seeking a share in power' increased and were followed by hung Houses and coalition politics. The Commission also took serious note of increase in political mobilisation of the electorate on the basis of social cleavages based on ascriptive ideologies, in particular of religion and caste. Casteism, communalism and personality domination became the main planks around which the fragmentation of parties took place. The conclusion is inevitable: that our electoral and political party systems have proved to be most divisive of 'We, the people of India'. The Commission recommended that:

> There should be comprehensive law for registration, regulation and functioning of political parties and pre-poll alliances; the Election Commission should progressively increase the threshold criterion for eligibility for recognition so that the proliferation of smaller parties is discouraged; only parties or a pre-poll alliance of parties registered as national parties or alliances should get a common symbol to contest election for the Lok Sabha while State parties could contest for State Legislatures and the Council of States (Rajya Sabha).

Today, with more than 2000 parties registered, all entitled to contest elections to Lok Sabha, majority of Members are elected with minority of votes cast, ie. more votes are cast against each one of them than for them, rendering their representational legitimacy extremely doubtful.

The Representation of People Act provides for registration of parties and the Election Commission accords recognition as National or State parties in accordance with the norms laid down in the Election Symbols (Reservation and Allotment) Order. This is for the limited purpose of allocation of symbols. While there is nothing wrong or anti-national in the appeal or influence of a party being limited to a region, to be in the

House of the People of the Union Parliament, one must have a national perspective and agenda. Also, howsoever eloquent we may wax about the 'increasingly positive role and greater appeal' of the so-called regional parties, the fact remains that in terms of the Constitution and the law, there is nothing like a Regional Party. It is very difficult to appreciate a statement to the effect that today, in India, 'national parties are on decline and are being relegated to the background as regional parties are gaining strength'. If true, it would be a matter of great concern and one calling for immediate initiation of remedial action. As a first step, the national parties must recognise the legitimacy of each other as democratic alternatives and not as enemies or adversaries to be banished from the political map.

While flagging what he considers to be the inevitability of coalition politics in India, RNP Singh recognises the many pitfalls and 'innumerable challenges' in it. Coalition governments, he says, always remain weak and indicate subordination of ideology to power. It may be added that the coalition situation highlights the relevance of the dictum that politics is the art of the possible and of compromise. But, if coalition partners, particularly the dominant ones, honour the limits to which they can stoop to compromise to stay in power, coalitions per se are not bad and may provide even stable government and good governance. Also, good and lasting coalition governments can emerge only from pre-poll alliances founded on some ideological affinity and programmatic agreement. On the other hand, if after the election, disparate parties with shifting loyalties come together to cobble a working majority for sharing the fruits of power and loot of public resources, the constituent parties and their leaders may indulge in blame-games, bargaining, brinkmanship, bluff and blackmail.

One consequence of the coalition era in Indian politics, according to the author, has been the weakening of the authority of the 'Centre' and widening of the institutional space for the States. It is astonishing why our government institutions and agencies and even our learned intellectuals insist upon using patently wrong terms like Centre, central authority, Central Government, Centre-State Relations etc. which were positively discarded by our Constitution makers. The terms somehow continue to be used as a colonial hangover from the 1919 Act.

The Constitution speaks of the Union, Union-State Relations etc. and there is a fundamental difference between the concepts of the Centre and the Union. Centre is a point in the middle of the circle, while the Union is the whole circle. The use of wrong terms has done tremendous damage to our psyche and Union-State relations. The relationship between the Union and the States has to be understood as the relationship between the whole and its parts and not as between the centre of authority and its periphery.

Indian polity is unique in many ways. It cannot be fitted fully into any of the existing moulds or models. It has been variously described as federal, quasi-federal, amphibian, federal in structure but unitary in spirit etc. The truth is that it has features of both – unitary and federal – and the Constitution describes India as a Union of States and not as a federation or one with federal polity.

The prime imperative today is that of fighting fissiparous tendencies and divisive forces and building a strong and united nation. We talk about the principle of Unity in Diversity and under its garb, diversity is sought to be celebrated as a great Indian virtue. While diversity has to be accepted as an existent reality and fact of our social life, the principle of unity in diversity can be no justification for lauding growth of separate divisive identities. The aim is unity and not diversity. Diversity must also lead to strengthening the unity and integrity of the nation.

I whole-heartedly commend this highly educative and thought-provoking book to readers – old and young.

Subhash C Kashyap
Padma Bhushan
Former Secretary-General, Lok Sabha
President, Indian National Bar Association
Hon Professor, Centre for Policy Research
January 2019, New Delhi

Coalition Drawback: Ideological Incompatibility, Opportunism

As India heads towards general elections in 2019, the ruling National Democratic Alliance (NDA) is looking to renew its mandate for further five years. At the same time, the opposition parties are struggling to put together a *mahagatbandhan* or a grand alliance against the NDA. Regional parties play an extremely important role in the formation of political alliances. Multi-party coalitions are now an incontrovertible feature of Indian politics.

In his latest book, *Politics of Opportunism: Regional Parties, Coalitions, Centre-State Relations in India*, RNP Singh, Senior Fellow in the Vivekananda International Foundation, traces the evolution of the coalition era in Indian politics and the role of regional parties in the formation of the political alliances. He argues that coalition politics has gained salience because of the failure of the national parties to win even simple majority in Parliament (with the exception of BJP in 2014) and due to their inability to articulate the regional voices and aspirations.

Coalitions can be messy and breed instability. The author

identifies ideological incompatibility and the politics of opportunism as the main drawbacks of coalitions. For stability and effective governance, coalitions should follow the coalition dharma which allows the member parties to retain their identity but also enforces discipline on them to work as a team.

The book is based on meticulous research and delves into a wide range of issues such as the impact of coalitions on Centre-State relations, national security etc. It also examines in detail the behaviour of different political parties in different situations.

Being published on the eve of the 2019 general elections, I am confident that the book, which is an objective study of India's political reality, will be received well by the readers.

Dr Arvind Gupta
Director
Vivekananda International Foundation
January 2019, New Delhi

Preface

India has a multi-party system. According to the Election Commission there are 2,095 registered parties in India, a ten-fold increase from 2010. There are seven national parties, 24 State parties and 2044 unrecognised ones plus several others ingovernment data available till April 2018. Earlier the regional parties were unable to play any major role at the Centre due to the dominance of the Congress party. But in the lst few decades, State-based and region-based parties have posed the most powerful challenge to India's 'One Dominant Party System'. Since 1967, the regional parties have brought greater appeal to India's political theatre. The regional parties control most of the State politics and they have thus emerged as a powerful force and now play a vital role in the formulation of all governments at the Centre.

The presence of a number of ethnic, cultural, linguistic, religious and caste groups within Indian society is greatly responsible for the origin and growth of regional parties. Though the regional parties operate within limited area and pursue only limited objectives, they have played significant roles, both in State as well as in national politics and continue to do so in, the second decade of the millenium. These parties have formed governments in several States and have tried to implement their policies and programmes through control over governments. Some of the regional parties are also partner in the coalition government at the Centre. In the eighth Lok Sabha elections (1984), the Telugu Desam, a regional party from Andhra Pradesh, emerged as the main opposition party in Parliament. Now, no single party is able to form a government at the Centre. This demonstrates that in India, the era of a single party rule has ended and a new phase of multi-party coalitions has set in. The regional parties have made a strong impact on the nature of Centre-State relations and now, they strongly uphold the cause of Indian unity and integrity, along with upholding of their respective regional interests. In remote areas, they have also drawn the country's attention to various political and economic issues of concern to people of such areas and contribute to a sort of socio-political awakening.

The regional parties have provided a new dimension to the process of national integration and nation building. Regionalism has lost its aggression due to the positive role of regional political parties. The leaders of regional parties have started playing an active and even deterministic role in the organisation of the Central government. Since 1996, 24 regional parties have been sharing power at the national level. Their outlook now appears to be changing from a confrontationalist attitude to a cooperative bargaining tendency in respect of Centre-State relations.

Further, in this new era of coalition politics, regional parties have emerged as active actors in the Indian political system. Since 1996, coalition politics has come to emerge as a reality of Indian politics and, has brought home the fact that the national parties must join hands with State parties for strengthening their role and position in the Indian political system. Even the once-thought-to-be-indomitable Congress has now realised and accepted the necessity of forging alliances with the regional parties and was able to form a coalition government at the Centre with the help of regional parties in 2004 and 2009.

A coalition government means the coming together of more than one political party or group on the basis of common understanding or agenda. Coalition government can have framework within which all the parties function. This is because no major party gets any decisive vote after a general election. In the post-independence period, the first coalition government came to power in the State of Kerala (1960). At the Centre, the first non-Congress coalition government came to power in 1977. This coalition was a collective of the non-Congress parties and forces opposed to Indira Gandhi's party, that is the Congress (I), which itself was a splinter of the Grand Old Party.

A coalition government suffers from some major pitfalls. It finds difficulty in solving major problems, because major problems require agreement and support of various coalition partners. Also, in day-to-day working of the government and administration, different party leaders and critics bring in objections and difficulties. They often oppose and obstruct the process of decision-making and conduct of decision implementation. As a result, the government finds it difficult to work smoothly. In coalition politics, adjustment is required at the national and State levels and also at the local level. Stability and governance are both important to maintain the strength of any political system.

After emergence of regional parties and coalition politics, Centre-State relation has been one of the important areas of concern and cause of tension in India. In the early years since the written Constitution of India was unveiled, the relations were smooth primarily because they operated largely under the umbrella of one party, both at the Centre and in the States. But since 1967, the interpretation of the various Articles in the Constitution connected with the federal system and the way they are looked upon by various actors and parties in these areas have created irritants in the Centre-State relations.

The most serious situation is that non-ruling parties at the Centre and the States, in various conventions and resolutions, have come out with demands seeking not only changes in Centre-State relations but in a way calling for the dilution of the very concept of federalism itself. Financial problems in the Centre-State relations are the main focus of attention. Today, in India, the national parties are on decline and are being relegated to the background as regional parties are gaining strength. The phenomenon of growing regional tensions in Indian society is one of the most conspicuous developments in the political culture of this country.

It is unfortunate that matters like national security have also fallen under the debate of Centre-State relations. The laws relating to containing serious problems like terrorism, naxalism and increasing violence have also fallen into the Centre-State storm. After the Mumbai attack on 26 November 2008, the government of India proposed setting up of two security agencies, namely the National Investigation Agency (NIA) and the National Counter Terrorism Centre (NCTC) for proper investigation and intelligence integration, and collation in respect of such crimes. After lot of objections and debate, the NIA could get through but the NCTC could not see light of the sun due to the debate that law and order falls under the jurisdiction of the State. The parliamentarians and States should realise that in view of the present security scenario globally, the governance of India poses enormous challenge and safeguarding the country's security is truly a colossal task. Now, the security problems have gone beyond the reach of State governments. Hence, security problems need to be addressed in coordination by the Union and the States. Unfortunately, constitutional division of power creates barriers between the Union and the State for addressing most important issues like internal and national security jointly.

THE PARTIES

Regional Political Parties in India

Definition of Regional Parties

MANY SCHOLARS HAVE defined regional parties in their own way. According to KR Bombwall, 'The generally accepted distinction between "national" and "regional" parties, legitimised though it is by the Election Commission, is rather unsatisfactory'.[1] He says, it is used 'with considerable looseness as an omnibus designation for all manner of political formations'.

In determining whether a party is national or regional, two factors are taken into consideration: (1) the number of States in which it enjoys popular electoral support, and (2) the percentage of votes polled by it in the State Assembly and the Lok Sabha elections. The first criteria is territorial and the second one relates to the popularity of the party. Further, some scholars seek to identify a regional party in terms of ethnicity or religious-cultural identity. The Dravida Munnetra Kazhagam (DMK) and the All India Anna Dravida Munnetra Kazhagam (AIADMK) are regional political parties because these parties represent 'Tamil Culture' and 'Tamil Nationalism'. Shiromani Akali Dal too is a regional party and like the Panthic Party of the 1940s and '50s gets almost the whole of its support from the Sikhs in Punjab and, to a limited extent, also in Haryana and Delhi. Telugu Desam, Asom Gana Parishad, Sikkim Sangram Parishad, National Conference, Biju Janata Dal of Odisha, Jharkhand Mukti Morcha, Bangla Congress, Oriya Congress, Kerala Congress, PDP in J&K, Trinamool Congress in Bengal, Meghalaya Democratic Alliance, Harayana's Indian National Lok Dal (INLD) etc are all regional parties.

A Regional party or a Local party, writes Stanley A Kochnock, is 'primarily concerned with exploiting local resources of discontent or preserving a variety of primordial demands based on language, caste or community or region'.[2] The fact is that a regional or a local party is one which enjoys its popularity in one or two States and or which mainly identifies itself with the interests of a particular area or community or a linguistic or cultural or religious group.

Keeping in view the importance of political parties in governments, sociologist Robert Morrison Maclver has said that, 'without political parties there can be no unified statement of principle nor orderly evolution of policy, no regular resort to the constitutional device of parliamentary elections, nor of course any of the recognised institutions by which a party seeks to gain or to maintain power'.[3] Samuel Huntington has gone a step further when he said, 'a partyless regime is a conservative regime'.[4] A modern form of representative democracy increases the need for a party system. India being no exception, developed a multi-party system wherein a number of national and State-based parties exist because of the regionally concentrated diverse groups found in the country. One of the specified classifications made by the scholars of the Indian polity is the division of Indian political parties into two broad categories – national and regional or State parties. The regional parties play an important role in Indian politics.

Maurice Duverger's minor party – 'Minority Minded' party – seemingly includes regional, local and such other smaller parties formed on the basis of linguistic, religious, ethnic and cultural interests. According to him, there are two distinct types of minor parties. They are 'personality minor parties' and 'permanent minor parties'.[5] Personality Parties are purely legislators' groups,[6] not based on any real organisation. They mostly originate as dissident groups and subsequently appear as separate organisations. These parties are centred around influential personalities. It is for these reasons that such parties lack a true social sub-structure and also, they are neither strong nor stable in character. In the absence of any discipline and precise doctrine they turn out to be the most recalcitrant of all parties.[7]

On the other hand, 'Permanent Minority Parties' have organisations in the country which is either national or local.[8] They represent a modern variety of minor party and in this respect, they stand in sharp contrast to the personality party which is more of an archaic type.[9]

Myron Weiner has observed that the term 'regional' should not be narrowed down to include in it only those parties which function exclusively in a particular State or section of the country but it should be broadened so as to include such national parties which although they claim a national character, outlook and philosophy, yet are pragmatically concerned primarily with the region in which they function. A regional party, therefore, can be defined precisely as an organised group of people having consciousness of their customs and ideals in set homogenous physical area, and thus possesses a sense of political identity distinct from the rest of the country. It endeavours to share power at the national level, and tries to control government at regional level, promotes local and regional interests through militant and agitational approach and articulates a regional identity and particularism based on religion, language and culture etc.

Rise of Regional Parties in India

Ever since independence many regional political parties have emerged in India and gained significant influence in some regions. Some political observers have hailed the resurgence of regionalism on the ground that the more regional parties come to power; the less will be the imbalance between the Centre and States. It is claimed that regional parties are better able to understand regional hopes and aspirations. India is a multi-lingual and multi-cultural nation. The linguistic and cultural diversities give rise to separatist tendencies. The people living in a particular linguistic region tend to identify and attach themselves to that region. Political parties also try to exploit the ethnic and cultural factors. In a different sense, uneven development of regions also brings a sense of discrimination and alienation leading to the formation of regional parties.

Regional parties in India were at first generally formed due to factionalism in the Congress or other parties and were dissolved when accommodated in the power circles or absorbed by the parent organisations. Some of them had no particular ideology except to gain power. Most such parties were headed by disgruntled leaders of the major parties without any cadres or proper organisation. These major parties included the Left parties that split early in their existence. A few regional parties like the Dravida Munnetra Kazhagam grew out of other regional dispensations (like the Justice Party) and not the Congress or Communist bloc. Since the first general elections in 1951-52, the Indian political system has experienced the emergence of several regional and sub-political parties. In a majority of cases these parties have come into existence because of the excessive centralism and monopolistic politics of the Congress. Particularly after the fourth general elections in 1967, the rise of regional political parties to power and the crucial role played by those parties in some of the States is noteworthy.

After her independence, while recognising the nature and extent of her social, political, cultural and economic diversities and taking cognisance of the fears, suspicions and prejudices that were subsisting among the different religious, regional, cultural and linguistic communities, India consciously opted for a democratic setup. Political parties are prominent features of such democratic setups wherein they play a vital role in the effective working of a political system. In fact, they supply the motive power, which keeps the wheel of administration moving. As such, the growth and development of political parties are considered as an indispensable part of modern statecraft. And in a parliamentary democracy, their importance need hardly be emphasised.

In a democratic system, people have got the right to devise their own system of governance without any outside interference. People enjoy the inalienable right to frame their own Constitution, a Constitution most suited to their country's peoples' genius, ethos and aspirations. Generally, the task of framing the Constitution of a sovereign democratic nation is performed by a representative body elected by the people for the purpose of considering and adopting a Constitution and is known as Constituent Assembly.

Framing of the Indian Constitution

Twenty six January 1950 marked a great event in the long and chequered history of India. On that particular day, the present Constitution of India was brought into force and the birth of a new Republic was announced to the world. It was, in fact, the rebirth of an ancient country after a very long period of subjugation.

The Constituent Assembly consisted of 389 members which included 292 representatives of the States, 93 represented the princely States and four from the chief commissioner's provinces of Delhi-Merwara, Coorg and British Baluchistan. Prominent Congress leaders included Pandit Jawaharlal Nehru, Sardar Patel, Maulana Azad, Rajagopalachari, Sarat Chandra Bose, Sachidanand Sinha, Rafi Ahmed Kidwai and Vijaya Lakshmi Pandit. The Constituent Assembly also included sections of Christians, Anglo-Indians and other minority communities. Rajendra Prasad was elected as permanent president of the Constituent Assembly and BR Ambedkar, chairman of the Drafting Committee.

In the AICC session of the Congress held at Faizpur, in 1936, the party had declared that it stood for a genuine democratic India where political power is transferred to the people as a whole and the government would be under their control.[10] According to a resolution adopted earlier, the Congress stressed its demand for democratic India, which was the cornerstone of its policy. After threadbare discussion on the issue of democracy, the Constituent Assembly finally passed the draft drawn up, on 26 November 1949, amidst prolonged cheers from the members. The Constitution was formally signed and authenticated by the president. The members of the Assembly also signed the Constitution.

Speaking immediately after the adoption of the Constitution, Rajendra Prasad as the Assembly president, stated that, 'I desire to congratulate the Assembly on accomplishing a task of such tremendous magnitude. It is not my purpose to appraise the value of the work that the assembly has done, or merits or demerits of the Constitution which it has framed. The future generations indeed owe a great debt of gratitude to all the founding fathers of the Constitution for making a Constitution most suited to the needs of independent India. Its successful working since 1950 compels us to bow our heads to the maturity, wisdom and political sagacity of the founding fathers of the Constitution'.[11]

This is how the rights of the States to exist as independent federal units of India, on the USA model, was established post-independence.

In India, the rise of different regional parties in different States became, harbinger of politics of religionalism as after her independence the regional parties better organised themselves and many new ones were born. The regional parties organised themselves primarily on the basis of four kinds of regionalism, viz:

1. Demand of secession of State from the country as demanded by the DMK party in Tamil Nadu and the regional parties of Nagaland and Assam.
2. Demand for separate statehood as made by master Tara Singh, the leader of the Akali party in Punjab.
3. Demand for more autonomy with regard to financial and administrative matters at local or regional level, like in the case of the Telangana Rashtra Samithi.
4. Demand for concessions on the basis of language, religion and culture so as to protect the rights and interest of a particular community. For example, the Akali party stands for the protection of the rights of the Sikh community and the DMK for non-Brahmins in Tamil Nadu. Thus, a regional party confines itself to the problems of its region and tries to fulfill the local needs of the people.[12]

In the light of the above criteria, many parties claim to be called as 'regional' parties on India's political stage. To name a few: Akali Dal, DMK, AIADMK, All Jammu and Kashmir National Conference, Telugu Desam, Karnataka Kranti Ranga, Sikkim Sangram Parishad, Asom Gana Parishad, APHLC, National Democracy Party and Maharashtra Gomantak Party. All these parties were formed in the in the context of State politics.

Elections in India in 1989, 1991, and 1996 have underlined the rise of regional parties not only in electoral strength but also in terms of political influence. Regional parties in the south have established themselves as powerful political groups not only at State level but also in the Parliament. Similarly, the regional parties in the north-east part of the country as well as the parties in the north-west have indicated that none of the major national parties can do without their active support and participation.

The national parties have lost their political influence in the outlying regions and have generally become unable to gather such support from the electorate that would enable them to form a government on their own. In a general sense, the regional parties have highlighted the weaknesses of the main national parties, particularly of the Indian National Congress. Such weaknesses of the Congress party first became visible in 1967 when the party lost its prime position in several States and had a reduced position in Parliament.

The Early Indian Parties

Today, the Indian Parliament has a sanctioned strength of 545 in Lok Sabha including 2 nominees from the Anglo-Indian Community by the President, and 245 in Rajya Sabha including the 12 nominees from the expertise of different fields of science, culture, art and history. Elections are held every five years and a member has to be of 25 years of age to contest for a Parliament seat. To form a government 273 MPs in the lower chamber of Parliament are required for a party to be acknowledged as a majority position-holding party. The upper house of the Parliament is called Rajya Sabha and the lower, Lok Sabha.

Before independent India went to the polls in 1951-52, two former cabinet colleagues of Nehru established separate political parties to challenge the supremacy of the Indian National Congress. Shyama Prasad Mukherjee went on to found the Jana Sangh in October 1951 and India's first Law Minister, BR Ambedkar, revived his Scheduled Castes Federation (which was later named the Republican Party). Other parties which started coming to the forefront included the Kisan Mazdoor Praja Parishad of Acharya JB Kripalani; the Socialist Party, which had Ram Manohar Lohia and Jayaprakash Narayan's leadership to boast of; and the Communist Party of India. However, these smaller parties were unable to make an electoral stand against the Congress in the first general elections in 1951-52. The participating parties then were:

Table 1: India's First Elections

Party	Abbreviation	Votes	%	Seats
Akhil Bharatiya Hindu Mahasabha	ABHM		0.95	4
Akhil Bharatiya Ram Rajya Parishad	RRP		1.97	3
All India Republican Party	REP		0.04	0
All India Republican Party	RPP		0.05	0
All India United Kisan Sabha	UKS		0.06	0
All Manipur National Union	AMNU		0.02	0
All People's Party	APP		0.03	0

Party	Abb.	Votes	%	Seats
Bharatiya Jana Sangh	BJS	3,246,288	3.06	3
Bolshevik Party of India	BPI		0.02	0
Chota Nagpur Santhal Parganas Janata Party	CNSPJP		0.22	1
Cochin Party	CP		0.01	0
Commonwealth Party	CWP		0.31	3
Communist Party of India	CPI	3,484,401	3.29	16
Forward Bloc (Marxist)	FB(M)		0.91	1
Forward Bloc (Ruiker)	FB(R)		0.13	0
Ganatantra Parishad	GP		0.91	6
Gandhi Sebak Seva	GSS		0.01	0
Hill People's Party	HPP		0.02	0
Historical Research	HR		0.00	0
Hyderabad State Praja Party	HSPP		0.01	0
Independents		16,817,910	15.9	37
Indian National Congress	INC	47,665,875	44.99	364
Jharkhand Party	JKP		0.71	3
Justice Party	JP		0.06	0
Kamgar Kisan Paksha	KKP		0.13	0
Kerala Socialist Party	KSP		0.1	0
Khasi-Jaintia Durbar	KJD		0.03	0
Kisan Janata Sanyukta Party	KJSP		0.01	0
Kisan Mazdoor Mandal	KMM		0.01	0
Kisan Mazdoor Praja Party	KMPP	6,156,558	5.79	9
Krishikar Lok Party	KLP		1.41	1
Kuki National Army/ Kuki National Organisation	KNA/KNO		0.01	0

Party	Abb.	Votes	%	Seats
Lok Sevak Sangh	LSS		0.29	2
Madras State Muslim League Party	MSMLP		0.08	1
National Party of India	NPI		0.00	0
Nominated Anglo-Indians		–	–	2
Peasants and Workers Party of India	PWPI		0.94	2
Peoples Democratic Front	PDF		1.29	7
Praja Party	PP		0.02	0
Punjab Depressed Class League	PDCL		0.01	0
Pursharathi Panchayat	PURP		0.01	0
Revolutionary Communist Party of India (Tagore)	RCPI		0.06	0
Revolutionary Socialist Party	RSP		0.44	3
Revolutionary Socialist Party (Uttar Pradesh)	RSP(UP)		0.02	0
SK Paksha	SKP		0.13	0
Saurashtra Khedut Sangh	SKS		0.03	0
Scheduled Caste Federation	SCF		2.38	2
Shiromani Akali Dal	SAD		0.99	4
Socialist Party	SP	11,266,779	10.59	12
Tamil Nadu Congress Party	TNCP		0.03	0
Tamil Nadu Toilers Party	TNTP		0.84	4
Total		**105,944,495**	**100**	**489**
Travancore Tamil Nadu Congress Party	TTNC		0.11	1
Tribal Sangha	TS		0.11	0
Uttar Pradesh Praja Party	UPP		0.2	0
Zamindar Party	ZP		0.27	0

Open Source Information

So powerful was the Congress at that time that it not only swept 364 seats, it also managed to ensure defeat of powerful political stalwarts like Ambedkar and Kripalani. Ambedkar was defeated in the Bombay (North Central, reserved seat) constituency as a Scheduled Castes Federation candidate by his little-known former assistant and Congress candidate Narayan Sadoba Kajrolkar, who polled 138, 137 votes compared to Ambedkar's 123,576 votes. Ambedkar then entered Parliament as a Rajya Sabha member. He contested the by-poll from Bhandara in 1954 to try to enter Lok Sabha but again lost to Ansuyabai Bhaorao Borkar of the Congress. Acharya Kripalani lost from Faizabad in UP as KMPP candidate, but his wife Sucheta Kripalani defeated the Congress candidate Manmohini Sahgal in Delhi.

Victories of the Congress party in 1971 and 1972 re-established its position as the dominant party in such a way that it appeared that the regional parties had lost their position of advantage. The situation changed again in 1977 when, for the first time, a non-Congress government was established at the Centre by the Janata coalition. This change again brought the position of the regional parties to the forefront, indicating the importance of the regional parties and their support to the government at the Centre.

But this situation continued only for the couple of years of non-Congress coalition, and from 1980 to 1987 again, the Congress party held sway over the whole country including a large part of the regional areas. It was in 1989 that the Janata Dal coalition gave an impetus to the regional parties for the anti-Congress position taken by them. The regional parties got an opportunity to become important contributors in the formation of the government at the Centre. But this situation was short-lived and in 1991, the position of the Congress party was re-established with a reduced numerical strength in the Lok Sabha. Due to this general ebb and flow of electoral politics, the regional parties at once became aware of their crucial position of advantage for political bargaining in national politics.

This became clearly evident after the 1996 elections when the Congress party could not secure sufficient number of seats to form the government at the Centre. It was the Bharatiya Janata Party, which secured the largest number of seats in the Lok Sabha, and the Congress became the second party. But neither the BJP nor the Congress could muster sufficient support to constitute the government. This made the position of the regional parties inevitably important in the formation of a coalition government at the Centre with other national parties, who also had only a contributor's strength.[13]

Thus, a coalition of 13 parties was formed and became the United Front that then formed a government at the Centre with the support of the Congress. This situation established the position of strength gained by the regional parties and it appeared that no national party could do without their support at the Centre. In the States of their respective regions, their position was clearly established in the formation of State governments.

The existence of regional parties was nothing new but their entry into national politics was, however, a new phenomenon. In 1977, the Akali Dal and the DMK were partners in the Janata government, although the Janata Party had a clear majority of 295 seats on its own. This was the first time that regional parties shared power at the national level. There were 51 members in the Lok Sabha belonging to various regional parties in 1977. In 1980, regional parties lost their newly found moment of glory when Congress returned to power. DMK managed to win 16 seats but the Akalis were reduced to one seat and the total tally of regional parties including the smaller Left parties of West Bengal remained only 35 in the seventh Lok Sabha. The elections to the eighth Lok Sabha (1984) were held in the backdrop of Indira Gandhi's assassination. At the time regional parties increased their share in the Lok Sabha. There were 76 members belonging to different regional parties in the eighth Lok Sabha. The rise of Telugu Desam in Andhra and Asom Gana Parishad in Assam were the main factors responsible for this performance of the regional parties. However, with Congress having 415 seats in Lok Sabha, the role of regional parties was bound to be insignificant in national politics.[14]

Non-Congressism brought many regional parties together in the National Front (NF) in 1988. These included TDP, DMK, AGP and Congress (S) apart from the newly formed

Janata Dal. But in the elections in 1989, these regional parties did not meet with success. In the ninth Lok Sabha, 48 members belonged to regional parties, but the regional allies of NF had only two seats, won by TDP. In spite of their disastrous performance, these regional parties became partners in the NF-led government of 1989. In 1991, the strength of regional parties in the Lok Sabha was at 57 but this time around TDP had a fair share of 13 seats. AIADMK, Janata Dal (G), Indian Union Muslim League (IUML), Sikkim Sangram Parishad (SSP) and Kerala Congress supported the Congress government of PV Narasimha Rao. However, these parties were not part of the government. In any case, both in 1989 and 1991, regional parties were playing a crucial role at the national level in making or unmaking the Central government. Thus, the 1977 elections not only speeded up the demise of the Congress system but also inaugurated a new era of partnership between All-India parties and regional parties – something which never happened in the pre-1977 period.

Since 1996, regional parties have become indispensable in the formation of government at the national level. They have been important partners in the coalitions that came to power after 1996. Besides, the numerical strength of the regional parties has considerably increased, with a sizable vote share being captured by regional parties. The experiment of United Front (UF) government first underscored the centrality of regional parties to national politics. In the 1996 Lok Sabha,

137 MPs belonged to various regional parties. At that time, it appeared that most regional parties were gravitating against the BJP. Thus in 1996, 95 out of 137 MPs belonging to regional parties were part of the United Front coalition. This gave rise to the impression that regional parties were occupying the 'third' space outside of Congress and BJP. This picture, however, disappeared almost as quickly as a rainbow disappears. And the United Front was actually described as a rainbow coalition. Rainbows are ephemeral. They make a good view but do not last long. The United Front proved to be similarly short-lived, although its supporters drew satisfaction from the fact that a large number of parties agreed to block an allegedly communal party from coming to power.[15]

The regional forces, at least some of them, quickly switched over to the BJP-led National Democratic Alliance (NDA) in 1998. The Lok Sabha in 1998 included 162 MPs belonging to regional parties: 92 of these were part of the BJP-led NDA. TDP, which was one of the leading parties of the UF, chose to join the NDA, which proved crucial for the survival of the government. However, another regional party, AIADMK, played a decisive role in defeating the NDA government. The thirteenth Lok Sabha (1999) had 168 MPs who belonged to regional parties. The NDA included 109 MPs from different regional parties.

In all, 32 regional parties were represented in the 13th Lok Sabha (1999) of which 15 were part of the NDA, four were constituents of Left Front (6 MPs), six were Congress allies (23 MPs) and seven parties had not joined any front or alliance (38 MPs). It may be noted that the discussion of the 1999 elections does not treat Janata Dal (U) as a regional party although this party consisted of four regional groups – Samta Party of Bihar, JD of Bihar, Lok Shakti of Karnataka and one JD faction from Karnataka. There was little coordination between the Karnataka unit and the Bihar unit of JD. Also, relations between the Samta faction and JD faction in Bihar were only nominal. The JD(U) won 17 seats in Bihar and 3 seats in Karnataka.[16]

In 2004 elections, 24 regional parties were represented in Lok Sabha with combined strength of 137 MPs. In 2009 General elections, the tally of regional party MPs further increased to 157. But the total number of regional parties represented in Lok Sabha was reduced to 21. The sixteenth Lok Sabha (2014) was represented by 34 regional parties with 217 MPs.

Vote Share

It can be observed that since 1996, the BJP and Congress together got only a little over fifty per cent share of the total votes. The Communist parties, Bahujan Samaj Party and JD were the three other non-regional parties. Together, they did not have more than 20 per cent votes. Thus, at least one fourth of the electorate voted for regional or State level parties. In

1999, the share of votes polled by regional parties showed an increase. While BJP polled 23.5 per cent votes, its regional allies polled 18 per cent votes. The regional allies of the Congress polled only 5 per cent votes. Other regional parties polled more than 15 per cent votes. Thus, if we look at the votes polled by All-India parties and State-level parties, their vote share was almost 60:40. The rise in the vote share of regional and State-level parties was mainly due to the broad range of alliances forged by BJP with various parties since 1998. In 1998, the BJP had allied with 15 regional parties, while in 1999 it allied with 19 regional parties. This also indicates that since 1998, most regional parties have been gravitating towards the BJP in contrast to the situation in 1996. In 2004 the Congress had allied with 12 regional parties. In 2009, the Congress had taken support of 8 regional parties. In the 16th Lok Sabha elections in 2014, the BJP had allied with 11 regional parties.

Party-wise Distribution of Seats in 2014 General Elections

Table 2: Parties in Lok Sabha in 2019 up to May

Party	Abbr.	Seats	Leader in Lok Sabha
Aam Aadmi Party	AAP	4	Bhagwant Mann
All India Anna Dravida Munnetra Kazhagam	AIADMK	37	Ponnusamy Venugopal / M Thambidurai
All India Majlis-e-Ittehadul Muslimeen	AIMIM	1	Asaduddin Owaisi
All India NR Congress	AINRC	1	R Radhakrishnan
All India Trinamool Congress	AITC	34	Sudip Bandyopadhyay
All India United Democratic Front	AIUDF	3	Badruddin Ajmal
Apna Dal	AD	2	Anupriya Patel
Bharatiya Janata Party	BJP	270 (269 + 1 Speaker)	Narendra Modi
Biju Janata Dal	BJD	19	Bhartruhari Mahtab
Communist Party of India	CPI	1	CN Jayadevan
Communist Party of India (Marxist)	CPI(M)	9	P Karunakaran
Independents	IND	3	-
Indian National Congress	INC	49	Mallikarjun Kharge
Indian National Lok Dal	INLD	2	Charanjeet Singh Rori
Indian Union Muslim League	IUML	2	ET Mohammed Basheer
Jammu & Kashmir National Conference	JKNC	1	Farooq Abdullah
Jammu and Kashmir Peoples Democratic Party	JKPDP	1	Muzaffar Hussain Baig
Janata Dal (Secular)	JD(S)	2	HD Deve Gowda
Janata Dal (United)	JD(U)	2	Kaushalendra Kumar
Jharkhand Mukti Morcha	JMM	2	Shibu Soren
Lok Janshakti Party	LJP	6	Ram Vilas Paswan

Party	Abbr.	Seats	Leader in Lok Sabha
Nationalist Congress Party	NCP	6	Supriya Sule
Nationalist Democratic Progressive Party	NDPP	1	Tokheho Yepthomi
Nominated Anglo-Indians (Bharatiya Janata Party)	NOM	2	Richard Hay and George Baker
Pattali Makkal Katchi	PMK	1	Anbumani Ramadoss
Rashtriya Janata Dal	RJD	4	Jay Prakash Narayan Yadav
Rashtriya Lok Dal	RLD	1	Begum Tabassum Hasan
Rashtriya Lok Samta Party	RLSP	3	Upendra Kushwaha
Revolutionary Socialist Party	RSP	1	NK Premachandran
Samajwadi Party	SP	7	Mulayam Singh Yadav
Shiromani Akali Dal	SAD	4	Ranjit Singh Brahmpura
Shiv Sena	SS	18	Anant Geete
Sikkim Democratic Front	SDF	1	Prem Das Rai
Swabhimani Paksha	SWP	1	Raju Shetti
Telangana Rashtra Samithi	TRS	11	AP Jithender Reddy
Telugu Desam Party	TDP	16	Thota Narasimham
Vacant	21 (There were 21 Lok Sabha seats vacant at the time of publishing this edition of the book.)*		
YSR Congress Party	YSRCP	4	

Open Source Information

* https://loksabha.nic.in/members/vacant.aspx

As many as 36 political parties are represented in the 16th Lok Sabha which has 545 seats today, 56 seats more than in 1951-52.

Types of Regional Parties

Often, a party is easily identified as 'regional' if it propagates the ideology of regionalism or thrives on invocation of regional pride. Parties like Asom Gana Parishad (AGP), Telugu Desam Party (TDP) and Dravida Munnetra Kazhagam (DMK) were quickly recognised as regional parties. However, yet another type of parties needs to be incorporated in the category of regional party. These are parties which enjoy considerable support only in one State of the Indian union. Such parties may not emphasise their regionalist outlook. They have, in fact, an All-India perspective but only a regional reach. Forward Bloc (FB) and Revolutionary Socialist Party (RSP) in West Bengal or Peasants and Workers' Party (PWP) in Maharashtra may be cited as examples. The nineties have witnessed the rise of such parties in Bihar and Uttar Pradesh. In fact, together with the 'regionalist' parties, these parties were also playing an important role in the political developments that unfolded in the nineties.

The first criterion of distinction between the types of regional parties is its *territorial differential*. By its very nature, a regional party restricts its area of action to a single region, which, in the prevailing Indian situation, means a State. A party which extends its organisational network and electoral concerns over more States than one, becomes 'cross regional' and, in proportion to its territorial extension, its regional commitment gets diluted since it may have to sort out the conflicting interests of its various State units. A cross regional party does not have an exclusively, or even predominantly regional commitment per se, though no political party, cross regional or all-India, can always be indifferent to regional pressures. At times and particularly in respect of electorally sensitive area-specific issues, every party is prone to swim with the regional tide.

The best example of a cross regional party is the Communist Party of India-Marxist (CPI-M), which is firmly entrenched in three States ie. Tripura in the northeast, West Bengal in the east and Kerala in the south. It was particularly well entrenched in West Bengal where it continuously ruled for three decades from 1977. The party has a noticeable presence in a few other States too, such as in the Punjab, while in the east, especially in the Hindi heartland its electoral support is marginal or non-existent. The Communist Party of India (CPI) falls in the same category even if it cannot claim a single State as its bastion. It is nevertheless, a 'cross regional' party since its electoral appeal is thinly but firmly spread over several States. Similarly, some other Left parties like Forward Bloc, Revolutionary Socialist Party and Peasants and Workers' Party, which have achieved some sort of a toe-hold in more States than one, are 'cross-regional' rather than regional parties as they lack the regional specificity, which is the hallmark of a genuine regional party.

The erstwhile Janata conglomerate, which was an all-India party, fell apart in 1979. Even though, its electoral strength lay primarily in the States north of the Vindhayas, it had a varying thin sparkle of support in the four southern States. What remains of the Janata experiment after its fragmentation can only be categorised as a cross-regional party. It is politically effective in only one State – Karnataka – but has a sizeable following in some others, such as Uttar Pradesh and Gujarat. Whether or not its two factions are able to reunite, the Lok Dal remains a 'cross regional' party with a fairly strong base in a number of States – Haryana, Uttar Pradesh, Rajasthan and Bihar.

The Bharatiya Janata Party was until recently, essentially, a party of north and west India. It enjoys considerable and committed support in several States of the Hindi belt – Himachal Pradesh, Haryana, Uttar Pradesh, Rajasthan, Bihar and Madhya Pradesh. It has only recently succeeded in its determined endeavour to cut across the north-south divide and made significant inroads in Karnataka and Kerala; where it has been able to put together a workable organisational infrastructure with a growing and dedicated cadre. Thus, the proposition that opposition parties – that is, parties other than the Indian National Congress – are, in effect, cross-regional and regional parties because they have cross-regional and regional pockets, held currency till recently. For 50 years, the INC was the only archetypal all-India party.[17] However, the speed with which, particularly after the 2014 Lok Sabha elections, the BJP is spreading its pan-India tentacles, and the Congress is losing its grip, it will not be a surprise if the BJP soon becomes an all-India party and the Congress is reduced to being a 'cross regional' party.

The second criterion of a regional political party is that *it articulates and seeks to defend a regionally based ethnic or regional-cultural identity.* Thus, the Dravida Munnetra Kazagham (DMK) and the All India Anna Dravida Munnetra Kazagham (AIADMK) act as the voices and champions of Tamil cultural nationalism, against the inroads of what is perceived as the Aryan imperialism of the north. The shrill and confrontationist idiom in which the two parties conducted their politics until the mid-seventies has been substantially softened in recent years but the concern for Tamil identity and opposition to the introduction of Hindi continue to be the main planks in their platform.

NT Rama Rao, a former matinee idol like his Tamil counterpart, MG Ramachandran, and his Telugu Desam burst into politics under the banner of Telugu 'gauravam' or self-respect. The Akali Dal, in its various incarnations, has stuck tenaciously to its claim to be the defender of interests of the Sikh Panth and Punjab. Asom Gana Parishad was born out of a fierce popular movement, which sought to stem and reverse the tide of immigration from other countries and States such as Bangladesh and from West Bengal. At stake was the survival of the Assamese identity, it declared.

The third criterion is, *demands based on language, caste, community or religion.* It is in the very nature of a regional party to be 'primarily concerned with exploiting local sources of discontent or pressing a variety of primordial demands based on language, caste, community or religion'.[18] This is so because the electoral destiny of these parties is inseparably linked with their respective regions. With no hope of capturing power or being able to play a decisive role at the Centre, they perceive their essential role as pressure groups for protecting and promoting the interests of regional communities and, to that end, mobilising local support by playing up real or imagined feelings of discrimination and deprivation.

When NT Rama Rao opposed a 'national policy' on water resources which proposed to treat an entire river basin rather than the territorial limits of a State as a unit, his opposition resulted from the perception that the principle, if implemented, will trim his freedom to push on with his Telugu Ganga Project, despite the objections raised by neighbouring States like Karnataka. A similar perception characterised the Akali claims in respect of the distribution of the Ravi-Beas waters among Punjab, Haryana, and Rajasthan and the party's insistence on the upper riparian winner principle. To sum up, a regional political party has a regional support base, a regional perspective and a regional issue orientation.

Reasons for Emergence of Regional Parties in India

The emergence of several regional political parties in India has been a natural development because of the presence of socio-economic, religious and cultural pluralism. Several scholars like KM Panikkar even advocated the view that 'no one can conceive of India except in terms of the great regions'. Rasheeduddin Khan describes India as 'an aggregation of regions and sub-regions'. As such, the development of regional political parties is natural and may well have been anticipated in a vast and variegated country like India.[19] There are India-specific factors that have influenced and propelled the emergence of regional political parties in India, among them are:

Anti-Centralism of 1950-96 Period

Indian political system has a federal structure with a unitary spirit. The Union enjoys a predominant role in the Indian federalism. As a reaction against the spirit of centralism or unitarianism, several regional parties have not only come into existence in India but also have been in a position to earn popularities. The DMK, Telugu Desam, Akali Dal, Asom Gana Parishad and some others have been using anti-centralism as a means for securing popularity and support. But after 1996, there appears to be a change taking place in their perceptions. Now regional parties want more autonomy for States but at the same time, do not pursue anti-centrism. Therefore, there is power sharing at the Centre between a national party with an alliance of regional/local parties, eg. NDA and UPA governments. Besides, there are coalition governments in some States like with the Biju Janata Dal in Odisha, which earlier enjoyed the support of the BJP, the SAD and BJP share power in Punjab, JD(U) and BJP in Bihar and some other coalitions which have given a new look to federal politics in India. Anti-centralism is getting replaced by Centre-State cooperative-bargaining federation. It appears to be a healthy development in Indian politics.

Religious Factors

Though the framers of the Indian Constitution declared India to be a secular state, which is completely detached in matters of religion, religion has continued to be an important factor not only in Indian politics but also for emergence of regional parties in several States. The existence of several religions within India has helped the emergence of several regional parties like the Shiromani Akali Dal of Punjab which is mainly a religious party and stands for the preservation and promotion of Sikh religion and Punjabi language. Similarly, the Muslim League is a Muslim Party which aims at securing a respectable place for the Muslims in Indian politics. The Hindu Mahasabha and Shiv Sena are Hindu parties based on religion.

Regional Imbalances

The emergence of regional economic imbalances in India has also been a factor in the emergence of regional parties. Several regions of the country have registered a relatively high level of economic development while many others continue to lag behind. The local leaders, particularly those who belong to economically backward or lowly-developed regions, often exploit the local feelings and form regional parties for representing the regional interests as well as for strengthening their bargaining power vis-à-vis the national leaders. The emergence of Asom Gana Parishad is such an example.

Cultural Pluralism

The presence of several distinct cultural-ethnic-religious-linguistic-caste groups within Indian society has greatly helped the process of growth of regional political parties like the DMK in Tamil Nadu, the Jharkhand Mukti Morcha in Jharkhand and similar parties in Mizoram, West Bengal and other States.

Political Splits

Splits resulting from the emergence of sizeable dissident local groups in several national political parties have also been responsible for the emergence of some regional political parties. The emergence of Kerala Congress, Bangla Congress, Trinamool Congress, Janata Dal, Janata Dal (Secular), Janata Dal (United), Lok Janshakti Party, Pattali Makkal Katchi, BJD, Oriya Congress, Forward Bloc, Tamil Maanila Congress, AIADMK etc as regional parties in the Indian political system can be explained in terms of this factor of political disagreements with parent parties.

Personality-cult Politics

Another reason behind the emergence of regional political parties in India is the presence of personality-cult politics.

The ability of a leader to muster committed support from a group of followers because of his personal relations with them often encourages him to form a regional party as a means of showing his personal power. Bansi Lal's Party, Devi Lal's Party, Congress (J), Congress(S), Bharatiya Kisan Union, BKKU, TDP, Rashtriya Janata Dal, and some other parties came into existence because of this factor.

Caste Factor

Though the framers of the Indian Constitution adopted a document which is wedded to the ideals of democracy and social justice and aimed to establish a casteless and classless society in India, caste continues to be an important factor in Indian politics and it has also been responsible for the emergence of several regional/local/sectorial parties. DMK emerged as an anti-Brahmin party in Tamil Nadu, Republican Party of India, Bahujan Samajwadi Party etc are examples of caste-based regional parties.[20]

Developing Nature of the Indian Party System

The Indian party system has been developing. It has been regularly undergoing important political and constitutional changes. The party system too has been changing in accordance with the changes in the socio-economic environment. The transformation of several national political parties from a position of strength to weakness and vice-versa has been taking place. The Congress, which dominated the Indian political scene in the past, has suffered a decline and many a splinter. It has been the source of the birth of several regional political parties in India.[21]

Lack of Strong Ideological Differences

National-level political parties in India have been working as different political groups with different ideological commitments. Presence of leftist and rightist groups within several national parties have been at times responsible for the emergence of several regional parties in several States. Moreover, even some of the national level political parties behave as regional parties because they enjoy real support and popularity in only some States, may be one or two. For example, CPM is a national party but for its popularity base, and therefore, its operational base, stands confined to the States of West Bengal, Tripura and Kerala. Even the Bahujan Samaj Party, a pro-Dalit party, enjoys support only in some States, though Dalits are votebanks in all States. Several regional parties have emerged as splinter parties of a national party and are working as regional or State or local-level parties.

Besides these factors, there have been several other considerations for the emergence of regional parties in the Indian political stage, mainly after the 1980s.

Where Regional Parties Thrive

Let us look at the geographic regions in which regional parties are predominant. In the States of Rajasthan, Gujarat and Madhya Pradesh regional parties do not have much presence. Gujarat had two small breakaway groups originating from the splits in Janata Dal and BJP. But both were short-lived and finally gave way to a bipolar contest between Congress and BJP. Karnataka has a potential for regionalised politics since the two JD factions together garner a quarter of the votes. Finally, politics in Kerala is clearly divided between the two fronts, Left Front and the United Democratic Front. In both these alliances, smaller State level parties are important partners, but Congress and the Communist parties dominate politics.

In terms of seat share, regional parties dominate eleven States out of the 29 States and 7 union territories the country is divided into. The size of the State and its population determine the number of the Lok Sabha seats/constituencies that is allocated to a State or UT in the Lok Sabha. Half of the MPs from these States in the present Lok Sabha belong to regional parties. These include the smaller States of Manipur, Meghalaya and Sikkim. Besides these, other States in this category are Andhra Pradesh, Telangana, Tamil Nadu, Odisha, Maharashtra, Haryana, Jammu and Kashmir, Bihar and Uttar Pradesh. Another test of the prominence of regional parties is their vote share. In 13 States, regional parties had 30 per cent or more share of the votes in the 1999 elections. They include the smaller States mentioned above. In Manipur and Sikkim, regional parties polled 67 and 95 per cent votes respectively. Other States where regional parties polled around 30 per cent or more votes are J&K, Haryana, Punjab, Maharashtra, AP, Telangana, Tamil Nadu, Odisha, West Bengal, Bihar and Uttar Pradesh. In Tamil Nadu, various regional parties together polled 75 per cent votes. In Maharashtra, Telangana and Andhra, regional parties polled 42 to 44 per cent votes respectively. The vote share of regional parties in West Bengal, Punjab, Odisha and Haryana was between 33 and 35 per cent in the 1999 elections while in other States, regional parties polled between 29 and 31 per cent votes. Considering multipolarity of electoral contests, this performance is certainly impressive.[22]

In 2004 general elections, in the States, the regional parties secured more than 30 per cent of votes. In Mizoram, Sikkim and Tamil Nadu regional parties secured more than half of the total votes polled. In 2009 Lok Sabha elections, in 10 States the regional parties secured more than 30 per cent of votes. In Sikkim, Tamil Nadu and Tripura, they secured more than 50 per cent of votes.

Before the 1990s

Even before the rise of regional parties during the nineties, regional parties dominated State-level politics in many States. Apart from the States of northeast, politics in J&K, Punjab, Tamil Nadu and Odisha had witnessed rise of regional parties at the State level. The National Conference has been central to politics in J&K. In Punjab, the role of Akali Dal was limited till 1966. Since then however, Punjab politics has revolved around Akali politics. The Akalis established themselves politically by winning 43 of 104 seats in the legislative elections of 1969. Similarly, DMK in Tamil Nadu rose to prominence in the 1962 Assembly elections, winning 50 seats. It came to power in 1967 with 138 seats. The AIADMK replaced the DMK in 1977. Thus, Tamil politics has been regionalised since 1962.

Although Odisha has now joined the group of States dominated by regional politics, regional political parties between 1952 and 1975 also dominated the State. The Ganatantra Parishad won 31 seats in 1952, 51 seats in 1957 and 36 seats in 1961 Assembly elections. Later, the Jan Congress won 26 seats in 1967; Utkal Congress won 33 seats in 1971 and 35 seats in 1974. The two regional parties, Maharashtrawadi Gomantak Party (MGP) and United Goan Party (UGP), too, dominated Goan politics. Local parties of Karnataka had captured 41 seats along with independents in the State legislature in 1967 while local parties of AP won 70 assembly seats along with independents. The Forward Bloc and RSP together won 22 seats in 1962, 13 seats in 1967 and 33 seats in 1969 West Bengal Assembly elections. The eighties saw the rise of the AGP in Assam and TDP in Andhra. To sum up, regional parties dominated State-level politics in many States in the pre-1990 period.

Ideological Positions

A variety of regionalist and non-regional ideological positions are taken by the regionalist and State-based parties. Many such parties are personalistic and centered around one leader. Yet, formation of a party requires an ideological position even if it is only like a fig-leaf as far as legitimisation of the party's existence is concerned. Besides, the compulsions of electoral politics forces a party to present some arguments. The regional parties frequently combine the regionalist and non-regional arguments in order to explain their *raison d'etre* to the electorate.

Regional parties extend a broad range of regionalist arguments. These surround invocation of regional pride and marks of regional identity. Regional arguments involve demands pertaining to regional culture, history and language. The demands for formation of a State, as in the case of Chhattisgarh, Jharkhand, Telangana, or inclusion of certain territories into a State are potent weapons of mobilisation. Yet, another aspect of regional ideology is the demand for more autonomy to the State. Finally, regionalist ideological positions take the form of demands for State's development. Such regionalism deals less with issues of identity and more with issues of backwardness, investment and industrial progress. Regional parties variously use these arguments – identity, Statehood, autonomy, regional interests and development.

The National Conference, Akali Dal, DMK often combine identity and autonomy arguments. Parties like Biju Janata

Dal (BJD) or Trinamool Congress (TMC) emphasise the development arguments. The TDP emerged under the leadership of NT Rama Rao on the basis of the identity argument but Chandrababu Naidu has led the party quietly to the development argument. Many parties originate in the demand for Statehood. The Jharkhand Mukti Morcha, Chhattisgarh Mukti Morcha, Vishal Haryana Parishad are examples of parties demanding Statehood. Most of the parties of the northeast continue to combine identity issues with autonomy or Statehood demands. By invoking regionalist arguments, a regional party can easily identify with the different sections in the regional society. Its language of identity appeals to the intelligentsia and the masses alike. Besides, identity discourse also benefits the materially dominant sections of the society.[23]

However, it is not always necessary that a regional party will confine itself only to regionalist arguments, many times it also showcases non-regionalist ideological positions. While Akalis tend to define regional identity in terms of religion, the Shiv Sena uses the two ideologies of regionalism and religious communalism according to exigencies of electoral politics. Regional parties also rely on caste for their ideological formulations. Thus, the DMK originally combined Dravidian identity with non-Brahminism. By employing anti-caste ideological resources, the DMK strengthened its claims pertaining to a separate Dravida identity vis-à-vis the Aryans. More recently, the PMK in Tamil Nadu has also combined the regional rhetoric with an anti-caste social position on behalf of the OBCs. Such ideological formulations should not be seen cynically only as marriage of convenience. There is also a broader implication involved in such formulations. They tend to restate the meaning of 'regional' identity.

Thus, the Akali Dal claim implies that the Punjabi identity is not merely a territorial and linguistic identity, but being a Punjabi is implicitly equated with Sikh also. Similarly, the Shiv Sena keeps on shifting its rhetoric from Maharashtrian pride to Hindu pride. It believes that there is no contradiction between these two identities. On the other hand, the latter is the extension of the former. The symbol of Shivaji employed by Shiv Sena embodies both these ideological assertions. Shivaji – a seventeenth century Maratha chief – is portrayed both as saviour of 'Marathi' pride and protector of Hindutva. The Dravida parties, particularly the DMK, originally also defined the regional identity in the context of two factors. Firstly, the regional identity was defined in terms of the juxtaposition between outsiders – aggressors vs indigenous pride, ie. the Aryans vs Dravidas. Secondly, it was claimed that Dravida identity belongs to the masses – non-Brahmins. Thus, regionalist ideology disinherited the Brahmins from Dravidian legacy. If regionalism is exclusionary in the sense that it excludes persons belonging to other regions then, *some regionalist formulations involve a double exclusion of outsiders and exclusion of certain communities.*[24]

Some State-based parties employ only the second variety of exclusion/inclusion. There are parties which seldom explicitly rely on regionalist exclusion. Instead, the primary locus of exclusion/inclusion is caste/community/tribe. Secondly, because the principle of exclusion/inclusion has a regionally-specified political salience, the party becomes a single State party. Although examples of such parties are more prominent in the late eighties and nineties, regional parties did exist earlier also which did not rely on regionalist ideology. The Republican Party of India was conceived as an all-India party. But it operated in the framework of exclusion/inclusion on the basis of caste. In the late fifties, Dalit mobilisation on such basis could take place only in Maharashtra. So, the party became confined to Maharashtra. The same constraint impinges on growth of BSP outside the typical context of UP. More recently, in 1993, the Bahujan Mahasangh (BMS) has emerged in Maharashtra as a party of OBCs favouring Dalit-OBC cooperation and unity. But the more dramatic examples of this type of parties are the Samajwadi Party (SP) and Rashtriya Janata Dal (RJD). Both aspire to be national, ie. all-India parties. Both are non-regionalist in their ideology. They have reached the regional station through the caste-route of exclusion/inclusion.

In principle, the ideology of Dalit and OBC uplift can have all-India applicability. But the RJD and the SP have defined their ideological positions in the specific context of their respective States. As a result, their ideology is translated into ideology of the upwardly mobile OBC communities. The rhetoric of protecting the minorities does not attract people outside of UP, nor does Laloo Prasad Yadav's rhetoric about Advani's ignorance about milking the cow, appeal to OBCs outside of Bihar. In other words, the meaning of pro-OBC ideology becomes State-specific in the case of Bahujan Mahasangh of Maharashtra, Samajwadi Party of UP and RJD of Bihar. Yet, it is undeniable that these parties cover a very significant ideological terrain. Caste and Tribe exist both at all-India level and at the State level. An ideology based on those factors may claim all-India status but such ideology becomes relevant and meaningful only in specific contexts. Discussions of peasant castes has to pin down whether we are talking about middle castes like the Jats, Marathas etc or if we are talking about peasant OBCs like Yadavas or Malis. This peculiarity often forces anti-caste parties into State-specific or regionalised positions. Perhaps, this characteristic of anti-caste ideology may continue until the gap between caste-specific identity and supra-caste mega-identities is filled or overcome. Till then, caste ideology will keep on regionalising the forces claiming anti-caste space.

Social Bases of Regional Parties

It is noted by experts that initially, after the rise of regional parties, politics appeared to be becoming triangular.[25] The growth of regional parties also upset the established patterns of voters' preferences. Not only new segments of voters were ushered into the electoral arena, but traditional loyalties too were put under strain. The regional parties succeeded in mobilising greater share of voters. Congress was the obvious loser in most of the States, notably in Andhra Pradesh, Assam, Kerala, Punjab, Tamil Nadu and West Bengal. While this description is factually accurate, it captures only one aspect of the reality. The second aspect is fragmentation of non-Congress and non-BJP votes. This happened in Bihar, Karnataka and Uttar Pradesh where the so-called Janata Dal was divided into regional fragments.

The third aspect of the political reality was readiness of regional parties to enter into alliances with the BJP rather than with the Congress. Since most of the regional parties had a tradition of anti-Congressism and a social base, which was mobilised on a non-Congress ideological basis, these parties were constrained in choosing electoral allies. This electoral arithmetic produced two results. Firstly, by aligning with the BJP, these regional parties made it possible for the BJP to take over State power. Secondly and more importantly, alliance with the BJP signalled new social equations. For instance, Lok Shakti practically facilitated the entry of BJP into Karnataka in 1998 by breaking the Lingayat and Vokkaliga (Gowda) axis. It isolated the Vokkaligas and turned the Lingayats towards the BJP.[26] Samta Party in Bihar accomplished almost a similar task. In Maharashtra, The Nationalist Congress Party went ahead with the consolidation of Marathas in 1999 and facilited the efforts of BJP-Shiv Sena to garner OBC votes.[27]

Role of Regional Political Parties in Indian Politics

Commenting upon the role of regional parties in Indian politics, KR Bombwall remarks that these 'have catalysed a re-alignment of political forces and their impact on the structure and process of politics has been multi-directional and far reaching'.[28] Bombwall identifies several distinct dimensions of the growing regionalism of politics in India. In the first place, regional parties have posed the most powerful challenge to India's 'one party dominant system'.

Secondly, the regional parties have made a strong impact on the nature and course of Centre-State relations. In the past, several tension areas in Centre-State relations in India and the intensity gathered by the demand for grant of greater autonomy to the States emerged largely due to several active and powerful regional actors like the DMK, the AIADMK, the Telugu Desam and the Akali Dal. The State leadership tried to become more and more vocal in their dealings with the central leadership and the Centre began becoming more responsive to the needs and demands of regional actors.

Finally, within the liberal-democratic frame of reference, regional parties made politics more competitive and popular participation in the political process more extensive at the grass roots.

After 1996, several regional parties emerged as key players in national politics. Today, as many as 23 regional parties, as partners of NDA, have been sharing power at the Centre. Some of the regional parties are ruling the States like AIADMK in Tamil Nadu,

JD (U) in Bihar, BJD in Odisha, TMC in West Bengal and some other northeastern States. All this reflects the continued and ever-growing importance of regional parties in Indian politics.

Table 3.1 7 recognised national parties

Name	Abbr.	Foundation year	Founder	Party Supremo
All India Trinamool Congress	AITC	1998	Mamata Banerjee	Mamata Banerjee
Bahujan Samaj Party	BSP	1984	Kanshi Ram	Mayawati
Bharatiya Janata Party	BJP	1980	Shyama Prasad Mukherjee	Amit Shah
Communist Party of India	CPI	1925		Suravaram Sudhakar Reddy
Communist Party of India (Marxist)	CPI(M)	1964		Sitaram Yechury
Indian National Congress	INC	1885	Allan Octavian Hume	Rahul Gandhi
Nationalist Congress Party	NCP	1999	Sharad Pawar PA Sangma Tariq Anwar	Sharad Pawar

Open Source Information/Wikipedia

List of Recognised Regional Parties in India

Parties that have received certain number of votes or seats in a State might be recognised as a State party by the Election Commission of India which conducts elections across the country. Recognition as a State party gives the party the chance to reserve a particular election symbol in the concerned State. A party recognised in four States is automatically recognised as a national party. Here is the list of 51 recognised regional parties in 2019.

Tabel 3:2 51 recognised State parties till 2014.

Name	Abbr.	Foundation Year	Current leader(s)	States/UT	Symbol
Aam Aadmi Party	AAP	2012	Arvind Kejriwal	Delhi, Punjab	Broom
All India Anna Dravida Munnetra Kazhagam	AIADMK	1972	Edappadi K Palaniswami and O Paneerselvam	Tamil Nadu, Puducherry	Two leaves
All India Forward Bloc	AIFB	1939	Debabrata Biswas	West Bengal	Lion
All India Majlis-e-Ittehadul Muslimeen	AIMIM	1927	Asaduddin Owaisi	Telangana, Maharashtra	Kite
All India NR Congress	AINRC	2011	N Rangaswamy	Puducherry	Jug
All India United Democratic Front	AIUDF	2004	Badruddin Ajmal	Assam	Lock and key
All Jharkhand Students Union	AJSU	1986	Sudesh Mahto	Jharkhand	Banana
Asom Gana Parishad	AGP	1985	Atul Bora	Assam	Elephant
Biju Janata Dal	BJD	1997	Naveen Patnaik	Odisha	Conch
Bodoland People's Front	BPF	1985	Hagrama Mohilary	Assam	Nangal
Desiya Murpokku Dravida Kazhagam	DMDK	2005	Vijayakanth	Tamil Nadu	Nagara
Dravida Munnetra Kazhagam	DMK	1949	MK Stalin	Tamil Nadu, Puducherry	Rising sun
Goa Forward Party	GFP	2016	Vijai Sardesai	Goa	Coconut

Name	Abbr.	Foundation Year	Current leader(s)	States/UT	Symbol
Hill State People's Democratic Party	HSPDP	1968	HS Lyngdoh	Meghalaya	Lion
Indian National Lok Dal	INLD	1999	Om Prakash Chautala	Haryana	Spec-tacles
Indian Union Muslim League	IUML	1948	Panakkad Sayed Hyderali Shihab Thangal	Kerala	Ladder
Indigenous People's Front of Tripura	IPFT	2009	Mevar Kumar Jamatia	Tripura	Dao
Jammu & Kashmir National Conference	JKNC	1932	Omar Abdullah	Jammu and Kashmir	Plough
Jammu & Kashmir National Panthers Party	JKNPP	1982	Bhim Singh	Jammu and Kashmir	Bicycle
Jammu and Kashmir People's Democratic Party	JKPDP	1998	Mehbooba Mufti	Jammu and Kashmir	Inkpot and pen
Janata Dal (Secular)	JD(S)	1999	HD Deve Gowda	Karnataka, Kerala	Lady farmer carrying paddy on her head
Janata Dal (United)	JD(U)	1999	Nitish Kumar	Bihar	Arrow
Jharkhand Mukti Morcha	JMM	1972	Shibu Soren	Jharkhand	Bow and arrow
Jharkhand Vikas Morcha (Prajatantrik)	JVM(P)	2006	Babu Lal Marandi	Jharkhand	Comb

Name	Abbr.	Foundation Year	Current leader(s)	States/UT	Symbol
Kerala Congress (M)	KC(M)	1979	CF Thomas	Kerala	Two leaves
Lok Janshakti Party	LJP	2000	Ram Vilas Paswan	Bihar	Bunglow
Maharashtra Navnirman Sena	MNS	2006	Raj Thackeray	Maharashtra	Railway engine
Maharashtra-wadi Gomantak Party	MGP	1963	Deepak Dhavalikar	Goa	Lion
Mizo National Front	MNF	1959	Pu Zoramthanga	Mizoram	Star
Mizoram People's Conference	MPC	1972	Pu Lalhming-thanga	Mizoram	Electric bulb
Naga People's Front	NPF	2002	TR Zeliang	Manipur, Nagaland	Rooster
National People's Party	NPP	2013	Conrad Sangma	Meghalaya, Manipur, Nagaland, Arunachal Pradesh	Book
Nationalist Democratic Progressive Party	NDPP	2018	Neiphiu Rio	Nagaland	
Pattali Makkal Katchi	PMK	1989	GK Mani	Tamil Nadu, Puducherry	Mango
People's Democratic Alliance	PDA	2012	Bd. Behring Anal	Manipur	Crown
People's Democratic Front	PDF	2017	PN Syiem	Meghalaya	Candles

Name	Abbr.	Foundation Year	Current leader(s)	States/UT	Symbol
People's Party of Arunachal	PPA	1987	Tomo Riba	Arunachal Pradesh	Corn
Rashtriya Janata Dal	RJD	1997	Lalu Prasad Yadav	Bihar, Jharkhand	Hurricane lamp
Rashtriya Lok Dal	RLD	1996	Ajit Singh	Uttar Pradesh	Hand pump
Rashtriya Lok Samta Party	RLSP	2013	Upendra Kushwaha	Bihar	Ceiling fan
Revolution-ary Socialist Party	RSP	1940	TJ Chandra-choodan	Kerala, West Bengal	Spade and stoker
Samajwadi Party	SP	1992	Akhilesh Yadav	Uttar Pradesh	Bicycle
Shiromani Akali Dal	SAD	1920	Sukhbir Singh Badal	Punjab	Scale
Shiv Sena	SS	1966	Uddhav Thackeray	Maharashtra	Bow and arrow
Sikkim Democratic Front	SDF	1993	Pawan Kumar Chamling	Sikkim	Umbrella
Sikkim Krantikari Morcha	SKM	2013	Prem Singh Tamang	Sikkim	Table lamp
Telangana Rashtra Samithi	TRS	2001	Kalvakuntla Chandra-shekar Rao	Andhra Pradesh, Telangana	Car
Telugu Desam Party	TDP	1982	N Chandra Babu Naidu	Andhra Pradesh, Telangana	Bicycle
United Democratic Party	UDP	1972	Donkupar Roy	Meghalaya	Drum
YSR Con-gress Party	YSRCP	2011	YS Jagan-mohan Reddy	Andhra Pradesh, Telangana	Ceiling fan
Zoram Nationalist Party	ZNP	1997	Lalduhawma	Mizoram	Sun (without rays)

Open Source Information: valid upto May 2019

This is a list of unrecognised but registered regional outfits.

Table 3.3 Unrecognised registered notable parties

Name	Abbr.	Foundation year	Current leader(s)	States/UT
Amra Bangali	AMB	1983	Prabhat Ranjan Sarkar	West Bengal
Bharatiya Minorities Suraksha Mahasangh	BMSM	1994	Haji Mastan Mirza	Maharashtra
Bharipa Bahujan Mahasangh	BBM	1999	Prakash Ambedkar	Maharashtra
Hindustani Awam Morcha	HAM	2015	Jitan Ram Manjhi	Bihar
Bahujan Republican Socialist Party	BRSP	2015	Suresh Mane	Maharashtra
Indhiya Jananayaga Katchi	IJK	2010	TR Pachamuthu	Tamil Nadu
People's Democratic Front	PDF	2001	Ajoy Biswas	Tripura
Jai Samaikyandhra Party	JSP	2014	Nallari Kiran Kumar Reddy	Andhra Pradesh
Jan Adhikar Party Loktantrik	JAP	2015	Pappu Yadav	Bihar
Suheldev Bhartiya Samaj Party	SBSP	2002	Om Prakash Rajbhar	Uttar Pradesh
Jana Sena Party (Former Actor)	JSP	2014	Pawan Kalyan	Andhra Pradesh, Telangana
Janshakti Party of India	JSPI	2015	Gurjeet Singh Azad	Punjab

Karnataka Janata Paksha	KJP	2012	Padmanabha Prasanna Kumar	Karnataka
Kerala Congress (Jacob)	KC(J)	1991	Anoop Jacob	Kerala
Kerala Congress (B)	KC(B)	1989	R Balakrishna Pillai	Kerala
Kongunadu Makkal Desia Katchi	KMDK	2013	ER Eswaran	Tamil Nadu
Kongunadu Makkal Katchi	KMK	2001	AM Raja	Tamil Nadu
Lok Satta Party	LSP	2006	Jayaprakash Narayan	Andhra Pradesh, Telangana
Manipur Peoples Party	MPP	1968	Sovakiran N	Manipur
Makkal Needhi Maiam	MNM	2018	Kamal Haasan	Tamil Nadu
Manithaneya Makkal Katchi	MMK	2009	MH Jawahirullah	Tamil Nadu
Marumalarchi Dravida Munnetra Kazhagam	MDMK	1992	Vaiko	Tamil Nadu
Odisha Janmorcha	OJM	2013	Pyarimohan Mohapatra	Odisha
Param Digvijay Dal	PDD	2014	Adhyatmik Neta Krishna Mohan Shankar Yogi	Uttar Pradesh
Peace Party of India	PPI	2008	Mohamed Ayub	Uttar Pradesh
Puthiya Tamilagam	PTK	1996	K Krishnasamy	Tamil Nadu
Rashtriya Samaj Paksha	RSP	2003	Mahadev Jankar	Maharashtra

Rashtriya Ulama Council	RUC	2008	Aamir Rashadi Madni	Uttar Pradesh
Rayalaseema Parirakshana Samithi	RPS	2013	Byreddy Rajasekhar Reddy	Andhra Pradesh
Social Democratic Party of India	SDPI	2009	A Saeed	Delhi, Uttar Pradesh, Rajasthan, Gujarat, Bihar, Madhya Pradesh, Jharkhand, West Bengal, Assam, Manipur, Telangana, Maharashtra, Goa, Andhra Pradesh, Tamil Nadu, Karnataka, Kerala
Tamil Nadu Kongu Ilaingar Peravai	KIP	2001	U Thaniyarasu	Tamil Nadu
Tamil Maanila Congress	TMC	1996	GK Vasan	Tamil Nadu
Uttarakhand Kranti Dal	UKD	1979	Kashi Singh Airy	Uttarakhand
Viduthalai Chiruthaigal Katchi	VCK	1972	Thol Thirumavalavan	Tamil Nadu
Vishva Shakti Party	VSP	2013	Tarun Kothari	Delhi
Welfare Party of India	WPI	2011	SQR Ilyas	Kerala, Tamil Nadu, Karnataka, West Bengal, Gujarat, Rajasthan, Maharashtra
Hindu Sena		2011	Vishnu Gupta	New Delhi

Gorkha National Liberation Front	GNLF	1980	Subhash Ghisingh	West Bengal
Gorkha Janmukti Morcha	GJM	2007	Roshan Giri	West Bengal
Revolutionary Communist Party of India	RCPI	1934	Saumyendra-nath Tagore	Assam
Akhil Bharatiya Gorkha League	ABGL	1943	Bharati Tamang	West Bengal
Praja Socialist Party	PSP	1952		Kerala
Rashtravadi Loktantrik Party	RLP	2018	Manoj Kumar Singh	New Delhi
Swaraj India	SI	2016	Yogendra Yadav	New Delhi, Karnataka
All India Mahila Empowerment Party	MEP	2017	Nowhera Shaik	Telangana, Karnataka
Rani Channamma Party	RCP	2016	MB Desai	Karnataka
Bahujan Azad Party	BAP	2018	50 IIT Alumni	
All Indian Public Freedom Party	AIPFP	2016	V Siva Kumar	Tamil Nadu
Naam Tamilar Katchi	NTK	1958	Senthamizhan Seeman	Tamil Nadu
Peoples Party United	PPU	2013	Ghulam Rasool Doolwal	Jammu and Kashmir
All India Hindustan Congress Party	AIHCP	2015	Buddh Prakash Sharma	Gujarat, Rajasthan, Karnataka, Madhya Pradesh, Chhattisgarh
Indian Gandhiyan Party	IGP	2012	Aashin US	Kerala

Open Source Information

Table 3.4 Recognised Major Regional Parties in India up till 2009

Name of the Party	Year of Formation	State/States
Siromani Akali Dal	December 1920	Punjab/Haryana
All India Forward Bloc	May 1939	West Bengal/Tripura
National Conference	June 1939	Jammu and Kashmir
Revolutionary Socialist Party	March 1940	Tripura/West Bengal
DMK	September 1949	Tamil Nadu
AIADMK	October 1952	Tamil Nadu
AIMIM	March 1958	Andhra Pradesh
Mizo National Front	1961	Mizoram
Maharastrawadi Gomanthak Party	1961	Goa
Kerala Congress	Oct-64	Kerala
Siva Sena	June 1966	Maharastra
Arunachal Congress	Sep-66	Arunachal Pradesh
Manipur Peoples Party	December 1968	Manipur
Jharkhand Mukthi Morcha	1972	Jharkhand/Odisha
Mizoram People's Conference	April 1975	Mizoram
Utharakand Kranti Dal	July 1979	Utharakhand
Sikkim Sangrama Parishad	1979	Sikkim
Kerala Congress (M)	1979	Kerala
Pattali Makkal Katachi	1980	Tamil Nadu
Telugu Desam Party	March 1982	Andhra Pradesh
Assam Gana Parishad	October 1985	Assom
Samajwadi Party	October 1992	Uttar Pradesh
Samta Party	1994	Bihar
MDMK	April 1994	Tamil Nadu
Biju Janata Dal	December 1997	Odisha
Rashtriya Janata Dal	1997	Bihar/UP
All India Trinamool Congress	January 1998	West Bengal
Janata Dal (Secular)	April 1999	Karnataka
Peoples Democratic Party	1999	Jammu Kashmir

Name of the Party	Year of Formation	State/States
Lok Jana Shakthi	2000	Bihar
Telangana Rastra Samithi	2001	Telangana
Janata Dal (United)	October 2003	Bihar/Jharkand
Maharastra Nava Nirmana Sena	March 2006	Maharastra
Jharkand Vikas Morcha	September, 2006	Jharkand
Lok Satta Party	October 2006	Andhra Pradesh
Haryana Janhit Congress	2007	Haryana
Praja Rajyam Party	August 2008	Andhra Pradesh

Source: Compiled from respective Party websites

The growing number and popularity of regional political parties have helped the emergence of a new thinking which admits a positive role that regional political parties can play in the process of nation building, ie. in the realisation of the often-quoted principle of unity in diversity. As can be seen from Tables 3.2 and 3.4, in the last twenty years, at least twenty new parties have come into being.

Registered Unrecognised Regional Parties

A large number of political parties are registered at the Election Commission, without having gained any recognition as national or State parties. In many cases registrations remain, although party in question might have been disbanded or merged into another formation several years ago.

Dominance and Decline of Indian National Congress

Congress in Pre-independence Era

THE ENTRY OF India into modern political arena may be said to be coincident with the founding of the Indian National Congress, on 27 December 1885, by a retired civil servant of the British Administration from Poona, Allan Octavian Hume.[1] He was a British citizen. In 1885, INC was a small body of self-elected men of less than hundred members. In 1886 it consisted of 434 delegates, a year later it was a body of 607 delegates. The emergence of INC, its development and its character has been one of the dominant subjects of modern historiography. In recent years, a number of regional studies have realised that the Congress did not, as was once supposed, represent the interests of any particular class, caste or interest group.[2]

The Indian National Congress was not a political body in the beginning. Long before the emergence of the Congress, there were many social organisations actively working in India for bringing social transformations and effecting sweeping social reforms. In the beginning, the formation of the Indian National Congress was never viewed as congregation of political forces in the country, which might act as an effective political organisation for demanding political rights and liberties. When Lord Dufferin granted permission for the formation of the Indian National Congress, he was aware of the social consciousness which had dawned in India and, by his favourable gesture, he wanted to meet challenges of the elite and to recognise their work in the sphere of social uplift.

The INC promoted social uplift with the support and cooperation of the British and wanted to be a forum for promoting friendly relations among the educated class. A policy of 'break away from England' or instances of political activities was alien to the Congress during the formative period and independence was never clearly outlined officially till 1930. The founder of the INC, AO Hume had unquestionable loyalty towards the English and he could never have dreamt of making India free from British rule. Out of 18 people who held the office of the president of the Congress, besides Hume, there were four Englishmen – George Yule (1888), Sir William Wedderburn (1889), Alfred Webb (1894) and Sir Henry Cotton (1904). They were loyal to the British government in India as their own interests were involved in perpetuation of the rule.

The leaders, who were responsible for shaping the policy and programme of the Congress during first two decades of its existence (1885-1905), came from the higher strata of society and most of them were the products of western education.[3] The year 1905 was remarkable in the history of development of political extremism in the country. Being unmindful of the reactions of the people, Lord Curzon partitioned Bengal into two parts in this year. The extremists provided a new dimension to India's struggle for freedom. The old begging policy of the Congress was rejected by the new generation of leaders like Bal Gangadhar Tilak, Bipin Chandra Pal, Lala Lajpat Rai and Aurbindo Ghose.

The development of extremism in 1905 made the political atmosphere highly vulnerable and the alien rule made it still worse by its unwise action. It failed to solve the economic problems of the people. The nationalists were excluded from attending the Congress convention held on 28 December 1907. The nationalists' convention was held afterwards under the name of the All-India Conference. December 1906 marked the beginning of an open split between the 'old party' of the 'veteran conservatives' and the new party of the nationalists led by Tilak, Lajpat Rai, Bipin Chandra Pal and Aurbindo Ghosh. They held the 22nd session of the Congress in Calcutta.[4] This was the first split in a recognised political outfit in India, where splits today are a part of life. After a long political career of thirty-five years, the INC led the first non-cooperation movement in 1920 under the aegis of Mohandas Karamchand Gandhi, who had just returned to India from South Africa.[5] In 1930, the independence pledge was drawn up, and the party working committee decided to issue the new pledge for independence on 26 January 1938, and described in some detail the moral and material harm done to India by British imperialism.[6]

The Indian National Congress is one of the oldest political organisations in Asia. Like the Republican Party in the USA, it is sometimes called the Grand Old Party, GOP. It was, in fact, a coalition which already in the 1920s influenced the main national regions in the country and large section of the Indian people, office employees, the intelligentsia, workers, peasants, craftsmen, propertied classes and part of the landlords. The INC's dominant position was ensured by its traditional influence on the leading force of the national liberation movement against colonial oppression, and the immense prestige of its leaders like Mahatma Gandhi, Jawaharlal Nehru and others. The Congress, which at that time united diverse classes and social groups of India's multi-structural society in the context of the freedom struggle, should have remained multi-structural in social class's terms also in its new avatar later. During the British period, INC did well under the old constitution, winning 44 of the 88 elected seats in assembly elections held in 1934.

Their greater triumph came in 1937 elections to the new provincial legislative assemblies, when they won 716 out of 1,583 seats having clear majorities in five provinces – Madras, Bihar, Odisha, Central Province and United Province. The INC was also strong in Bombay, Assam and the North-West Frontier Province, though a coalition of opponents could outnumber it. Non-Congress ministries were formed in Bengal, Punjab, Assam and Sind, and throughout this period the constitution functioned in those areas. The new machinery went rapidly into smooth working order, proving more than adequate to its task confirming the commitment of an increasingly wide range of Indian political opinion to this political style.[7]

Congress in Post-independence India

The INC forced the British rulers for freedom of India. On the eve of India's independence (1947), one of the major questions that the INC faced was whether or not the INC, which had successfully, albeit at great cost, won freedom for India, should be dissolved. The question became all the more pressing since Mahatma Gandhi advocated its dissolution. He was apprehensive that the tendency of Congressmen to use state power for advancing their own interest would be further aggravated if the Congress party, which stood for serving the people, undertook the responsibility of managing the affairs of the country. Mahatma Gandhi thought to keep the Congress out of unhealthy competition with political parties and communal bodies and allow it to flower into a 'Lok Sevak Sangh' and work for the social, moral and economic independence of the country in terms of its 700,000 villages. Most of the members of the Congress high command were not convinced of the 'politics' that made Gandhi's advice to disband the Congress party viable. They were also not sure if they could win elections in competition with other political parties and retain the upper hand in 'moulding the destiny of India' which was rooted in this different concept of politics and the role of the state in social transformation.[8]

The post-independence dominance and decline of the Congress focuses on the Congress party, which dominated Indian politics for the first four decades after independence. Post-independence India exhibited a unique phenomenon of resurgence and decline of the Indian National Congress. The vision of a new, economically-developed, socially integrated and politically dynamic India has dimmed in the mist of mounting difficulties. Even today, almost eighty years on, infighting, particularly in the States, always poses a threat to its cohesion and coherence. The key source of strength of the Congress party in all the States and the Centre, under Nehru, was precisely the tolerance the Centre had for local adaptations and adjustments to national policies. Nehru died on 27 May 1964 and an epoch in independent India's history came to a close. A new one opened with India's second Prime Minister taking office. The death of Nehru was marked by an intensification of the struggle for power within the grand old Congress party and mounting concern over its future electoral prospects due to an aggravation of the economic crisis.

The supremacy of the Congress had been a distinguishing feature of India's party system, both before and after the split into Congress (O) and Congress (I). The Congress never faced any real challenge from outside. Even before independence, different political parties or groups existed within the Congress. The Congress Socialist Party (CSP) was formed in 1934 and Subhas Chandra Bose's Forward Bloc was established in 1939. The Communist Party of India (CPI) was formed before independence. During Nehru's period, the only opposition party that assumed office in a State was CPI (1957-59) in Kerala, but it was dismissed from office in the wake of the liberation movement in the State. The Congress dominated a the Indian States till 1967.

The one-party dominant politics of the Indian Natio Congress was weakened at the State level in 1967 gene elections, as Indira Gandhi maneuvered to establish contro over the Congress party (after the death of Lal Bahadur Shastri) as against opposition alliances on the one hand and internal dissidence on the other.[9] Indira Gandhi was elected leader of the Congress parliamentary party on 19 January 1966 after the sudden death of Lal Bahadur Shashtri at Tashkent (USSR). In a straight contest, she defeated Morarji Desai by 355 votes to 169. Eighteen months after Nehru's death his daughter stepped into his shoes. On 24 January 1966, she was sworn in as the third Prime Minister of India.

The fourth general elections in 1967 was fought under the leadership of Indira Gandhi, and this election constituted a watershed in Indian politics. The results of these elections were bad for the Congress party. In several major States, the party was defeated, and in three more States, the party faced defection. The defection game – which the Congress had been playing since independence to weaken the opposition parties – boomeranged on it. Since 1967, the internal Congress conflict became aggravated. Eventually, the Congress broke up on 16 November 1969 when Morarji Desai split. He was elected chairman and formed the separate Congress-O (Organisation) Parliamentary Party, reducing the party to a minority in the Lok Sabha.

Earlier, Morarji Desai was dismissed from the Congress and had resigned from the office of Deputy Prime Minister on 19 July 1969. On the same night, Prime Minister Indira Gandhi had promulgated an ordinance, nationalising 14 commercial banks. Acute policy differences arose between Indira Gandhi and the old guard in the party, the Congress Syndicate group, and this accelerated over the selection of the candidate for the post of the President of the Indian Republic.

On 20 August 1969, Indira Gandhi's candidate, labour leader VV Giri was elected President of India with the combined support of the Left parties, including both the SSP (Samyukta Socialist Party) and the PSP (Praja Socialist Party). Thus, Indira Gandhi defeated Sanjiva Reddy, the official candidate, who was supported by the Congress dissidents (Syndicate) group, the Swatantra Party and the Jana Sangh. On 13 November 1969, the Indian National Congress formally split when Indira Gandhi was expelled by the working committee by a majority of one.

On the issue of Presidential candidate, the Congress Parliamentary Party had in the past, twice acted in defiance of Jawaharlal Nehru's wishes. Rajendra Prasad was a veteran nationalist leader. He was popular with the rank and file of the Congress Parliamentary Party. The names which Nehru sponsored were, comparatively, unacceptable to the Congress Parliamentary Party. C Rajagopalachari had let down the nation in 1942. Radhakrishnan, though an eminent philosopher, came nowhere near Dr Rajendra Prasad in terms of sacrifice. He did not even give up his knighthood as Rabindranath Tagore had done. Nehru was, therefore, unable to disregard the strong sentiment in the Congress party on the issue of Rajendra Prasad's candidature for the office of the president, both in 1950 and 1957.[10]

However, Nehru's position as the Congress leader was unchallenged. He was anointed successor of Mahatma Gandhi.

He suffered neither from a sense of insecurity nor inferiority. He could afford to yield graciously without loss of face. Indira Gandhi's case was different. The Congress Parliamentary Party, in voting her as leader, had voted for the Nehru name. She was the daughter of Jawaharlal Nehru. Her contribution to the building up of the Congress organisation was insignificant. On the other hand, each of the Syndicate bosses had spent his whole lifetime in the service of the Congress. However, they were not attractive figures in the party and no one possessed the charisma which Indira had inherited. Nevertheless, Indira Gandhi, politically, was still an unknown personality. She had yet to prove her capacity for independent leadership.[11]

Regretting SSP's role on that presidential election, veteran SSP leader Madhu Limaye opines that the presidential election had been a great divide. 'I think the SSP made a mistake in committing itself to "Giri" at so early a stage. It should have only reaffirmed its desire for a consensus opposition candidate. But this is being wise after the event. The truth is that nobody knew that Mrs Gandhi would act the way she did. All the middle-of-the-road and progressive parties became victims of Mrs Gandhi's amoral action. The SSP, PSP, BKD, Bangla Congress, CPI, CPI-M, everybody was duped and exploited by Mrs Gandhi. Whether Mrs Gandhi's move was pre-planned or whether it was a gamble suggested by the changing course of alignments in the presidential election and its success is just a windfall which will continue to be debated forever.'[12]

Coming back to Indira's move, the opposition leaders (Jana Sangh leader AB Vajpayee, in particular) repeatedly challenged Indira Gandhi to go to the country. Mrs Gandhi did not relish much the dependence on the CPI, DMK and other small parties' support for her minority government, after the Congress split. She took strong and more popular steps, abolished the privy purses and ICS' privileges and her confrontation with the Judiciary over the privy purses issue brought her mass support and she decided to dissolve the fourth Lok Sabha mid-way, soon after its winter session in 1970,[13] and fresh mid-term elections were held in 1971.

In these elections, Indira's strong current successfully reversed the process of Congress decline by regaining her dominance (and therefore her party's) by capturing a big majority in the Lok Sabha. She was again elected as the Prime Minister. Following India's victory in the Bangladesh war, in the 1972 assembly elections, she snatched all the States from opposition parties and maintained Congress' dominance in Indian politics, which continued for about six years. In June 1975, she imposed a state of Emergency in the country. After twenty months of Emergency, a combined opposition, named as the Janata Party, won the majority seats in the Lok Sabha. The Janata Party emerged due to wide reactions to the Emergency imposed by Indira Gandhi.

The dominance of Congress in Indian politics reduced after its 1969 split, following Lal Bahadur Shastri's death and

Indira's bid for power. In fact, the GOP had been disowned by the entire nation excepting a few loyal-to-Indira southern States. After Emergency, in 1975, the Congress lost the 1977 general elections to a multi-party alliance named Janata Party. In that election, only southern States saved the Congress party from getting vanquished completely. Except for a brief period of Janata Party rule, the Congress, however, remained in India's Central governments till 1989, having returned to power, thanks to a sympathetic votebank, following Indira Gandhi's assassination. While it had vacated the space in some important regions of India, the opposition parties realised in 1989 that their struggle against the Congress had just begun.

Emergence of Janata Party, First Non-Congress Government

After the elections of 1977, held under the leadership of Jayaprakash Narayan, the first non-Congress government was formed at the Centre with Morarji Desai as Prime Minister. With Indira defeated at the hustings, the Congress, now a headless chicken, suffered a further serious blow when senior leaders such as Jagjivan Ram, Nandini Satpathy and HN Bahuguna deserted it and formed a new outfit, the 'Congress For Democracy' (CFD).

Just before these polls, on the initiative of Jayaprakash Narayan, the Janata Party was formed in January 1977 with the merger of the Congress (O), Jana Sangh, Bharatiya Lok Dal (BLD) and Socialist Party. With this coalition at the Centre, the

State-level parties were for the first time seriously exposed to national issues that needed decision-making as members of the union government. At the same time, the bigger national level parties got a taste of politics in the distant States, played often at much lower levels. Regionalisation of Indian politics was perhaps inevitable when the politically all-pervasive Congress system appeared to have lost its all-India appeal.

Coalition politics in India did not have an easy birth. At the very outset, the Janata Party coalition suffered a crisis when there arose a question as to who would become the Prime Minister. There were three aspirants – Morarji Desai, Charan Singh and Jagjivan Ram. However, with the intervention of Jayaprakash Narayan (JP) and JB Kripalani, the issue was resolved with Desai being chosen by the octogenarian leaders because not only was he age-wise senior among the three but was the most experienced administrator as well.[14]

The Janata Party government was the product of Emergency imposed when the Allahabad High Court judgement on an election petition by the socialist leader Raj Narain convicted Indira Gandhi and declared her election 'invalid' for having indulged in corrupt practices. The High Court judgement and the Gujarat poll results gave Indira the fillip to impose the state of Emergency on the nation. The Emergency was promulgated under Article 352 of the Constitution to provide legality as further deterioration of the law and order situation in the country had to be stymied.

During Emergency, the senior opposition leaders were arrested, strict censorship on the press was imposed and fundamental rights were suspended. During this period, nearly 111,000 people had been detained under the Maintenance of Internal Security Act (MISA) and the Defence of India Act. Only under MISA 35,000 individuals were detained of whom only 13,000 were related to political parties or banned organisations. The overall purpose of such large-scale arrests and banning a number of organisations was, obviously, to silence all opposition.[15] However, India had not seen such country-wide detentions after independence, and a shocked nation, for the first time realised the value of democracy and the power a vote wielded. The Janata experiment soon failed, and its government fell within two years due to internal bickering and ideological incompatibilities based on group loyalties of yesteryears. The constituent units never really ceased to exist within the party (Janata Party). The first of the failure was due to individual bickering and the Jana Sangh's dual membership of the RSS (the Rashtriya Swayamsevak Sangh). This led to a serious crisis when both, the BLD and the Socialists, decided to leave the coalition. The defecting group and one of the founders of Janata Party, BLD, formed a minority government at the Centre with the outside support of the Congress Party. But the BLD leader, Chaudhary Charan Singh, (who was more a regional satrap rather than a national leader), failed to face the Lok Sabha a single day as Indira Gandhi withdrew her party's support from Charan Singh's government and the 6th Lok Sabha was dissolved in August 1979. Clearly, in the early days of coalition politics, a two-party system failed to find root in India.

Return of the Congress

General elections were held for the 7th Lok Sabha in 1980. In these elections, one party's dominance, under Indira Gandhi, came back with a thumping majority in the Lok Sabha. For the first time since independence, the Indian Congress fought the election in the name of Congress (I), ie. Indira, in 1980. Her new symbol, the hand, emphasised stability. Indira smoothly ran her government till 1984. A series of dramatic events took place in 1984 with the 'Operation Blue Star' action against Sikh militants entrenched in the Golden Temple at Amritsar. Reaction to this strong-man action was Indira's assassination later in the year (31 October 1984) by two of her Sikh body guards. Thereafter, the Congress (I) elected her elder son Rajiv Gandhi as the new Prime Minister of India. The sympathy wave propelled her son Rajiv to a four-fifths Lok Sabha majority in the December 1984 elections. With a historical majority in the Lok Sabha, Rajiv Gandhi dominated the country till 1989. These five years leapfrogged India into the technological era, although Rajiv was believed to be politically naïve.

The position of dominance of the Congress (I) was changed abruptly, as the 1989 elections drew near. Charges of corruption, true or not, provided new content to the short hand expression 'Congress Culture' in high place.[16] The allegations had a certain amount of credibility as they came from personalities like VP Singh, themselves standing on a high moral pedestal. It was a current the 'Mr Clean' Rajiv did not know how to stem. The corruption issue involved in the alleged payment of commission to secure the contract for guns, manufactured by the Swedish company Bofors, was exposed in the press and Parliament. VP Singh, a former cabinet colleague of Rajiv Gandhi, played a crucial role in giving a sharp edge to the fight against this corruption issue and resigned from the cabinet only to mount a fearless attack on corruption in high place.

Appearance of National Front

The National Front (NF) made its appearance on the Indian political scene in October 1988. The idea of such a front was first voiced when on the occasion of JP's birth anniversary, on 11 October, the Janata Dal was formed with the merger of the Jan Morcha, Congress (s), Janata Party and Lok Dal. Later, with the BJP as partner, it became the National Front. The Janata Dal-led National Front and the BJP agreed not to contest against each other in about eighty-five per cent of the Lok Sabha seats. The 1989 general elections results were unexpected for Rajiv Gandhi-led Congress party. With only 197 out of 539 Lok Sabha seats, Rajiv gave up his claim to form the government and the stage was set for the National

Front to stake its claim. With 146 Lok Sabha seats, the National Front secured a majority with outside support of BJP, with its 86 members in the Lok Sabha, and the left parties, with 52 members. Arithmetically, the front was well placed with 284 seats in the House of 539.

Apart from the anti-Congress stand, no parallel can be drawn between the sixth national poll in 1977 and the ninth national elections in '89. The regional parties that challenged the Congress electorally maintained their regional profile even within the National Front by paying equal attention to region-specific issues that had catapulated them to power in the States. By adopting a two-pronged strategy to highlight both the national and regional issues, the regional parties devised a political agenda to sustain their claims both at the national and State level. One can say, this was the beginning of the phase in Indian politics, when coalition politics began to mature.

Notwithstanding its pan-Indian identity, the BJP also agreed to pay attention to regional issues, presumably to sustain its organisational base in the provinces. The national issue was corruption which forced Congress to leave the government to opposition parties. VP Singh replaced Rajiv Gandhi as 'Mr Clean' and almost created a new 'catch all' political party and became a highly popular leader of a new opposition grouping – though for a very short time. Two important issues, however, made the 1989 elections significant. The Congress was ousted from power for the second time since the 1952 elections, and secondly for the first time, India came to be governed by a minority government representing the political parties that constituted an alternative force.

The dramatic decline in Congress' parliamentary seats was illustrative of a shift from a majority Congress to a minority non-Congress national government. The opposition mobilised the electorates primarily around issues of corruption, rising prices and the perceived ineffective leadership of Rajiv Gandhi. Another noteworthy trend is that since 1989, whenever the Congress has won a seat, it has won with less than 50 per cent of the vote, the opposition candidate in every constituency has played havoc with Congress' electoral fortunes. In 1989, there was a small but significant decline in Congress' normal level of support and the opposition (National and Regional parties) cashed in on the situation by fielding one-on-one contests, across India.

Mandalisation, countered by Hindutva forces on the streets, prevented Singh's caste strategy from succeeding as a national policy. As PM, he was attempting to implement a long-dormant Mandal Commission's Recommendations on caste reservations, which unleashed a storm of protest. Religion in large measure trumped caste as a political tactic. The BJP, which had facilitated the formation of the National Front, brought it to its feet in a year's time.

In 1990, under the leadership of BJP, a nation-wide movement mobilised Hindu supporters behind the call for a

Ram Mandir in Ayodhya, where a 16th century mosque stood at the site of a temple where the popular Hindu deity Ram was supposed to have been born several thousand years ago. LK Advani, a senior leader of the BJP, personally led a Rathyatra from Gujarat to Kanyakumari to promote the cause of the mandir. His arrest by the Bihar Janata Dal government, led by Lalu Yadav, at Samastipur, contributed to the withdrawal of BJP's outside support to the VP Singh government in 1990.

Congress Comeback and Start of Segmentary Politics

The UP leader Chandra Shekhar of the Samajwadi Janata Party became India's 8th Prime Minister in November 1990, following VP Singh government's fall. While Singh was supported by the BJP, Chandra Shekhar was supported by the Congress. This is when it started becoming clear that there were two king-makers emerging, the BJP and the Congress. The Congress, from being king realised that all was not lost yet and moved to become the fiddler very quickly. Within six months, the Congress withdrew its outside support to the Chandra Shekhar government in March. The mid-term Lok Sabha elections began in May 1991. Earlier all elections were held in the month of November. Timings changed with the 10th election to Parliament. Earlier, the general elections were held on the same day for the entire country. In this election, the polling was held in three phases. No elections were held in Jammu and Kashmir and Punjab, a total of 19 Lok Sabha seats in a House of 545. On 20 May, the first phase of voting took place. On 21 May, Rajiv Gandhi, campaigning in Sriperumbudur, was assassinated. The 12 and 15 June voting immediately saw a sympathy swivel for the Congress. Yet, in these elections, the Congress (I) failed to get a clear majority.

Since independence, India has been largely monopolised by the Nehru-Gandhi family. Rajiv Gandhi's position, as Congress leader, may not have been totally secure, but until his assassination in 1991, the possible challenges to his supremacy in the party remained unclear. Rajiv did not have much knowledge about the party and its senior leaders even after remaining general secretary for more than three years and Prime Minister and party president for five years.[17]

In 1991, the Congress sans Rajiv got 227 seats and PV Narasimha Rao became the 11th Prime Minister of India with the support of the AIADMK, Muslim League, Kerala Congress (Mani), Janata Dal (Gujarat) and Sikkim Sangram Parishad. Rao led the minority government, also obtaining support from TDP and Jharkhand Mukti Morcha (JMM). The regional parties now began to assume great importance in national politics and for the GOP. Though he lost credibility in December 1992, when the mosque in Ayodhya, known as the Babri Masjid, was demolished by Hindu mobs, somehow Rao pulled the first minority government of the Congress to a full span of five years.

Coalition becomes Fashionable

The coalitional tendency first appeared at the States level in 1967, when the Congress rule continued at the national level with reduced dominance. The Congress party led by Nehru was a much more institutionalised party, organisational elections were held and federally segmented from the work of power in the sense that the Congress chief ministers of that period enjoyed greater regional or federal autonomy. In the Indira and Rajiv Gandhi period (1966-1991), for quarter of a century, the Congress dispensed with internal organisational elections and turned the party into a pack of personal followers and dynastic loyalists. Besides, the State parties were turned into neo-patrimonial entities, with even the chief ministers nominated by the so-named 'high-command' – from the top rather than they being a representation of the structure of interests and opinions in the State legislatures. Only those in the good books of Indira-Rajiv could become State chief ministers, not the one the State party chose.

The decline of the Congress dominance did not result in the immediate dominance by an alternative party. Instead, a heterogeneous set of parties replaced the Congress. Broadly speaking, three or four types of parties filled the spaces vacated by the Congress. The Left parties, Janata Party, Janata Dal and a few others. In the 1990s, the Congress suffered hopeless fragmentation, when the BJP and some regional parties tried to fill the spaces vacated by the Congress.[18]

The Congress split in November 1969 was the result of polarisation between younger socialist radicals and the older conservative party bosses.[19]

The tenure of Indira Gandhi had suffered from the pulls and pushes of regional aspirations, as appendages tried to handle local problems. The results were the emergence of separatist movements in Punjab and the northeast and alienation of the people of Jammu and Kashmir, after Farooq Abdullah was dismissed in 1984. Because of such types of disruptive Congress tactic, non-Congress parties began to work together. Castes as the category of political mobilisation, never absent from the Indian scenario, came to the centre stage. This is how, since the 1990s, the Congress rapidly fell to a position where it had to face most trials and tribulations in its long chequered political history, which began in 1885.

The Congress was the most important single political institution in India displaying most of the important features of Indian political life and in a great measure determining the course of Indian politics.[20] It was the party that had struggled for national freedom and the factions within it subordinated their sectional and regional interests to the goal of national independence, because it was a necessity. So, the Congress proudly claimed that legacy, placing under the carpet the history that Gandhi had wanted the party dissolved, fearing corruption in its leaders.

While the Akali Dal, CPI, DMK, TDP emerged outside

of the Congress party, Swatantra Party, Bharatiya Lok Dal, Bharatiya Kisan Dal and the Janata Party were formed by the leaders who were initially connected with the erstwhile Congress. At the regional level also, many parties were the outcome of the factional struggle within the Congress. All parties at national level emerged after independence, except INC, and the Communist Party which was formed in 1925.[21]

Before independence, the party system in India was characterised by an identifiable centre, which was represented only by the INC. The Indian National Congress was the only party which had developed nationwide organisation and leadership. After independence, INC promised nationwide party reforms and for this it enjoyed massive support in the rural areas of some States and regions. In urban areas, the Congress faced main opposition from the Communist Party, Praja Socialist, Jana Sangh and other small and regional parties.[22] For about two decades after independence, the political discourse on caste was dominated by the left-radical parties, liberal modernist and intellectuals who saw some naive changes in the hoary caste system as suggesting its transformation into a system of polarised economic classes.

The Emergency crashed the dream of the rich principle of India's democracy. It was declared in the early hours of 26 June 1975 and became a marker for the so-far most severe setback in the political evolution of India. The rule of law was drastically compromised. The unchallenged leadership of Indira Gandhi gave her an exaggerated sense of power, and Congressmen began to depend on Indira Gandhi's charisma rather than on their own work among the people. Emergency was a major watershed in the contemporary history of India.

The emergency regime not only generated a new political sensibility toward parliamentary democracy and the question of democratic right in the country, but it also gave rise to, and in certain cases renewed, the demand for regional autonomy and re-drafting of Centre-State relations in the context of India's multi-linguistic nationality scenario. The re-emergence and consolidation of regional parties in opposition to the Congress is a significant aspect of the post-Emergency political reality.[23] In the immediate aftermath of the Emergency, power brokers and national parties engineered setting up and toppling of Central governments like a game of nine pins. Post-Rajiv, this was no longer possible.

The decade of 1990s and the beginning of the 21st century have witnessed growing fragmentation of society because India's political class has openly taken recourse to sectarian social mobilisation. The all-catch party politics is challenged by sectional and segmentary party politics.[24] The dominant role of the Congress party and its internal coherence has gradually declined. The ascendance of new leaders, organisations and definitions of interests and their national implications have found a more valued voice in the progressively maturing institutions and procedures of the wider political system. Also, with a more sophisticated votebank.

The Big Picture

All the national elections of the 1990s, even including the one in 1991, made the weak Congress come back. But, more and more decisively the 1998 and 1999 Congress electoral setbacks registered a clean message of change that made this transforming promise more credible. If the 1996, 1998 and 1999 elections leading to multi-party governments made the political centre look weaker compared to the early Congress-dominance years, actually, the increasing confidence of the regional voices speaking for the nation must have contributed a new measure of coherence to the nation as a whole. At the same time, in the 1996, 1998 and 1999 general elections, the BJP's national stature was rising and that of the Congress steadily falling. The more important fact was that neither party could ignore the compulsion of combination with regional parties. The fact of the matter is, the BJP managed to retain an overall unity in a more coherent way during and after the 1999 elections than its Congress counterpart did.

On the eve of the 1999 general elections, the revolt of the Maharashtra strongman Sharad Pawar, against Sonia Gandhi's leadership in May 1999, was symptomatic of the deeper problems that faced the Congress since 1967. It had so long ignored the fact that it needed to include regional leaders who represented the emerging forces. These alone could appeal to the region-based, vernacular-speaking, rural but rapidly urbanising lower caste groups.

The Congress still enjoyed a distinct advantage over sectional and regional parties. It was still a party that managed to garner the largest amount of support from the underprivileged. Congress leaders had undertaken such moves at a provincial and national level in the past. This emerged clearly in the early 1930s, when Mahatma Gandhi negotiated with the Dalit leader BR Ambedkar to create the system of joint electorates. In a similar vein, despite his own inclinations against linguistic units, Nehru eventually acquiesced in the creation of linguistic States in much of the peninsular and western India. For a long period, from around 1920s when it was re-shaped by Mahatma Gandhi till the end of the Indira-Rajiv period in 1989, the Congress was able to evolve with the times. It was the first pressure group to spearhead a mass movement. The party remained in office in seven provinces of British India for a couple of years (1937-39). It was at the head of an uneasy compromise during the British-led interim government (1946-47), and eventually became the party that led the first government of free India. Its attitude towards popular upsurges were simultaneously those of containment and that of assertion of its leadership role.[25]

One major change since the days of Indira and Rajiv Gandhi was the rise of anti-Congressism that has a substantial base in at least half of the States in the Indian union. In the case of both Rajiv Gandhi and Narasimha Rao, a five years spell in office was followed by the erosion of the Congress' own base. In both instances, it was the BJP that was a direct beneficiary, initially as a result of anti-Congress alliances and later from around 1999 with its ability to by itself redefine the parameters of politics. In 1996, 1998 and 1999 general elections, the BJP had the largest number of MPs in the Lok Sabha. It was able to expand its core votes to one in five voters. From the mid-1990s, it had managed to turn the ears of anti-Congress segments or regional parties to its ideological appeal for a coalition government. Congress is a grand old party, it may regain its 1970s, 1980s votebank but its politics in UP and Bihar will decide its performance in the future.

The Congress party has declined due to the alienation of traditional social constituencies and fragmentation of India's electoral mass along the lines of social justice and cultural nationalism. Another important factor in the Congress party's decline has been the reduction in intra-party coalition and centralism in the party, leading to non-accommodation of the demands of new social-cultural groups. These patterns are also evident in the emergence and fragmentation of the Janata Dal and also in the multiple fragmentations of many other parties which have since emerged as region-specific parties in UP, Bihar, Odisha, West Bengal, Maharashtra etc.[26]

On the basis of the 1999 Lok Sabha elections, India's Election Commission has determined that there are seven national parties, and over fifty regional and State parties. The major parties can be broadly categorised into the right wing, centrist and left-wing parties, the right wing parties in electoral politics are the BJP and Shiv Sena, the centrist parties are the Congress and the Janata Dal. Since 1991, the Congress has shifted its position to right-of-the centrist by introducing neo-liberal economic reforms with emphasis on market forces. The left-wing parties are the CPI, CPI(M), Forward Bloc and the RSP. This is the basic structure today of Indian political parties with their respective politics and programmes.[27]

The Indian National Congress, which was the party of Mahatma Gandhi, Jawaharlal Nehru, Sardar Patel etc, was India's party of governments since independence till 1996 (except the brief periods of 1977-79 Janata Party and 1989-90 Janata Dal rule). It governed India after eight parliamentary elections – that was following the 1952, 1957, 1962, 1967, 1971, 1980, 1984, and 1991 general elections. Since 1996, it had to sit on the opposition benches and it was only after the 2004 general elections that it became a ruling party once again. But this time, it governed India with a coalition system with other regional parties and outside support of the Communist parties. In particular, the Congress has faced sharp decline from the 1996 elections onwards.[28]

Since 1984 Lok Sabha elections, a single-party majority does not seem possible in India any longer, a combination of parties will continue to rule at the Centre. *Ideology appears to play insignificant role as partners are mostly selected not on the basis of ideological compatibility, but due to realistic seat and power calculations.* With the fragmentation and regionalisation of the party system in the coalition era, the inter-party alliance has obviously assumed significance in holding or breaking winning coalitions.

Didactic Dilemmas

According to a 1998 declaration, the Congress did not favour the idea of allying with other parties to form a government at the Centre. In the Panchmarhi conclave, the then leader of the party, Sonia Gandhi, said that 'coalition politics was a passing phase' and the Congress would come back again with full force and on its own strength. However, after Congress' sharp decline, the party thought it wise to join coalition politics for its survival. Within six years, in May 2004, the Congress formed its first coalition government at the Centre which was named as UPA (United Progressive Alliance). This government was led by Manmohan Singh, under the chairmanship of Sonia Gandhi. The Congress-led alliance was formed prior to the elections.

The decline of the Congress is, in many ways, the story of Indian politics in the 1990s. The decline has been swift and decisive. Inspite of the party's slippery position, its leadership did not realise the importance of coalition politics. The Congress considered these regional parties and forces as threat to the survival of India as a nation-state. The 1967 general elections marked the beginning of the end of the Congress dominance and show the emergence of the first non-Congress governments in the States.The Congress suffered significant losses in 7 States which included: Gujarat where it won 11 out of 24 seats while Swatantra Party won 12 seats. Madras where Congress won 3 out of 39 seats and DMK won 25 seats. Odisha where it won 6 out of 20 seats and Swatantra Party won 8 seats. Rajasthan where the Congress won 10 out of 20 seats and Swatantra Party won 8 seats. West Bengal where Congress won 14 out of 40. Kerala where it won only 1 out of 19. In Delhi, the Centre's seat of power, the Congress won 1 out of 7 seats while remaining 6 were won by the Bharatiya Jana Sangh. The decline in support for Congress was also reflected by the fact it lost control of six State governments in the same year.

The year 1989 marked the total collapse of the Congress dominance and it never recovered afterwards. The Congress wanted to come to power on its own in the 2004 Lok Sabha elections. Ultimately it realised that it could not do so and hence had to make an alliance with 14 parties.

POWER HUNGRY COALITIONS

Dawn of the Coalition Era in Indian Politics

Ending One-Party Rule

PARLIAMENTARY AND PRESIDENTIAL democracies in modern India can function only with the presence of political parties. Constitutionally, India is a quasi-federal structure with a parliamentary form of government. The heterogeneous nature of Indian society and the complexity of problems it faces has nurtured a large number of political parties at the national, regional and local level. For over five decades since independence, there has emerged a number of political parties with very little ideological difference.

In India, the coalitions and minority governments are the

outcome of the failure of the parliamentary system to satisfy the norm of getting the absolute majority of seats in the lower House (Lok Sabha) to form the government. This means, out of the **total 545 seats** in Lok Sabha, one party **has to win 271 seats** at least. Out of these, 2 members are nominated from the Anglo-Indian community. A just-majority after election is when you have 1 more than half of the total seats to be elected (543). Since 1989, no single party has succeeded in winning a comfortable majority in the House except in the 2014 parliamentary elections, when the BJP secured 282 seats by itself. In 2014 elections, BJP-led NDA claimed a historic victory when it secured 336 seats (including 282 of BJP) in coalition.

When we take the Indian National Congress as a 'National Movement' in the freedom struggle, we find it representing variety of interests, classes, communities and castes. However, the sole aim of the Indian National Congress, during the pre-independence days, was to achieve freedom for India. As and when that aim was achieved, the Congress transformed itself into a political party to take up the challenge of running responsible governments at the Centre as well as the States.

India had a period of stable governments at the Centre despite all the social and economic problems, primarily because of certain charismatic leaders like Sardar Patel, Rajendra Prasad, Jawaharlal and Indira Gandhi who were supported by a galaxy of selfless leaders like Lal Bahadur Shastri, Kamaraj, Chavan and so on. Now such charismatic personalities are small in number, what we have is what Churchill calls 'men of straw' who are supported by a team of professional politicians, some of whom are downright villains.

During the uninterrupted rule of Jawaharlal Nehru, which lasted for about a period of 16 years, the Congress enjoyed monopoly in power both at the Centre and in various States. The charismatic personality of Nehru with his magnetic power to attract people at home and abroad brought India to an enviable position in political circles. The death of Nehru was a shock to the people and the Congress Party. Surprisingly, more than 50 years old, the party had not prepared for a time without Nehru.The gap created then was, to a certain extent, filled by his daughter Indira Gandhi. But the process of degeneration of the Congress party started during her tenure and it culminated in the break-up of the party during her time. The disintegration of the Congress party resulted in the winding up of the one-party dominant system as commonly described, paving the way for the mushroom growth of political parties. The emergence of a multi-party system creating new dimensions for the structure and functions of governments in the Indian political space began.

The framers of our Constitution consciously adopted the British model of parliamentary democracy with a cabinet government, with its attendant concept of collective responsibility, as best suited to the conditions of India. Coalition is a direct descendant of the exigencies of a multi-party system in a democratic set up. It is a phenomenon of a multi-party government where a number of minority parties join hands for the purpose of running the government, which is otherwise not possible in a democracy based on a one-party system. A coalition government is framed where many political parties in a House agree to join hands on a common platform by striking down their broad differences and form a majority in the House. It is an astonishing chorus of discords.

The term coalition has been derived from the Latin word 'coalition', meaning to grow together. Thus interpreted, the term coalition means an act of coalescing or uniting into one body or alliance. It indicates the combination of a number of bodies or parts into one body or whole. In the political sense, the term coalition is used for an alliance or temporary union between various political groups for the exercise or control of political power. Prof Ogg, in the *Encyclopedia of Social Science,* defines it as the cooperative arrangement under which distinct political parties or all members of such parties unite to form a Government or Ministry.[1] A coalition is thus an alliance between two or more hitherto separate or even hostile groups or parties formed in order to carry on the business of government and share the principle offices of the state. A coalition government is formed when more than one political party or group come together on the basis of common understanding or agenda. Thus, the government can have a framework within which all parties function.

The emergence of coalition governments has become a

world-wide phenomenon. Although the coalition's nature, composition, life expectancy etc. vary from country to country, depending on particular political circumstances, the basic reasons for the rising popularity of a coalition remain more or less the same.

However, there are generally three types of situations which give rise to the emergence of coalition government. Firstly, when a single party is not in a position to form the government, then it joins with other political parties and forms the government. This is a phenomenon of a multi-party system. Secondly, when there arise differences between the two political parties. Under such circumstances, one party makes compromise with any minor group such as neutrals or defectors and forms the government. Finally, a national crisis or war gives rise to coalition government.

The first type of situation is found most frequently in Europe. This trend is also found in many States of India, ie. in Kerala, West Bengal, Uttar Pradesh, Rajasthan, Odisha and Bihar. The second and third types are most commonly found in the history of Britain, a classic land of bi-party system.

In a parliamentary democracy, coalitions arise mainly as a result of political compulsion. Coalition might result from racial, communal, religious, economic, social or political conflicts. It may also be formed due to a national emergency. The policies that are adopted by the coalition government are made by the coalescing parties and merely finalised by the leader of the coalition. In a conflictual coalition game, each party opposes every other party and each party seeks its own maximum ministerial advantage.

Rooted in Swaraj

The roots of coalition politics in India can be traced back to the nationalist movement, especially to the Gandhian conceptualisation of Swaraj. Gandhi avoided the idiom of nationalism since he was aware that the Congress' flirtations with nationalist ideas in the first quarter of the twentieth century repelled not only the Muslims and other minorities, but also sections of lower-caste Hindus.

Yet, nationalism appears to be the most pragmatic idea conceivable for a country such as India, which is united in terms of religions, race, culture and common historical memories of oppression and struggle. Although the 1947 Great Divide of the Indian sub-continent was articulated in terms of religion, the nationalist language, drawing upon the exclusivity of Islam which appeared inadequate for sustaining Pakistan, resulted in the creation of Bangladesh in 1971.

The first instance of 'Coalition Government' in India began with the British regime, when under the leadership of Jawaharlal Nehru an 'Interim Government' was formed with the Muslim League, on 2 September 1946, with Liaquat Ali Khan as Finance Minister.

In independent India, after the third general elections, Ram

Manohar Lohia emerged as the most staunch supporter and leader of 'coalition politics'. Time and again he remarked, 'the unchallenged leadership of Congress Party in the past general elections is the mere outcome of lack of unity of non-Congress political parties in the country'.[2] The success of the Congress system was attributed to its 'central role in maintaining and re-structuring political consensus'. The system continued almost uninterrupted till 1967 elections, when non-Congress governments came to power in several States introducing a new trend of coalition politics in India. The transition toward a new party system is not a sudden development but the cumulative end product of changes taking place over time and shifts in the party system since the mid-1980s. More specifically, it arises out of the decline and breakdown of the Congress in the 1980s, and parallel process of regionalisation of politics and consequently of the party system that has operated since independence.

Shift in India's Political System after 1989

Since 1989, a set of coalitions and minority governments in New Delhi is an important aspect of the paradigmatic shift that then occurred in the Indian political system, in terms of political federalisation and economic liberalisation in the 1990s. The coalition and minority governments at the Centre appeared after a long spell of Congress dominance. Although, coalition governments at the Centre formally began in 1989 and have continued, but the Janata Party (1977-79) in New Delhi also was a de facto coalition. The decade (1989-99) featured a series of unstable coalitions and minority governments, following each other like a game of musical chairs.

Among these governments, the one headed by PV Narasimha Rao (1991-1996) eventually turned into a single-party minority government as a result of internal parliamentary re-alignments and elections in the State of Punjab. It also lasted its full term, although it had to struggle for its survival against a parliamentary vote of no confidence. The end of Congress party dominance and the lack of a clear single party majority after the assassination of Indira Gandhi, in December 1984, ushered in an era of coalition politics in the context of a fragmented party system. The growth and increased prominence of State-based or regional parties introduced a new element in the working of the federal system.

Ending One-Party Rule

Indian society is moving in the direction of social fragmentation on the basis of identity and sub-identity politics and multiple political parties for the representation of social identity and segmentary interests of diverse social groups have been established to participate in politics. It is logical that the ongoing process of fragmentation of the society is accelerating the process of fragmentation and multiplication of parties also. It was not without reason that the BJP-led NDA (1999-2004) had as many as 24 constituent parties and groups with a purely regional party like the TDP of Andhra Pradesh extending support to the BJP-led NDA from 'outside'. These Lok Sabha elections had been contested by forty-five parties and groups.

The fragility of such alliances of 'opportunism' became clear when Mamata Banerjee, or Ram Vilas Paswan walked out mid-way from the NDA, George Fernandes was made to quit on the *Tehelka* episode but later brought back to the NDA council of Ministers. The DMK had extended full support to the Vajpayee-led NDA government but walked out midway because it felt that the NDA government had not proved beneficial to the party in the following elections in the State because every State has its own diverse political reality.

In the 2004 Congress-led UPA government at the Centre, DMK was a major ally of the coalition. A pretentious philosophy propounded by the contemporary politicians is that there can be no permanent friends or permanent enemies in politics or there is nothing right or wrong in politics.[3] In the emergence of coalition politics in India, the party system transformation from one-party dominance to a multi-party configuration is at least one desirable consequence. The regionalisation of the party system has articulated the federal features of the Indian political system that had remained suppressed during the Congress dominance. Some influential sections of political opinion have painted a rather gloomy picture of India's experiments with coalition and have expressed conviction that the only answer now lies in the total restructuring of the Constitution so as to usher in a second Republic.

In the current situation, the roots of coalition politics can be traced to India's immense social and regional diversities and the decline of the one and only Congress party dominance. Coalition governments in India have by and large remained stable under conditions of polarisation of parties in a coalition with a dominant partner.[4] India has four types of coalition: right-dominated, left-dominated, centre-dominated and amorphous. In India, regional parties in coalition politics and governments have become players of a game of selfish, opportunist, power hungry and unscrupulous politicians who look after nothing but their personal interests.[5]

Politics of Opportunism

The regional political parties and their coalition politics have resulted in furthering the criminalisation of politics. The problems of persons with criminal records entering the electoral politics and through them, the representative bodies, have received a big boost with the proliferation of regional political parties. The national parties have no control over who gets a regional party Parliament seat ticket to contest. Coalition politics has given criminal politicians a national exposure at the cost of the credibility of the political system. Today, there are several leaders who are playing important roles in the regional and national politics and have some or other criminal cases pending against them.

Coalition politics has helped in spreading the malady of political corruption much more comprehensively throughout the Indian political system with the help of regional parties.[6] Regional political parties do not give up their parochial approach and therefore, are narrow in their outlook. These regional parties tend to get support through populism. In this system, power shifts from the Centre to the States. All regional partners of the coalition have their priority agendas and there is no national agenda. As a result, the States tend to become strong and the Centre becomes weak and often practices policy captive to the needs of coalition partners.[7] A case in point would be the DMK-BJP partnership of 1999-2003, when the regional partner managed to steer the digging of the Sethu Samudram sea canal despite the BJP's reservations regarding digging up the Ram Sethu, a holy Hindu religious symbol and pilgrimage site at exorbitant costs to the national exchequer and the environment. For the Congress, alliance with the same DMK has resulted in the burden of the 2G scam.

Under the influence of self-seeking politicians, coalition politics becomes vulnerable to opportunism, inefficiency and depravity. As they shift loyalties of their respective parties only under personal, selfish and narrow consideration, the stability of the coalition government and parliamentary democracy itself may be put in danger. It is vulnerable to the excessive personalisation of politics, apart from relegation of ideology and political ethics to the background. *One of the most important drawbacks of the coalition system is that it is the worst manipulator of the popular mandate. Coalition politics and the influence of the regional parties, in the process of forming the government, often undermine the mandate given by the people.*[8]

The *mandate theory* differs from situation to situation. The US mandate theory is not applicable in India. The British theory is equally irrelevant, since we do not have a two-party system yet. European practices differ from country to country.[9]

India is a multi-party democracy. The multi-party system in India is adopted by the Representation of People Act 1951; but now the party system for parliamentary democracy is significantly recognised by various statutory provisions and the tenth schedule of the Constitution of India, which was inserted in 1985. The tenth schedule regulates in detail the situations arising from splits and defections. The Representation of the People (Amendment) Act of 1988 also gives statutory recognition to the political party system, when it provides for registration of political parties with the Election Commission. A party may be registered as 'National Party' or 'State Party' or 'Unrecognised Party'.[10]

Political parties are the very lifeblood of democracy. The multi-party parliaments predominate in western parliamentary democracies. They constitute over 75 per cent of all peace time parliaments, formed from 1918 to 1974. There is no parliamentary regime that has not experienced multi-party politics.[11] In India, the presence of a large number of political parties always provide the possibility of the emergence of coalition governments, yet it could not take place so long as the Indian National Congress continued occupying the Indian political space.

The Indian National Congress which spearheaded the freedom struggle for independence automatically became the major ruling party during the transfer of power. It remained as all-India dominant party till 1967. In the post-independence period covering more than three decades, one finds that it dominated Indian politics since 1952 to 1967 in the States, (except in Kerala, 1957-59). The election of 1967 was a kind of watershed for the Congress party because the party got defeated in important States of the Indian union. For the first time, the non-Congress parties got an opportunity to assume office in many States and it struck home that the Congress was not invincible, nor could the States be ignored any longer.

The period from 1967 to 1977 witnessed the passage from one-party dominance to multi-party politics. Several States have moved towards a two-party system, though the two parties vary from State to State. In Kerala, government is either Congress-led or Left-led. In Bengal, it is Left-led or Trinamool-led. In UP it is BJP-led or SP/BSP-led. This change, since 1989 elections, may mark the beginning of a new era in the party system.

Caste and Class Politics

Political development over the last decade of the 20th century makes it clear that Indian politics now has a strong lower class thrust. This development is a result of the increased influence of regional and State-based parties and mirrors the paradigm shift in politics. They have increased their vote share to 8-9 per cent of the popular vote. Two factors have contributed to the multiplication of parties. One has been the growing power of regionalism and regional parties, and the other, the intensified pursuit of political power rather than disagreement over any principle. This explains the fracturing of the Janata Dal in 1999, the formation of the NCP on the eve of the 1999 general elections in Maharashtra and the splits in the Congress and BSP in UP in 1998.

The leadership of the Janata Dal forced a disintegration of the party. This had an adverse impact on all its constituents who lost heavily in the bargain. In the pursuit of this power game, the JD had given birth to a few more regional parties, making national politics much more complex. The demise of the JD had, for instance, shifted the votes to the share of SP, RJD, Lok Janshakti, JD (U), JD (S) and Biju Janata Dal. State power is seen now as favouring castes and communities. Social status has a crucial role in gaining political power. So, today, the fight for power is a battle of the castes.

The intensification of competitive politics changed the party system from being a rivalry between national parties and regional parties. The nineties witnessed a succession of minority or coalition governments. The coalition governments were formed in 1989, 1990, 1996, 1997, 1998, 1999 and 2004-

2009 by several political parties. From 1989 to 1999 eight governments were formed. Many small parties have acquired disproportionate influence because the few seats they held were crucial to forming a coalition government. Since 1977, 138 State governments were formed, 40 were coalitions and their average life was not more than 26 months. At the national level, right from 1977 many parties have emerged to form the governments, but they were not real coalitions.

The BJP's Emergence as a Second Option

From 1998 onwards, under the leadership of Atal Behari Vajpayee, experiments in coalition politics had been carried on, with 24 constituent political parties giving a strong and stable government at the Centre in 1999. The Congress also led the UPA coalition at the Centre in 2004 and 2009.

In April 1999, when its partner, the AIADMK walked out of the coalition, the Vajpayee-led government fell by a single vote (that of Saifuddin Soz of the NC who voted against his party whip) when it lost the confidence motion and the fabric of coalition politics, shared by Indian politicians, unfortunately did not stretch till 1999.

The 1999 mid-term elections were the product of the Congress' aversion to share power with other political parties in the workable condition,[12] but the party did not succeed in mustering opposition parties in its favour and failed to give an alternative government at the Centre.

Coalition a Conundrum

The Indian experience with coalition governments, both in the States and at the Centre, however, suggests a more differentiated and complex set of findings. As compared to the plurality of the electoral system, more commonly known as the 'first-past-the post' system, where even a minor electoral swing can wipe out the smaller parties, the Proportional Representation System has shown to be more conducive to stability.[13]

Stable government is an important element in the success of representative democracy. The durability of government is a particular problem among parliamentary democracies.[14]

The ground realities in Indian politics also indicate that some sort of method needs to be evolved for effecting a harmony between political and social coalition which refers to creative combination of culture and power within the broad multi-ethnic national matrix of India.[15]

The plethora of parties in Tamil Nadu exemplify the fragmentation process – with the Dravidian ideology in retreat, many groups that formerly supported the Dravidian movement have formed parties of their own. The MDMK, PMK and Puthiya Tamizhagam are breakaway groups from DMK and AIADMK. The smallest party, even one with a member or two, can drive hard bargains with the large parties which need their support[16] to form the government. An example would be Thol Thirumavalavan and his Viduthalai Chiruthaigal Katchi, which entered electoral politics in alliance with GK Moopanar. In 2009, the party occupied a single Lok Sabha seat and was considered very important by both the Congress as well as its opponent, the AIADMK.

The political shops clearly reveal that caste, sub-caste, region, sub-region have emerged to have a share of power in the Central government on the basis of spurious claims of representing group identity aspirations. Today, the party system in India typically mirrors the complexity of social cleavages along lines of religion, caste, language and region to produce a multi-party system.[17] Multi-party politics has inevitably led to multi-cornered contests and it has seriously undermined the popular mass base of the dominant party, the Congress, which ruled India from 1952-1989 with majority status, but not with a majority support base.

This also played a crucial role in erosion of a single dominant party and as a result of multi-party system, became competitive since the 1990s. India's party system has undergone a transformation and beginning of the 21st century has witnessed the growing fragmentation of society because the political class has openly taken recourse to sectarian mobilisation.

Awakening of Regional, Linguistic & Cultural Identities

This shift from one-party dominant ideology of a 'nation state' to the political ideology of building towards the assertion of ethno-religious identities, resurgence of newly empowered social groups and realignment and reconfiguration of castes over the last decade of 20th century, is a process that has been going on continuously in multiple forms and through layers of identity in India.[18] India is a multi-cultural, multi-language, multi-religious, plural secular democratic and federal country, where social diversity has been given a legal space to celebrate its existence as a secular country of the world. India's political scenario is known for its pluralism and the entire society exhibits various levels of pluralism in different walks of life. Coalition politics in India is, therefore, the natural corollary of a system depicting pluralist tendency. One more reason highlighted by political scientists regarding the emergence of a coalition politics relates to the role played by the Congress party in the earlier decades after independence. Its dictatorial functioning is supposed to have suppressed the emergence of pluralist tendencies.

The most significant development in Indian polity began in the 1980s, when under the leadership of Atal Behari Vajpayee, there was rise of a rightist force, namely BJP, in the central stage. The rise of the BJP with its emphasis on Hindu nationalism, the leadership structure and recruitment patterns point to the continuation of its linkages with its Jana Sangh and RSS heritage.

Since 1990, the BJP has maintained its dominance in the Hindi belt with higher mobilisation figures in Bihar, Haryana, Himachal Pradesh, Madhya Pradesh, Rajasthan, Delhi and Uttar Pradesh. It also gained in Gujarat, Maharashtra, Karnataka and Odisha. The Indira period witnessed the emergence of regionally-based parties as an alternative to the national political parties.

During Nehru's time, Congress dominance was visible in entire Indian politics and after him, the Congress became the biggest loser in the Hindi belt. Regional parties mainly made their gains at the expense of the Congress.The 1980s finally is a testament to the political devastation of the Congress party. From early dominance over much of the country, Congress was able to mobilise voters in only three States in those years: Andhra Pradesh, HP and Kerala. In all other States of the country, Congress lost support and their position in Maharashtra, Punjab, Tamil Nadu and Uttar Pradesh got sufficiently weakened. In fact, the dominance of the Congress party was practically eroded mainly due to factors such as long spell of incumbency, lack of credible leadership, its failure to accommodate the newly mobilised sections and rise of another national party like the BJP and several strong regional parties like the TDP, AGP etc. Major regional parties in India pursue politics of identity in regional, linguistic, cultural or ethnic terms and they tend to have a populist orientation that is difficult to characterise in a simple ideological spectrum of just right-left orientations. In India major regional parties are DMK, AIADMK, TDP, AGP, NC, SAD, SP, RJD, JD(U), Shiv Sena, INLD, NCP, RSP, TMC etc. The Congress had not learnt anything from the experience of the Justice Party, Dravidar Khazagam, CPI and the Dravida Munnetra Kazhagam and played the cards of a novice in the game of coalition in the 1980s. This was surprising since the Congress and parties like the DMK have coexisted for more than half a century. The Congress' whimsical political game in the 1970s and '80s cost the nation a huge phase of political instability due to rapid fall of union governments and illogical dismissal of elected State governments by wrongful use of Article 365, just because the Congress in its blinkered wisdom thought it the right thing to do. It was a dark era in Indian politics when 'politics' became 'dirty politics'.

In the wake of the changing political scenario, the multi-party system with the dominance of a single party soon gave way to political plurality. This was destined to happen. This development was a natural consequence of the diverse Indian population. Awakening of regional, linguistic and cultural aspirations resulted in the coming to the fore of several political and social diversities articulating ethnic, caste, religious and other such factors. As a logical corollary, various new political identities came to thrive mainly on regional consciousness.[19] The regional consciousness differs from State to State and the coalition system is the one and only system that can comfortably accommodate the regional political parties.

Political coalitions, being compulsions of power-sharing and political accommodation, need to be seen as emergence of a new level of political consciousness and maturity of judgment, on the part of the voters.

Instead of treating coalitions as a path towards political instability, they have to be seen as a sign of the electorates' dissatisfaction with the dominant role of one single party, leading to dissents, protests and extremism. It is a symbol of the voters' maturity if they prefer political accommodation and power-sharing on the part of political parties, rejecting rigid postures and unitarian forces.[20] Coalition government consists of two or more political parties that serve the government and signifies the fulfilment of conditions of governance, political accommodation, power-sharing and socio-economic stability. To be noted here is that most Indian political parties unfortunately are not yet mature or committed enough to the requirements of parliamentary democracy.

Many State parties are new and adolescent in their behaviour. Tolerance, understanding, consultation and compromise for the sake of democracy are totally lacking. Politics has become quick business; the non-ruling party members cannot wait long enough for a share in the cake. Hence the frequent elections. The multi-party system leads to the shrinking of the size of the cake for each party. India's social and regional diversities are much better served by a pluralist and federal parliamentary regime as it allows, if required, greater concentration of political power in the federal parliamentary executive.[21] But average coalition governments are less stable than one party government. Under certain specific conditions they have shown more stability, the most important being the ideological compatibility among the coalition partners.

As we analyse coalition politics in India, we have to keep in mind the background of various experiments of coalition in different parts of the world. While in countries like France, Italy and Japan there have been unstable coalition governments, Austria, Germany, Netherland, Switzerland and Swedan have witnessed fairly stable coalitions. Thus, all coalition experiments have not displayed a uniform pattern. In India, the growing political, social, economic and regional tensions gave rise to different parties and new parties are still being born, which wield varying influences in the States.[22]

Multi-Party Politics: An Integral Part of Indian Politics

Coalitions have come to stay since 1989 which is obvious as no single party has secured a majority in the Lok Sabha except in 2014 elections when BJP crossed the half mark. In the coalition era, the politics of 'support from outside' has made the office of the Prime Minister a 'Lottery', and this phenomenon has decisively weakened governance at the Centre. The regionalists have come to play a very crucial role in national politics since 1989 by either aligning with any of the two bigger parties like the Congress and the BJP or by making calculations depending on the seats won by any of the two national parties in the Lok Sabha.

The 'unconditional support' offered to a coalition government by a regional or national party does, in fact, conceal a hidden agenda of the new recruits to the emerging coalition. This poor practice was started since 1977, which has done no good to politics in India. Coalition politics rules out homogeneity of composition, unity of perception and approach to the important problems of the nation. Party manifestos are showpieces, no longer relevant for analysing the output of the government under scrutiny. The BJP's Hindutva agenda has had to adjust to socialism. The communist parties have learnt to live with parties of federalism, social justice, economic liberalisation. The Congress has already shifted from its socialistic ideologies to a more capitalistic economy. Political parties based on firm ideology are changing their political line according to the changing situation in the country, even though they find it difficult to discard old attachments.

At present, the most crucial problem seems to be how to maintain the unity of a coalition after attaining power. In fact, coalition politics in India gives chance to every party or group to interpret the public mandate to suit its convenience. The regional parties, which play important role in the formation and power sharing of coalition governments, often have short-term goals before them. The parties under the coalition system suffer from the lack of a long-term vision. The coalition governments under Congress-led UPA and BJP-led NDA formulated common minimum programmes which are, however, accommodating both the short-term and long-term goals of the polity.[23]

In the context of the emergence of a competitive multi-party system and the inevitability of coalition politics, minor reforms are needed in the scheme of parliamentary governance to expand the democratic space and increase the effectiveness of government, as well as stability.[24] On government stability, Shivraj Patil, the then Speakers of Lok Sabha, had suggested, in April 1995, a Constitutional reform to ensure stability in government. The suggestions included:

I. The Prime Minister be elected by the Lok Sabha and resign only when an alternative leader is chosen.
II. The Prime Minister be elected by two-third majority of the Lok Sabha.
III. The Prime Minister can be removed only by two-third majority of the Lok Sabha and Rajya Sabha.[25]

In the Indian political arena, a unique phenomenon has emerged due to multi-party coalition politics. Besides the complications that arise due to multi-party coalition politics, dynasties have become an integral part of Indian politics. The Nehru-Firoze Gandhi family of the Congress, the Thackerays and Pawars of Maharashtra, Karunakaran of Kerala, Karunanidhi of Tamil Nadu, Patnaik of Odisha, Lalu Prasad of Bihar, Mulayam of UP, Chautala of Haryana, Badal of Punjab and the Abdullahs of J&K are a few examples. They present the people with a face that can draw the incremental vote in increasingly presidential-style elections, which has increased instability and confusion in Indian politics. However, the coalition and multi-party politics in India is indicative of the pluralistic tendencies in Indian politics. It seems that coalition politics has come to stay in India and one can only hope that with the passage of time, it will evolve in a manner which will help democracy to be more effective and representative.

Prominent Features of Coalition Politics

Disagreements and Bargaining

AFTER INDEPENDENCE, JUST one party, the Congress had dominance at the Centre and the States. It did not face any challenge till 1967 in the States and before 1977 at the Centre. *In 1977, a fragmented coalition, named as Janata Party, came to power and since then bargaining became the main feature of politics in India.*

The verdict of 1977 brought about a geographic north-south division which called for tactful handling to ensure that the larger national interests were not compromised. However, the Janata Party broke away soon in absence of the spirit of compromise. The squabbles and feud within the party resulted into disarray of the Janata Party. The feuding, which Morarji Desai described as 'foul stench', weakened the party in two ways. First, differences – over which many interest groups demanded priority – which widened the gap among Janata factions. Second, these disputes weakened the rapport between the national and State factions of the national party (in this case, the Bharatiya Jana Sangh) in respect of both, the party and the political system. The factions which dominated the party at the national level were antagonistic to those which had an upper hand in several key Janata controlled State legislatures.

Downfall of Janata Party Government

The most important issue in the downfall of the Janata government was the alleged 'dual membership' of the erstwhile Jana Sangh. The parties forming the coalition government, other than the Jana Sangh, raised the red flag and demanded that the Jana Sangh should break its ties with the RSS, an ideological and cultural organisation, which the Jana Sangh leadership refused to do.

The coalition government of Morarji Desai could not continue for more than 28 months due to the tug-of-war among the leaders of the Janata Party and the country was left to seek a fresh mandate. Again, in the ninth general elections, no party could get a majority and in 1989 VP Singh became the Prime Minister with the support of the BJP and the Left parties. Here again, the contradiction hits the eye. The BJP stands on a religious platform, the Left are anti-religion; how could this coalition ever happen, students of politics still wonder. However, the kind of support the National Front got from the Left parties and the BJP, provided it with all the trappings of a functional coalition. The collapse of the VP Singh government, in the first week of November 1990, was however, not surprising. The reasons for failure of the National Front government included the lack of effective hold its leaders exercised over their own respective parties, in particular, VP Singh's own hold over the Janata Dal. Singh did not prove to be as assertive a leader as he was expected to be. And when he did try to carve out for himself a political constituency over the Mandal issue, he was checkmated both by friends and foes, within and outside the Janata Dal.

The second imperative of organisational discipline was equally missing. This naturally raised doubts about the coalition leaders' capacity to deliver on whatever agreement and understandings they may have arrived at.

The third imperative of successful coalition politics, namely, ideological and programmatic loyalty was also missing. The vehemence with which the Janata Dal members disagreed and squabbled in public over Punjab or Kashmir or the economy, made the tasks of coalition agreement even more difficult. This requirement of ideological loyalty is necessary because increasingly, the polity will have to cope with a shift away from the status quo. In a society of extensive poverty and pervasive inequalities, vibrant politics necessarily generates social tensions. Coalition politics provides a setting for co-opting the newly emerging and assertive social groups, keen to have a place under the sun.

Above all, the VP Singh coalition arrangement failed because of widespread indifference to the rules of the games. Perhaps, it would be more correct to say that rules of the game had collapsed, and new rules were yet to be framed. The very shadows that doomed the Singh government also chased Chandra Shekhar.

Fall of the Chandra Shekhar Government

Defying history, Chandra Shekhar took over the reigns of the government with Congress support, from outside, with 211 members supporting the motely groups of 54 Samajwadi Janata Party-Rastriya (SJP-R) members. By all political logic, Chandra Shekhar's government was bound to fall. Once Rajiv Gandhi avenged his defeat against Chandra Shekhar, it simply remained a question of his choosing the right time to go to the polls by withdrawing support from the government. Here again is apparent, a deep political contradiction.

Chandra Shekhar and Rajiv Gandhi deeply distrusted each other since they both knew that it was only a matter of time that Rajiv Gandhi would withdraw support forcing elections, that he believed would return the Congress to power.

On 5 March 1991, the Congress members of Parliament

walked out in protest against a flimsy incident – the surveillance of Rajiv Gandhi by plain-clothed police officers from the Haryana State government led by Om Prakash Chautala, a part of the National Front. The Congress withdrew its support to Chandra Shekhar and he resigned and advised the President to call for elections. Thus, this stormy marriage of convenience came to an end.

The outcome of the 1991 elections can be seen as the emergence of the Congress as the single largest party mainly owing to the sympathy factor (due to the assassination of Rajiv Gandhi). Secondly, the rising crescendo of the BJP was due to positive votes on the Ram Mandir issue and its promise to curb corruption. Thirdly, the Left faced redundance due to the collapse of the Soviet Union and the non-acceptance of their ideological appeal by even the people of India, in general. Fourthly, due to unsatisfactory performance of the National Front, particularly because of its sectional appeal and flirtation with fundamental Muslims. Lastly, there was the growth of regional parties and their interaction with the parties at the national level. The cumulative effects of all these many factors were perceived as the likely cause of polarisation against the NF and increased articulation of the new forces in the changing Indian political spectrum.

The Congress government led by PV Narasimha Rao happens to be the only government since 1989 to have completed its full mandated term of five years, until 1999.

The United Front (UF) government (1996) led by HD Deve Gowda of Karnataka had once been described as the 'first true coalition government' at the Centre. The previous experiences such as the Janata Party government led by Morarji Desai, the Charan Singh-led Samajwadi Janata Party government, VP Singh's Janata Dal or the Chandra Shekhar government were not regarded as genuine coalition governments because in the Janata Party, the minority governments were supported by a major party from the outside which was a transitory phenomenon.

In the United Front, India had, for the first time in its post-independence history, thirteen political parties coalesced after the general elections to form a government at the Centre. The UF, despite the coalition, was dependent on external support from the Congress, the second largest party in the Lok Sabha, and this added another significant political dimension to the coalition.

The United Front, thus, represented a very significant development in Indian politics. Firstly, it broke the monopoly of a single party aspiring for power. The single party now had to do so in coalition with the regional parties. Secondly, the United Front imposed upon its leaders a new style of functioning.

Lack of Commanding Leadership

If the ten months of the United Front leadership are to be assessed, one can hardly ignore the new type of personalities who had come to occupy the seats of power. Unfortunately, the weakness of the United Front has been largely due to the incapacity of its leader, the Prime Minister himself. Personally, Deve Gowda may have all the virtues of a humble farmer but the Prime Ministership of India is something slightly more than the assignment and outlook of a good farmer. Nowhere did one find a touch of leadership quality in him, while the head of a coalition government in India has to command the confidence and respect of not only his ministers but also of the wide area of politics outside his government. Whatever might have been the folly of the Congress president in irresponsibly serving a notice to the government – it was indeed unbelievable (as had been revealed during the crisis) – that there had never been a mechanism of consultation and coordination of approach and action between the United Front and its life-saving ally, the Congress. It would be an exaggeration to claim that Deve Gowda's circle was immune from all corruption.[1]

Prior to extending support, there was an understanding between Deve Gowda and the Congress that there would be regular consultations between the leaders of the United Front and the Congress. In absence of a mechanism of consultation and coordination, the Congress lost no time in voicing its opposition and criticising several policies of the government. Since the UF government was a puppet whose gears and levers were in the hands of the Congress, it lost no time to withdraw its support from the Gowda government.

Thereafter, the Congress staked its claim to form an alternative government, it said, 'to protect the country from the communal forces, anarchy, chaos and destruction'.[2] It made an all-out effort to form a government with the support of pliable elements in the United Front. The United Front was not clear over supporting the Congress either from the outside or inviting it to participate in the government. The only possible remedy seemed to dissolve the Lok Sabha and hold fresh elections. However, no party was ready for it. The Congress knew that in the past few months its reputation had diminished, and it would not survive that elections with dignity. To pass the ball into the United Front's Court, the Congress announced on 14 April 1997 that it would continue to support if the United Front changed its leader.

The Congress president (Sitaram Kesri) formally wrote to the President of India, on 18 April 1997, 'Please refer to my letter dated March 31, 1997. The Congress Working Committee resolves to extend support to the formation of the government at the Centre by the new leader of the United Front other than Deve Gowda. Otherwise, my earlier letter stands'.[3] The United Front partners stood united and firm. They asserted that they would not desert Deve Gowda. They, however, fell to the last-minute machinations of the Congress. Some leaders of the United Front mooted proposals for rapprochement with the Congress for bargaining another lease of life and in the process, made Deve Gowda a sacrificial goat. The prospect of a mid-term poll apparently forced both the Congress and the United Front to come to an agreement. Deve Gowda also decided to support the collective decision of the United Front Steering Committee. The stage was, therefore, set for constituting a second United Front government.

To select the new Prime Minister, Harkishan Singh Surjeet (CPI-M) framed a criterion that a new leader must be from the Hindi speaking north with a mass base who might pose a formidable challenge to the BJP. This framework of understanding brought into focus United Front's three major north Indian leaders, Lalu Prasad Yadav, Ram Vilas Paswan, Mulayam Singh Yadav as possible candidates for the exalted office of the Prime Minister.

Lalu Prasad Yadav, the Chief Minister of Bihar, did indeed have a mass following in Bihar at that time. But Lalu Prasad had several crucial failings. The principal among them, the Left pointed out, was his implication in the fodder scam and the strong possibility of the initiation, by the CBI, of criminal proceedings against him. Although Paswan had none of those failings and had a clean, progressive Dalit image, he was relatively junior. He was also uncompromising with Lalu Prasad. In such a situation, the candidacy of Mulayam Singh Yadav, whose name was proposed by Harkishan Singh Surjeet, began to acquire powerful momentum. The Left pointed out that, in addition, to begin a fearless fight against the BJP's communalism in the real political battle field, he had a strong appeal among the minorities, particularly Muslims. But, as expected, Mulayam's candidacy ran into strong resistance from United Front constituents who were deeply apprehensive about his style of coalition management.

With Lalu Prasad Yadav, Janata Dal president, showing frontal opposition, it became clear that forcing a vote on Mulayam's candidacy would badly split the United Front, triggering another crisis. Tamil Maanila Congress (TMC) leader GK Moopanar was another forerunner, but he faced vehement opposition from the CPI(M) which told the United Front Standing Committee members that choosing Moopanar, would amount to inviting Sonia Gandhi to take over the reins of power. Moopanar was very close to 10 Janpath, and his Congress legacy went against him.

Chandrababu Naidu of Telugu Desam Party (TDP), who was a possible contender, had wisely ruled himself out of the contest. Ultimately, the core group of the United Front Steering Committee, comprising the then West Bengal Chief Minister, Jyoti Basu, M Karunanidhi of the DMK, Lalu Prasad Yadav, PK Mahanta of the AGP, Farooq Abdullah, Chandrababu Naidu, Harkishan Singh Surjeet, AB Bardhan of the CPI, Ram Vilas Paswan and Deve Gowda, authorised United Front convener, Chandrababu Naidu, to talk to various leaders of the constituents and evolve a consensus on the issue of leadership. It was at this point that the possible candidacy of IK Gujral took off.

First suggested by bed-ridden VP Singh from Apollo Hospital (New Delhi), Gujral met the Left's basic requirement of being a north Indian leader with no noticeable inclination to compromise with the Congress and had some experience at his back. By the late evening of 19 April 1997, all United Front constituents, barring the TMC, had come around to the candidature of IK Gujral. Finally, after a week's intense intrigue, practical wranglings and unprincipled jockeying, IK Gujral, external affairs minister and Janata Dal Rajya Sabha member from Bihar, became the accepted candidate.

Internal Quibbles and Dissolution of House

The role of the Andhra Pradesh Chief Minister, Chandrababu Naidu, as the key player in the protracted and painful process of leadership selection within the Front, served to demonstrate a new dimension of the ascendancy of the regional parties in Indian politics. The regional leaders were now seen as eager and willing to participate in decision-making at the national level. It did seem that regional parties were moving assertively into the political space vacated by the Congress. The high-profile activity of Naidu and other regional players in ensuring the United Front's continuance brought to life the idea of cooperative federation in the public imagination. It did seem that the concept of real federal political framework was becoming a credible reality.

However, within six months, the fate of the United Front

again hung in imbalance. In November 1997, in the wake of the leaked Jain Commission inquiry interim report on Rajiv Gandhi's assassination, the Congress insisted on the removal of the indicted DMK from the Front. Gujral finally resigned by November end, with the United Front refusing to ditch the DMK on the dictates of the Congress.

Following the Congress party's decision to withdraw from government, Gujral submitted his resignation and that of his council of ministers to the President of India, without recommending the dissolution of the Lok Sabha. He stated: 'For unjustifiable reasons, the Congress has been asking me to drop the three DMK ministers from my government. In my communications to the Congress president, I have said that it is unfair and unethical to tarnish the fair name of a party only because of the Jain Commission's interim report, without any substantiated data, (the Congress) has chosen to blame the party and I say with sadness, the entire Tamil people. While this is not acceptable to me, the honourable members of the Congress Party have not allowed Parliament to function and discharge its constitutional duty. Assigning high priority to the national interests, I have come to the conclusion that I should submit my resignation to you. My council of Minister and I hereby submit our resignation…'[4]

On the issue of recommendation for dissolution of the House, sharp differences in the Union Cabinet and members of the United Front Core Committee cropped up. The Union

Cabinet, which informally discussed the issue, failed to come up with a unanimous view on the dissolution aspect. It authorised the Prime Minister to take appropriate action. Several United Front leaders expressed their serious reservation in taking the country to another mid-term poll, while the leaders of the Left Parties, DMK and some of the cabinet ministers favoured submitting the resignation along with the dissolution of the Lok Sabha.

Since the House was not immediately dissolved, hectic political negotiation began for fresh alignments. Both Congress and the BJP were hoping that defectors from other parties would switch loyalty to help them to form another government to replace the Gujral ministry. The Congress managed the first formal assurance of support for its claim to form the government from the Rashtriya Janata Dal (RJD) and declared that it was talking to all United Front constituents, except DMK, to garner more backing.

The BJP and its allies met the President on 30 November 1997 and staked their claim to form a government at the Centre. But the hopes of the Congress and the BJP were dashed when 160 members of the United Front sent their individual letters to the President and candidly said, 'for 17 months the United Front has fought unitedly, on the basis of certain moral values and principles, (but now) we have resigned and no one can either use us or claim the support of our MPs'.[5] With this, it became clear to the President that no political combination in the Lok Sabha was in a position to offer or receive the lawfully valid support of the critical minimum number of MPs required by that combination to secure a majority in the House.

The BJP also conveyed to the President that it was in favour of early mid-term polls because till date it had secured the support of only 40 Congress MPs as against the 47 required to cause a split in the Congress. Later on, a United Front delegation led by the former Prime Minister and United Front chairman HD Deve Gowda urged the President to dissolve the Lok Sabha immediately to end the political crisis, as delay would lead to horse-trading. At last, the President dissolved the eleventh Lok Sabha and directed the constitution of the new Lok Sabha by 15 March 1998.

Emergence of BJP

After the 12th general elections (1998), the President had to make a choice as the BJP was the single largest party and its pre-poll alliance also was the largest. But unfortunately, even after the formation of the BJP-led coalition government at the Centre in March 1998, the infighting among its coalition partners continued to create an impression of instability.

The BJP-led coalition government (led by AB Vajpayee) was constantly kept under pressure by its regional allies like Jayalalithaa of the AIADMK, Mamata Banerjee of Trinamool Congress and a relatively more reasonable Samta Party led by Nitish Kumar and George Fernandes. All of them kept clamouring for the dismissal of their regional adversaries, namely the DMK government in Tamil Nadu, the Left Front government in West Bengal, and the RJD government in Bihar. Thanks to the Bommai Judgement of the Supreme Court, the Centre desisted from intervention under Article 356.[6] Finally, Jayalalithaa dramatically withdrew her party's support from the coalition government on 17 April 1999, after months of lobbying for the reinstatement of Admiral Vishnu Bhagwat, earlier sacked by the government for allegedly showing signs of defying the principle of cabinet control of the armed forces. It seemed, her real grudge was the reluctance of the government to slow down the judicial proceedings against her in corruption-related cases.

The 1999 mid-term elections were held after a delay of few months due to the Kargil war during which the Vajpayee government continued in the care-taker capacity.

BJP-Led NDA Government Constantly Under Pressure

General Elections for 13th Lok Sabha were held from 5 September to 3 October 1999, a few months after the Kargil war. The 13th Lok Sabha election is of historical importance as it was for the first time that a National Democratic Alliance, comprising thirteen parties, managed to attain a majority, thus, ending the period of instability at the national level. The government lasted a full term of five years. Atal Behari Vajpayee, elected as leader, was sworn in as Prime Minister on 13 October 1999.

A coalition government can face problems regarding consensus throughout its tenure. Parties joining the coalition can have different views and different stands on several domestic and foreign policy issues. Jayalalithaa (AIADMK) gave enough headache to Prime Minister Vajpayee and Defence Minister George Fernandes. They had to make several trips to Chennai to secure Jayalalithaa's support for the Central government policies. Railway Minister Mamata Banerjee had rocked the Vajpayee government several times. Shiv Sena leader Bal Thackeray, though not strictly in the government, was averse especially to the Indian policy towards Pakistan and sending Indian sports teams there while the TDP and INLD had objected to a Ram Temple at the Babri Masjid site.

On the eve of the government's first anniversary, Vajpayee came under extreme pressure from the Trinamool Congress. As the government reacted to the global surge in oil prices by imposing a major price hike on petroleum products, Mamata Banerjee and her party colleague, Ajit Kumar Panja, Minister of State for External Affairs, resigned from the Union Cabinet and announced a three-day deadline for the government to rollback the price hike, failing which, she said she would withdraw her party's support to the coalition.[7]

Vajpayee promptly rejected the resignations and deputed George Fernandes and Sudheendra Kulkarni, officer on special duty in his office, to go to Calcutta to mollify Mamata Banerjee. Both, Fernandes and Kulkarni met Banerjee for several hours and understood her compulsions to roll back the hike in the light of ensuing assembly elections in West Bengal. Although the Prime Minister was firm on not making any commitment, he wrote a personal letter and faxed it to Banerjee on 6 October 2000, shortly before her scheduled press conference in Calcutta, appealing to her to resume her ministerial duties.[8] There was nothing new in the letter but the personal touch and Vajpayee's public sharing of her concern for the poor, gave her the required exit route. However, she warned that she would revive her threat to resign if the Centre failed to roll back the oil prices.

Yet, after issuing a threat to withdraw support, Mamata Banerjee had soon realised that her own party cadre, not to speak of her party colleagues in the Lok Sabha, were against such an extreme step. Facing the Left Front in the State and the BJP at the Centre would have proved too big a challenge for the Trinamool Congress. Lack of support at the Centre could have further crippled the party in West Bengal. This left Mamata Banerjee with few choices but to accept the face-saving option that Vajpayee had extended. She eventually withdrew her resignation. The TDP and SAD also demanded a rollback, but they had not threatened to withdraw support to the NDA over the issue.

The NDA allies, particularly Trinamool Congress and the TDP, sought an explanation from the Prime Minister. Another problem arose when the Prime Minister indicated, on

7 December 2000, that he preferred the building of a temple at the disputed Ayodhya site. The VHP and BJP leaders not only welcomed the Prime Minister's statement but also went a step further, demanding the resolution of the Ayodhya issue through a parliamentary legislation. The Prime Minister talked about abiding by the court's verdict on the issue and explained that the court could resolve the issue by permitting the building of the proposed temple at the disputed site. The BJP allies, particularly the Trinamool Congress, the TDP and INLD, expressed their disapproval of the remarks, saying that it had sent a wrong message and that something needed to be done to correct the situation. They feared that such remarks would abet the growing communalisation in the country.

The NDA government adopted a tough and uncompromising line with the Vishwa Hindu Parishad mainly under the pressure of allies.[9] But the BJP as a party did not consider the demand of the VHP as illogical. Jana Krishnamurthy, BJP president, stated in an interview to *The Indian Express* that he did not consider the VHP's demand illogical because in his view, 'the actual dispute is over 80 ft by 40 ft where the structure known as Babri Masjid was located and the rest of the land was not disputed'.[10]

A major twist in the Ayodhya issue occurred when the Prime Minister categorically stated at a press conference in Lucknow on 16 February 2002, that his efforts to find a 'negotiated settlement' to the Babri dispute had failed and that the Ayodhya problem could now be resolved only in a court of law and nobody would be allowed to take the law in his own hands. The Prime Minister's statement created doubt in the BJP-led government's track record on this count. It became clear that Vajpayee was trying to run with the hare and hunt with the hounds. While on the one hand, he had lulled his partners in the NDA into inaction by declaring that the temple issue could only be resolved in the court, on the other hand, he kept the pot boiling by asking the Law Minister to see whether the so-called undisputed portion of the acquired land in Ayodhya could be handed over to the VHP.

As the VHP started ritual mobilisation at Ayodhya, a train carrying their kar sevaks (cadre who had volunteered labour to build the temple), the Sabarmati Express, was set on fire at a mid-way station called Godhra in Gujarat, on 27 February 2002, in which 58 VHP pilgrims were burnt alive. It led to communal riots in Gujarat which gave a fillip to the Ayodhya agitation. More than 600 people were killed in Ahmedabad alone, 20,000 were huddled into makeshift camps in these riots. The Prime Minister condemned the Gujarat riots as a 'blot on the image of India'.

By this time, the credibility of the NDA government had been seriously compromised by the series of controversies that put a big question mark on the integrity of some key functionaries. There was a furious controversy over abrupt changes in the telecom policy, a battle over a key official in the PMO (Brajesh Mishra, Principal Secretary) whose name cropped up in a media (*Tehelka*) transcript, whispers of irregularities in the BALCO privatisation and a stock market scandal are just a few examples. Arguably, these were functional hiccups, but they generated a stench. The *Tehelka* revelations were the proverbial last straw.[11]

Tehelka.com made revelations with support of video images about alleged irregularities in defence deals and involvement of top political leaders in them. The video tapes, which were first broadcast on a satellite television network, on 13 March 2001, showed among other things, the then Samta Party president, Jaya Jaitly, accepting a 'donation' from *Tehelka* journalists posing as middlemen, at the residence of the Defence Minster, George Fernandes, and the then BJP president, Bangaru Laxman, casually thrusting bundles of notes into a drawer.

The day the *Tehelka* tapes became public, the Union Cabinet met in an environment of confusion and disarray. George Fernandes, as the obvious focus of attention, had a dual strategy of relieving the pressure that was building upon him. On the one hand, he offered to resign if that would make the job of government easier. But on the other hand, he urged that a counter-offensive might bring greater rewards. With Vajpayee tending to tilt towards him, Fernandes retained his job. The cabinet finally came out with the rather rapid formulation that he was aware of the *Tehelka* tapes and would spare no efforts to arrive at the truth behind them, none of the guilty would be spared, and no innocent person's reputation would be unfairly damaged.

BJP president, Bangaru Laxman, on his part, responded to public outrage over his image of accepting bundles of notes with no sign of regret. He said that he indeed had taken a donation for the party. He alleged an anti-Dalit conspiracy behind the *Tehelka* story and that he had been framed.

Following a brief discussion in the party, it was agreed that Laxman had to go. Laxman's departure was the easy part of crisis management. It was, however, a difficult situation for Jaya Jaitly and George Fernandes. Captured in the self-incriminating act by the *Tehelka* camras, Jaya Jaitly had made herself scarce. Despite the media furore and the fiercely adverse publicity, she persisted with her stand of not having committed any offence by accepting 'donation' for her party's national convention.

As the public indignation grew, so seemingly did the BJP determination to sort out the crisis. On 14 May 2001, the leaders of the NDA's main constituents met to reaffirm their faith in Vajpayee's leadership. In a conspicuous display of unity, Commerce Minister Murasoli Maran of the DMK briefed the media after the meeting and waved away any suggestion that Fernandes should resign.[12] Fernandes repeated his offer to resign, but the NDA partners refused his offer. Outside the NDA, the TDP with its 29 MPs, angry with *Tehelka* for an earlier story on assets of Chandrababu Naidu, backed the government. Janata Dal (U) chief, Sharad Yadav, too was behind Fernandes despite his party men taking a few potshots. It was felt that after Laxman's departure, the government could ride over the storm.

Of course, there were a few exceptions within the NDA. Minister of State for Social Welfare and Empowerment, Maneka Gandhi, and Independent MP and Minister of State for Commerce, Omar Farooq Abdullah (National Conference) suggested that Fernandes should resign. They invoked the ire of Samta Party leader and Minister of Agriculture, Nitish Kumar.

Outside the meeting, another partner, The Trinamool Congress, was going through an existential dilemma. Always a great one for boycotts and strikes, Mamata Banerjee stayed away from the cabinet meeting and sent a communication to the Prime Minister urging that Fernandes' resignation be accepted. The reason was not her anguish over corruption. Actually, what had happened was that a fanatical stickler for honesty, Mamata flew into rage when she heard that the Samta Party treasurer, RK Jain, had described her as '70% manageable' in the *Tahelka* tapes.[13]

The Trinamool Congress leadership met in an emergency session and decided to pull out of the NDA. Mamata Banerjee sent her resignation as Railway Minister and the only other Trinamool Congress Minister, Ajit Kumar Panja, followed suit.

Mamata Banerjee's exit had more to do with electoral compulsions in West Bengal than any concern for ethics or morality. She might have felt it embarrassing to remain in alliance when leaders of some of its major constituents had been caught video tapped accepting money from fictitious arms dealers. The withdrawal of the Trinamool Congress, which came shortly after the Pattali Makkal Katchi pulled out of the NDA, considerably increased the parliamentary vulnerability of the Vajpayee government with core membership of the NDA now holding only 262 seats in the Lok Sabha. The government was now more than ever dependent on the external sustenance rendered by the TDP.

Vajpayee was initially reluctant to ask Fernandes to quit but had to do so, following pressure from some of the constituents and supporters of the NDA like Biju Janata Dal, The Janata Dal(U) and TDP. Moreover, the opposition made it clear that it would not let Parliament function as long as Fernandes remained a minister. The opposition prepared for a long battle that it believed would block the budget, create constitutional crisis and if lucky, even lead to the government's collapse.

Fernandes resigned as did Jaitly but government reputation was in shreds. Parliamentary Affairs Minister, Pramod Mahajan, said that Fernandes enjoyed unqualified trust of the NDA and would continue to function as its convener. In a gesture of loyalty that transgressed all norms of propriety, Mahajan also declared that Fernandes' absence from the Defence Ministry was a 'temporary inconvenience' that would be remedied following his exoneration by the Judicial Commission.[14] It was as if Mahajan knew before hand that the Commission would exonerate Fernandes.

The Union Cabinet recommended dissolution of the Lok Sabha eight months before its actual tenure till mid 2005. President APJ Abdul Kalam dissolved the Lok Sabha on 6 February 2004 and ordered fresh elections. The elections for the 14th Lok Sabha were held in May 2004. Both, the BJP and the Congress, were actually involved in forming alternative electoral alliances for the elections.

UPA forms Govt: Problems with Partners

The people of India voted decisively for the United Progressive Alliance (UPA) in the 14th Lok Sabha elections, for the promised (in its manifesto) secular, progressive forces, for the parties wedded to the welfare of farmers, agricultural labour, weavers, workers and weaker sections of society, for parties irrevocably committed to the daily well-being of the common man across the country. It was a huge mandate. In keeping with the mandate, the Congress, its pre-poll allies that included the RJD, DMK, NCP, PMK, JMM etc. came together to form a United Progressive Alliance. A 68-member Union Council of Ministers had been put in place with Dr Manmohan Singh at the helm; the first-ever Congress-led coalition government was at the Centre.

From controversies over a film about Hindu society's treatment of widows, *Water*, to the Right To Information Act to cricket controversies, the problems of the UPA coalition came into sharper focus from the first year of its term. The problems aggravated because of inclusion of tainted members as ministers. It was tragic that Manmohan Singh had to carry the baggage of Lalu Prasad Yadav who was facing charges in the court. The Congress was dependent upon the support of Yadav's party to stay in power.

The Telangana Rashtra Samithi (TRS) was the first party to quit the alliance. There was pressure also from the AIADMK and BJP in opposition. 'Ram Sethu is to Hindus what Mecca is to Muslims and Jerusalem is to Christians',[15] Bhartiya Janata Party president Rajnath Singh said on 18 September 2007, warning the UPA government not to play with religious sentiments of Hindus over the Sethusamudram Shipping Canal Project. The BJP would oppose the project tooth and nail as Ram Sethu was a matter of Hindus' faith and belief.

UPA's Problem with the Left

The communists who had chosen to support the Congress-led government from outside, were major sources of problems for the UPA. Remaining outside the government, they had the freedom to voice their dissent publicly, but their support in keeping the Congress-led coalition afloat was important enough to persuade the government to listen to their views and accommodate them as much as possible. *Coalition politics, by its very nature, is another name for instability in which a constant effort has to be made to keep the different players happy which involves a constant process of dialogue and an exercise to bring about compromise between players who have conflicting views.*

On 15 June 2006, the Left parties submitted a detailed note at a meeting of the Left-UPA Coordination Committee raising a number of issues on the two years of governance of the Manmohan Singh-led government.[16] The note categorically stated that the UPA government had not been able to better the material conditions of the vast majority of people. It also stated that issues and problems like price rise, the agrarian crisis, unemployment and the lack of access to education, health were not provided urgent attention by the government. It questioned specifically the policy direction and practical steps in various segments of governance – economic affairs, foreign policy, resource mobilisation, agrarian affairs, food security and planning process.

The relations between the Congress and the Left came under a heavy strain after the latter vetoed its move to impose President's Rule in Uttar Pradesh, in February 2007. On 14 February 2007, the Supreme Court disqualified 13 Bahujan Samaj Party (Kanshi Ram-Mayawati) MLAs who had defected to the Samajwadi Party in September 2003. The Congress argued that the Samajwadi Party-led government in UP was, therefore, unconstitutional and it had lost the majority support. So, the government should be dismissed under Article 356. But the Left parties strongly opposed this move of the Congress. They made it clear that if the Union government went ahead with its plan, it would cause a political breach between the UPA and the Left. Meanwhile, the Election Commission announced an assembly poll schedule in UP and the squabble came to an end. However, on this issue the Samajwadi Party withdrew its unwanted outside support from the UPA coalition government at the Centre.

Apart from these issues, there were many other problems on which the Left parties did not have agreement. In the beginning, there were occasional skirmishes, but these encounters turned into daily tussle. With its 61 MPs in the Lok Sabha, the Left parties supplied the oxygen that kept the minority UPA government alive. The working of the UPA clearly demonstrated that the Left virtually played the role of opposition and sometimes better than the BJP-led opposition. Prakash Karat, the General Secretary of the CPI(M) said, 'the UPA regime has shown that it is us (Left Parties) and not the BJP which is actually playing the role of an opposition party'.[17] Despite having a separate committee between the UPA and the Left, UPA found it difficult to understand the Left parties. Congress leaders found the Left's meddling irksome. National Advisory Council member Jairam Ramesh remarked, 'Dealing with the Left is like reading Upanishads. There are only questions and no answers'.

The task of running a coalition became even more difficult as two major factions – the Congress and Left parties – had serious ideological differences on economic issues as well as on foreign policy. The Congress was committed to economic reforms which had been initiated, in his capacity as Finance

Minister in the '90s, by Manmohan Singh, who became Prime Minister under the new setup in 2004.

Realising that a conflict was inevitable, the coalition partners tried to work out a Common Minimum Programme, but no amount of effort could have visualised the kind of conflict that arose on the issue of the Indo-US nuclear deal for the use of nuclear energy for civilian purposes.[18] The Prime Minister tried to prepare his partners and colleagues by taking the Parliament into confidence but no one could have prepared the members about the final details which emerged as a result of adoption of the Hyde Act by the US Congress and incorporation of conflicting clauses between the One-Two-Three agreement with India and domestic laws of the US. While some maintained that the nuclear agreement with India would prevail, others were of view that US could invoke the domestic laws to take action in case of conflict.

The parleys between the Congress and Left had helped in clearing the ground on some issues and both sides had agreed that the differences on the nuclear deal would not be allowed to reach a point where they become a threat to the UPA government. The Left had got an assurance that the Indo-US nuclear agreement would not be operationalised till differences were resolved and in return would continue to extend crucial support to the UPA. Such an agreement by its nature was temporary and would leave both sides to act independently when the elections would take place in 2009.

In any case, poll adjustment between the Congress and Left was almost impossible as the two were major contenders in crucial States like Kerala and West Bengal.

Troubles with Other Alliance Partners

Apart from Left Partics, MDMK, TRS, other parties within the UPA government had also created trouble in the working of the coalition government. RJD, DMK, LJP, all these regional parties had made a show of their strength at the time of ministry formation. These parties, while influencing the policies and decisions at the national level, did not forget to work for their regional interests. They did not hesitate to oppose those moves of the government, which in any way adversely affected their vote banks in their respective States. DMK, the main partner from Tamil Nadu in the UPA, questioned the proposal of UPA government to divest shares in the Neyveli Lignite Corporation (NIC), a profit-making public undertaking based in Tamil Nadu.[19] It threatened to review its participation in the UPA government, if the government continued with the disinvestment plan. DMK alone had 16 seats in the Lok Sabha, a number which the government could not ignore. Ultimately, the Prime Minister decided to keep aside all disinvestment decisions and proposals to keep the DMK in good humour.[20]

The clash between the two allies of the UPA, the DMK and the Left parties, over the issue of Indian Maritime University was another evidence of regional bias while working at the national level. On the presentation of the Indian Maritime University Bill 2007, the DMK and Left parties scuffled in the well of the House on 13 March 2007. The Left parties did not allow the Union Shipping Minister, TR Balu, to introduce the Bill in the House. The Left parties wanted the University to be set up in Kolkata.[21] Marshals were summoned, for the first time in the history of Parliament, to protect a Union Minister, that too from the government's own allies. After several rounds of negotiations, finally a compromise was brought on the principle of give and take. The Left parties then allowed the minister to pilot the bill, after which the bill was referred to the Standing Committee of Parliament.

Despite all intra-coalitional hiccups, the UPA I government completed three years in office on 22 May 2007, and on this occasion the Prime Minister presented a 72-page 'Report to the people 2004-2007'. It highlighted the various steps taken by the government to fulfil its pledges made in the Common Minimum Programme.

The function was attended by key coalition partners, except the Left parties, but they joined the celebratory dinner that followed. The Left parties regarded the government performance as a mixed bag of achievements and failures.

They regarded the Rural Employment Guarantee Scheme, the Tribal Rights Bill and the Right to Information Act as the positive measures of the government. They pointed out several areas like education, health and agriculture, which remained neglected despite the assurance of greater allocation in the CMP. Many promised laws like the Women's Reservation Bill, the Prevention of Communal Violence Bill, the Lokpal Bill, the laws on Protection of Unorganised labourers and Agricultural labourers were yet to be passed.[22] They warned the government to seriously introspect on areas it lagged behind against the target set in the CMP.

A peculiarity of the UPA coalition was Sonia Gandhi who, as the leader of the coalition United Progressive Alliance, handled most of the problems arising out of coalition politics at the party level and served the purpose of being something of a shock absorber. It was a far cry from the days of Congress supremacy.

UPA II Rocked with Scams and Scandals

When the United Progressive Alliance regime assumed office in 2009 for the second time, it had several apparent laurels to its credit. It had successfully fashioned a major welfare scheme, the Mahatma Gandhi National Rural Guarantee Act (MNREGA) in 2005, significantly restructured its relationship to the US by successfully negotiating the US-India civilian nuclear agreement and economic growth, after having faltered a bit in the earlier year, had managed to clock a respectable 7.4 per cent in 2009, letting the country to be the fastest growing economy in the world.

At a political level, Prime Minister Manmohan Singh had

also appeared to have secured his footing in the wake of his deft handling the US-India civilian nuclear agreement despite the stiff objection of his Communist coalition allies over the deal. Furthermore, the Indian electorate had rewarded the Indian National Congress, the principal party within the coalition, with as many as 206 out of 545 seats. Consequently, though part of a coalition government yet again, the Congress was now more safely established in office.

The hopes that the Indian electorate had reposed in UPA II, however, soon started to evaporate as various problems quickly came to the fore. In 2010, even as the preparations for the nineteenth Commonwealth Games (CWG) in New Delhi were underway, the government faced harsh criticism from a host of quarters but most notably, from members of India's civil society. The charges related to malpractice involved in the handing out of contracts for services, products, and infrastructure related to the CWG.

Shortly before the eruption of the CWG scandal, the government had already come under attack from civil society activists owing to the apparent involvement of elements of the Congress government in Maharashtra, in a corrupt housing deal – which saw land transferred for a commercial residential development benefitting key bureaucrats and well-heeled politicians – when it had been intended for the widows of Kargil war martyrs.

The government was already reeling under these corruption

charges when a far more significant scandal rocked it. This stemmed from the Comptroller and Auditor General of India's report that there had been widespread abuse in the auction of second generation (2G) mobile phone licenses to private telecom companies. Most disturbingly, the report asserted that the Indian exchequer had purportedly lost as much as $38 billion owing to a lack of transparent and fair rules in the allocation of the spectrum. The response from the Congress-led coalition regime was predictable; its members argued that the methods used by CAG were flawed and that there was little or no loss to the treasury. Despite the government's efforts to stonewall any further investigation including a Joint Parliamentary Committee (JPC) enquiry, the then Minister for Communications, Andimuthu Raja (DMK) was forced to resign from Parliament and formal charges were brought against him.

The misallocation of public resources to the private sector once again erupted in March 2012. This time it dealt with the flawed allocation of significant numbers of coal blocks to private companies without a competitive bidding process resulting in an estimated loss of $160 billion to the Indian exchequer. Most significantly, this process had taken place when Prime Minister Singh, who was otherwise known for his probity, was in charge of the coal portfolio.

Issues of corruption – at practically the highest levels of government – had obviously tarnished the image of the second incarnation of the UPA. To compound matters, the relentless campaign by the opposition, most notably by the Bharatiya Janata Party, had stopped the UPA II regime from making progress on a host of pressing domestic policy issues. Nevertheless, it made fruitful progress on some fronts.

Divide between Party and Government: PM Weakened

Another feature of UPA II was that the divide between the government and the Congress party had widened, which left Prime Minister Singh weaker. The Congress party and the government differed on vital issues of internal and external security. The Congress party's allies enjoyed power without subjecting themselves to any notion of moral conduct, discipline and accountability. In public eyes, it seemed that the Prime Minister was less assertive.

In his sixth year in power, even Singh's image of an honest leader was losing its sheen because he was increasingly seen as someone ready to tolerate dishonesty in the cabinet and in his government. The Congress party blamed it on its allies' lack of ethics and political opportunism. Top Congress leaders began to openly express their woes – that UPA II was not as stable as UPA I because their allies were opportunists. They felt that in the UPA II, though there had been ideological differences with the Left parties, but they were committed to the idea of satiability for the good of the country.

In the UPA I's term, the exclusive arrangement of dual centres of power worked well between Prime Minister Singh and party chief Sonia Gandhi; the former ran the government, the latter handled the political management of the coalition. But it did not work well in the later part of UPA II government. It seemed that the duo needed a new arrangement of power because the coalition had become very problematic. Partners positively embarrassed the government and their actions tarnished the image of an honest Prime Minister.

Pitfalls in Coalition Politics

The history of coalition politics in India shows the pitfalls of political alliances. Even though coalition system is the only system that can operate in Indian politics, it is also the system that is beset with innumerable challenges.

Every day, the fate of such coalition governments hangs in the balance, depending on the withdrawal of support by one or the other. The parliamentary system of government functions successfully with two political parties. But the political parties in India have increased in number, even at the State level. In Tamil Nadu, for instance, there are a dozen active parties – among them the DMK, AIADMK and TMC are very proactive, MDMK and the Left not far behind. In Andhra Pradesh, there are the TDP and the NTR-TDP and so on.

In such a situation, when a system of coalition operates, cabinet secrecy is also thrown to winds. To secure a consensus within parties is a very difficult task. The usual reason for detesting coalitions is due to the reason that they come together only for power. Since they are heterogeneous, they are both ineffective and unstable. Each coalition power tends to suspect the other. If the government is efficient, each constituent partner is worried that someone else will hog the credit. On the other hand, if it is ineffective, each partner will blame the other. And suppose the government has to take some unpopular decision, then each one will blame the other and keep the distance. It is neither possible to take credit for the achievement of the parties in a coalition, nor the blame for any kind of failure. Therefore, a coalition government always remains weak.

In such a system, there is the subordination of ideology to power.

Since in the Indian coalition system, there is one single party which is dominant in a coalition of several parties, there is every chance and also the absolute necessity that the identity, agenda and the ideology of that dominant party has to be merged with the remaining small parties. In other words, it has to dilute its ideology or keep some contentious issues in the freezer as has been done by the BJP, yielding to the wishes of the political parties joining it to form the government on three previous occasions. In view of such compromises, the BJP has lost its distinct identity, individuality and personality. The BJP, in fact, is a classic example of a party that has had to subordinate its ideology for the sake of power. The BJP feels that the contentious or controversial issues like abolition of Article 370, implementation of Uniform Civil Code and building the Ram Temple have to be shelved to widen support base of the BJP. In other words, compulsion of coalition politics necessitates such compromise by the BJP. This is clear to BJP watchers even on the eve of the 2019 general elections. Even the Common Minimum Programme of the National Democratic Front, promising the principles of Swadeshi ideology, has been diluted. The coalition parties led by the BJP had to show their commitment to the government by inviting foreign direct investment, opening up the Indian market and privatising many areas.

Coalition indicates the desire of political parties and personalities for maintaining power at any cost. These regional parties tend to get support through populism. In this system, power shifts from the Centre to the States. All the regional partners of the coalition have their stronger State agendas and there is no national agenda. As a result, the States tend to become strong and the Centre becomes weak.

Apart from this, the leadership of the Prime Minister is undermined. He cannot take strong decisions. Even the smallest party in the coalition can hold the PM to ransom. The PM has to deal with a heterogeneous group of power seekers who make no secret of their real intention. Such a Prime Minister cannot even choose his own cabinet. S/he has to consider the demands of so many parties, their leaders and then to select his team. Pressure is on the Prime Minister to allot certain portfolios to certain individuals. It requires lots of diplomacy to carry on in such a system. He frequently depends on the consent of the constituent parties to carry on the business of the government, which makes his position weak and pitiable.

In such a system, power shifts from the cabinet to an extra-constitutional authority like the coordination or the steering committee. Despite all these obvious concessions, a coalition government does not last long. A coalition is a weak and unstable government. Sometimes, the parties associate with other parties in spite of their ideological differences. The lack of ideological affinity and cohesion creates lot of problems. In such a loose association of political parties, there is bound to be hidden enmity between one another which may lead to antagonism of the worst kind in certain areas. The prime minister herself/himself finds it extremely difficult to carry the entire cabinet as one body due to their differences. Sometimes, the PM might have to give important positions to fence-sitters who may be insignificant otherwise. It is also not always that the chosen prime minister has the last word on the constitution of his/her cabinet. The prime minister may have to head a cabinet crafted completely out of compulsions of coalition politics, by the party chief (which is not always the chosen PM) and occupants of posts may not be the most competent, skilled or suited for the posts.

If fighting starts among the constituents either on the question of implementation of the Common Minimum Programme or the distribution of portfolios or offices etc; it leads to horse trading or defections, threat to quit the coalition and blackmail and ultimate downfall of the government. In some of the States, imposition of President's Rule become a distinct possibility due to non-cooperation of disgruntled coalition partners and State ruling parties and the Assembly may have to be dissolved.

Coalition Politics during Pre-NDA Period

Legacy of One-Party Dominance

DEVELOPMENT OF COALITION politics started in India with the general elections of 1989. But the truth is that coalition politics is older than the Indian Constitution itself.

Undivided India had its first experiment with coalition in 1937, when elections to the provincial legislatures, under the Government of India Act, 1935, were held. The Congress had a tacit understanding with the Muslim League when it was not fully confident of a decisive majority in the United Provinces Legislature. But after the elections, the Congress refused to form a coalition with the Muslim League.[1] However, when an interim government was formed, on 2 September 1946, there was a coalition with Muslim League.

The period of coalition of minority governments, since 1989 elections, was preceded by at least three phases of coalition governments in the past.

First of these were the non-Congress governments in the south Indian States after the 1967 general elections until 1971-72, when Indira Gandhi brought the Congress back to power in New Delhi and in a majority of the States. Second of these were the Janata Party governments at the Centre and in most of north-Indian States in the wake of the 1977-1978 elections. Thirdly, the Communist Party of India (Marxist) led Left-Front coalition governments and alliances, which were stable in Kerala and West Bengal because of the ideological factor cementing their relationship with allies. However, it would be incorrect to assume that all coalitions and minority attempts have been between the parties which were non-Congress by nature.

The Congress Party – One-Party Rule

Yet, one has to admit that Indian politics is reflective of electoral games in which there has been a historically dominant party – the Congress and a range of coalition experiments, especially at the State level. It's like a handicap in a ball game, an advantage. In fact, it has been argued that the Congress maintained its stature of a dominant party for nearly fifty years after independence only because it worked through a Congress system[2] of coalitions with its own set of mechanisms to accommodate diversified interests within its umbrella organisations. Thus, Congress in itself existed as a virtual coalition. By the late 1960s, the Congress was finding CPI and the DMK as its more or less stable partners, together with some floating ones choosing to join hands with it on issue to issue basis. During this virtual coalition, the Central government was already finding its options limited and freedom of action curtailed besides leading a hand-to-mouth existence. In this regard, relevant are certain examples which are cited as proof of the compulsions: decision to postpone the consideration of the Preventive Detention Bill, to withdraw the Criminal Law Amendment Bill and to withhold the discussion on the issue of compensation to the princes.

In the existent scheme of things, there was a change when the Congress system began to crumble. This deterioration had been underway for a while and the 1967 elections marked the end of one-party dominance and started a new era of political instability, coalition politics and political alignments. Significantly, to prevent the Congress from gaining from the splitting of opposition votes at that time of general elections, the opposition parties used the strategy of forming united fronts to avoid conflicts among themselves. At this stage, the parties were moving from the stage of temporary party coalitions to the stage of coalitional party system in which major political parties tried to enter into electoral alliance to join hands in a governmental coalition. The coalitions acquired names that defined its CMPs, had one or two anchor parties and lynchpin personalities and allowed partners to drift in and out.

The elections of 1967 replaced the single dominant party system by the multi-party system in which no particular party claimed absolute majority at any level of the political structure, and resulted in the model of intra-party, express or formal, coalition system.[3] In this sense, it has been noted that coalition politics in India is a direct legacy of the period when one party dominated the political scene. It represents a situation of political change in which major political parties enter into coalitions with a view to jointly fill the vacuum created by the Congress eclipse.

None the less, despite the debilitation of the Congress party in the post-1967 phase, it continued to be the most dominant party at the Centre till the ninth General Elections (1989) with the short interval of 1977-79, when a coalition ruled at the Centre as a non-Congress alternative.

It is an undeniable fact that the changed environment was most visible around the oldest party of India. New alliances centered around common interests and such situations had begun to emerge in politics by the late 1970s, due to the growing politicisation of vast numbers of the middle and lower peasantry and the middle caste groups. This led to a large-scale differentiation of the electorate, with diverse party identifications based on new interests and ideological alignments,[4] with the result, defections started in many States, primarily from the Congress. These defections were not only the means of fulfilling specific desires and goals but also were important for the supremacy of a party, and the multi-party system became the cradle of coalition governments.

The Janata Party – Two-Party Rule

The turning point in the history of coalition governments in independent India came about with the Janata Party rule (1977-79) which brought, for the first time, a group of non-Congress parties to power at the Centre. The formation of the first Janata Party government at the Centre, under the prime-ministership of Morarji Desai, was an example in Indian politics. Though, technically, the Janata Party government was not a coalition because its four constituents had agreed to merge and had fought the elections on a single manifesto and a common symbol. This was a unique phase of bipartisan tendencies. For the first time in India, a two-party system appeared, and it was the time (1977-79) when only two parties – the Janata Party and the Congress – together accounted for over 80 per cent of votes and seats.

The Janata Party had come into being soon after the release of opposition leaders from jails, when four major parties – the Jana Sangh, the Congress (O), Bharatiya Lok Dal and the Socialist Party – came together to contest the general elections with a common symbol and manifesto. The Janata Party obtained 43.17 per cent of the popular votes and captured 295 seats out of 540 (55.4 per cent seats).[5] The 1977 elections are described as *a political earthquake* in Indian politics, but the inherent contradictions within the Janata Party coalition soon appeared as a warning to its existence.

This was because the formation of this government was a result of an accommodative attitude of its constituent political groups. In this phase of India's political system, *bargaining politics* reigned supreme, replacing the characteristic of collective leadership of the pre-1977 era. Although the power struggle within the coalition was muted at the time of the formation of the council of ministers – in proportion to the strength of constituent groups within the Janata Party – very soon signs of demands for rights began to emerge on various grounds.[6] The over-ambitious attitude of some individuals, temperamental incompatibilities and the party's and its leadership's failure to appeal to the people were responsible for the split in the Janata Party.[7] The main reason of the collapse of this coalition was the very base of its existence. The plinth was fragile, and the house was top heavy.

In fact, the formation of the Janata Party is a historical event in the political history of India, which is unlikely to be repeated in the future. The event was the culmination of the national state of Emergency imposed by Indira Gandhi on 25 June 1975, when besides a number of tortuous activities, the press was censored, fundamental rights of the people were suspended and a large number of political leaders were arrested under MISA (Maintenance of Internal Security Act).

No sooner the Emergency was lifted on 25 March 1977 and elections were declared, all opposition parties, except the CPI, joined hands and decided to contest elections on a common symbol and manifesto.

Meanwhile, Jayaprakash Narayan had become the tallest and most popular political leader because of the anti-Congress movement led by him, prior to the Emergency, in 1974. As a result, no political party could dare to defy his political advice. Prior to elections in 1977, he asked all opposition parties to merge into one. Since there was no sufficient time to discuss and decide on formal modalities of merger, the BLD, Congress (O), Socialists and Jana Sangh merged together and contested elections on the informal Janata Party symbol. The Janata Party contested elections on the symbol of the BLD, ie. the 'Haldhar' or the plough.

It is a unique instance in political history that a party is formally formed *after* its massive victory in elections. *After formation of the government* at the Centre, under the prime ministership of Morarji Desai, the Janata Party was formally formed, and Chandra Shekhar was made its president.

Two of the strongest Janata Party constituents, the Bhartiya Lok Dal (BLD) and the Jana Sangh, engaged in a power tussle over the governing of the north Indian States. Whereas parties like the Jana Sangh had shed their identity to form the Janata conglomerate and abided by the cabinet decisions, Charan Singh's Lok Dal and George Fernandes' faction of the

Socialists could not adjust themselves to the new situation. As a result, on the one hand, Morarji Desai was accepted as the Prime Minister, while both Jagjivan Ram of the Congress for Democracy (CFD) and Charan Singh of Lok Dal remained unsuccessful candidates for this office. However, they were anointed as senior cabinet ministers. On the other hand, the Jana Sangh's rapid expansion irked the secularists who raised the question of 'dual membership' of the erstwhile Jana Sangh in the RSS.

The other troubles were that of corruption charges against Kanti Desai, the son of the Prime Minister. After YB Chavan of Congress-O brought a no-confidence motion against the government, in July 1979, the Morarji government became a minority government because of resignations and defections from the ruling party. This led to the resignation of Morarji Desai from the office of the Prime Minister of India.

A new coalition government was then formed with Charan Singh as the Prime Minister, in October 1979. This coalition included leaders and groups from one spectrum to another – the CPI, CPI (M) on the one hand, and on the other those who were alleged to be close to big business houses, ie. capitalists. The party headed by Charan Singh was a party of defectors and had no absolute majority. The constant presence and influence of the Congress party was reflected in its ability to manipulate the fall of the Janata government. By promising parliamentary support of the Congress to Charan Singh for prime ministership, it forced a split in the Janata government, and then it pressed for mid-term poll by refusing to extend further support to Charan Singh. It was humiliating politics at its worst.

Prime Minister Singh's advice to dissolve the Lok Sabha was accepted by the then President, N Sanjeeva Reddy and mid-term elections were announced. The failure of the Janata Party coalition was caused by personality clashes, ideological differences and defections. These drawbacks were further supplemented by the strategy of manipulations pursued by the Congress.

After parting with the Janata Party, the Jana Sangh constituent revived itself in the form of the Bharatiya Janata Party in 1980, and Atal Behari Vajpayee was made its president.

However, the major achievement for Indian democracy was that the 1977 elections showed the power of the ballot against authoritarianism. The failure of the mandated governments warned coalition-minded parties to iron out their differences first and then get prepared for governance. The Janata Party rule also showed the force and bargaining power of the coalition against the dominant Congress at the Centre which had never been challenged before.

After the Janata experience of coalition government in 1977-79, single party dominance re-emerged during the period from 1980-89. This phase was different from the earlier period of Congress dominance because it was set in a multi-party context. Many new opposition parties got established at the Centre and received electoral support in the States as well.

After the Ninth General Elections of 1989, the situation changed dramatically again in favour of a coalition arrangement at the Centre. From 1989 till 2014, six coalition governments have been formed on democratic principles. These represented the National Front Government led by VP Singh (1989-90), the BJP-led coalition under the prime ministership of Atal Behari Vajpayee in 1998-99, the second innings of the BJP-led NDA government (1999-2004), the Congress-led UPA governments in the 14th and 15th Lok Sabha and Narendra Modi-led NDA government in 2014. However, in 2014 elections the BJP had crossed the halfway mark, it could have formed a single-party dominant government but chose to form an NDA government because it had pre-election alliance with 14 parties.

The elections to the Ninth Lok Sabha, in November 1989, marked a watershed in national politics as for the first time since independence, a hung Parliament was thrown in with no party or group getting clear majority to form a government on its own. The Congress under the leadership of Rajiv Gandhi got the largest number, ie. 195 seats, in the House of 525, followed by Janata Dal with 141 seats and BJP with 88 seats. The Ninth General Elections of 1989 were held in an environment filled with emotions. There was a single dominating issue or slogan, political frustrations, factionalism and personality clashes which preceded the elections. The message of the 1989 elections was 'priority' and had a plebiscitary character.[8]

The National Front

The agenda had now begun to be defined through the interpretation of the vote. Two types of attitude prevailed, viz. one, that there was no alternative to Rajiv. It was counter-challenged by the fact that VP Singh was the alternative. Thus, just as the Janata Dal was a coalition of four parties, that is Janata Party, Lok Dal, Jan Morcha, and CFD of Jagjivan Ram which came under the banner of social justice, the National Front was also cobbled up in order to reach an understanding to oust the Congress government because of increasing corruption and a defence deal scandal plus the forced resignation of VP Singh, the then Finance Minister.

After the failure of the Congress to form government, National Front (NF) got the required support for formation of the government at the Centre.

The National Front, the BJP and the Left formed an alliance in some 400 constituencies on the eve of the November 1989 elections, to ensure that the opposition vote did not split. The most notable feature of the 1989 elections was the skillful deployment of the electoral arithmetic, which the opposition exploited to its best advantage. In their common pursuit to defeat the Congress at the Centre, the National Front became the axis with the strong support of the BJP and the Left. Singh played a crucial role in uniting the opposition parties – the Janata Party, Lok Dal (A), Lok Dal (B) and others to merge under the label Janata Dal and urged several other parties to fight against the Congress. Thus, the emergence of this colossal coalition against the Congress heralded polarisation of voters, with the maximum possibility of a coalition government being elected and formed.

The 1989 results, however, gave an ambiguous verdict against the dynastic rule though the results made a call for change. In 1989, the voter adjudged the Congress (I) to be incapable and inadequate but did not give enough strength to the National Front nor the Janata Dal. This resulted in a minority government at the Centre. The two emerging political forces – the BJP and National Front – defeated the Congress. Despite the Congress winning 39.5 per cent of the votes, it lost heavily in terms of seats from 415 in 1984 to 197 in 1989.

The Janata Dal alone had won 143 seats. While all the opposition parties agreed to come together to form a government under VP Singh, in December 1989, the Left parties and the BJP agreed to support the government from the outside.[9] The NF government had managed to bring the two poles of Indian politics – the Left and the Right/BJP – together. The issue of these groups supporting the National Front was explained by a common logic: the Congress (I) had to be kept at bay by any means.

The urgency of preventing the Congress (I) from forming a coalition government was important for BJP as its support to VP Singh's government at the Centre was part of a larger game plan. It was the time for BJP to play a waiting game, hoping to improve its position by showing power directly or indirectly in six States, and of course, at the national level. The BJP was, of course, dreaming to come to power at the Centre in the next parliamentary elections. This was a distinct possibility if it could take advantage of the dissentions within the National Front, limited political influence of the Left, the confused state of affairs in the Congress (I) and most important of all, the rising Hindu nationalism.

Support from the Left, however, was based on short term strategy. Its leaders realised that Left support was vital to make the National Front stronger than its numerical strength in the Parliament.

The National Front did not have any formal mechanisms of coordination. The JD, the Left parties and others, except the BJP, met every Tuesday.[10] VP Singh noted that the JD was the dominant partner in relation to the regional parties in 1989, it was more out of courtesy than because of the clout of regional parties.[11] The alliance, as it appears in retrospection, had not given any serious thought to the need of coordination between allies and maintenance of cordial relations.

Common Minimum Programme

Although there was the talk of a Common Minimum Programme for the alliance, there was no formal declaration. When VP Singh was asked about how he planned to deal with allies who were *diametrically opposing his ideologies*, he replied that they were committed to provide a *clean and stable government at the Centre*. On the Common Minimum Programme, as such, he said, it was a fight against the influence of money over politics.[12] It has been noted earlier that the Left Front and the BJP had decided to support the alliance on the manifesto of the JD.

Ministerial Coordination Panels

The National Front began well on this count. Soon after taking over, the Prime Minister constituted cabinet panels to deal with crucial and basic issues like price rise, panchayati raj, autonomy to the electronic media, right to work, problem in Punjab, Jammu and Kashmir and the right to information.[13] However, the government itself did not last long for the results of this experiment to fructify. In this attempt, there was the idea that there should be coordination between ministers and the role of the cabinet was recognised. The NDA made the best use of this coordination and maintenance mechanism later, during its tenure.

Mandalisation – Failure of the National Front

This was a minority coalition and had the inherent risk of a pre-mature collapse. Squabbles within the Janata Dal surfaced soon after it came to power. The JD's internal affairs were no different from in 1977-79, ten years ago.

Hard pressed in the internal power struggle, VP Singh, on 7 August 1990 announced 27 per cent reservation for jobs in the Central government and PSUs for socially and economically backward castes, ie. the OBCs to further consolidate his and his party's base among them. While this hastened the disintegration of Janata Dal, it also sent alarming signals to other National Front partners who were facing the onslaught of the pro-Mandal leaders. According to George Fernandes, it was a deliberate political move which went wrong and brought the government down. VP Singh thought that by doing a favour to a segment of the population, he would get support of this population and therefore, he could win. His government failed because it implemented the recommendations of Mandal Commission without taking the coalition partners into confidence.[14] Also, it was under tremendous pressure from the BJP to pursue a soft policy towards the hardcore-rightist forces on the Ayodhya issue.

Further, during the eleven-month rule of the National Front government (Nov 1989-Nov 1990), the Janata Dal was rocked by intense factionalism between its Jan Morcha and the Lok Dal constituents, the latter led by Devi Lal. Subsequently, the JD became entangled in the controversies created by the Prime Minister's decisions to reserve Central government and public sector employment for the OBCs. The National Front government was finally deserted by the BJP, following the triumphant Hindu revivalist rath yatra undertaken by LK Advani, the then BJP President. The National Front government, deprived of the BJP support, fell in a no-confidence vote in the Lok Sabha. Simultaneously, the National Front coalition suffered another defeat when Chandra Shekhar engineered a split in the Janata Dal for becoming the Prime Minister – that too with the support of the Congress. He too lost after six months when the Congress withdrew its support. Nevertheless, the 1989 elections and the National Front formation showed there is an alternative to both, the Congress and the BJP, which can provide democratic governance. However, the NF failed to realise that its strength was rooted in alliance and coalitions which are if not impossible, a very difficult task.

The Tenth Lok Sabha (1991-1996) was a minority government formed by the Congress party under the premiership of Narasimha Rao with some dubious support resulting from *horse trading with the Jharkhand Mukti Morcha*. The Rao government was able to complete its full tenure. Subsequetly, after five years of Congress rule, with the electoral verdict for the next Lok Sabha, coalition governments began to settle as a reality for Indian politics.

Cards Turn for the BJP

The Eleventh Lok Sabha of 1996 witnessed the emergence of the BJP with 161 seats, as the largest single party in another hung Parliament, followed by the Congress and the Janata Dal. The BJP and its allies, as the largest political combine in the Parliament, were invited by the President to form the government on the condition that it will have to win a vote of confidence on the floor of the Lok Sabha within 13 days of its swearing in, on 16 May 1996. Atal Behari Vajpayee took charge as Prime Minister. On 28 May, the BJP failed to prove its strength in Parliament and the Vajpayee government resigned. During the debate over confidence motion, Vajpayee declared that his party was ready to freeze its controversial stand on the construction of Ram Temple, abrogation of Article 370 and the implementation of a Uniform Civil Code in the interest of evolving a consensus in the country.[15]

The United Front Government

Following the failure of the two-week-old BJP minority government, the NF-led Left Front alliance formed a fragile United Front (UF) coalition government consisting of 13 national and regional parties, headed by HD Deve Gowda, a Karnataka overlord, with the outside support of the Congress. The UF consisted of various parties divided on various issues but aligned for the sake of power politics.

The UF government actually emerged in the complicated post-election negotiations among the parties. This was in clear contrast to the formation of the Janata Party in 1977 and the National Front governments in 1989. Both were formed prior to elections. Moreover, both were marked by joint manifestos and comprehensive seat adjustments to avoid mutual contest, and with an understanding of common campaigning.

One of the significant political developments, as an outcome of the eleventh Lok Sabha elections (1996), was strengthening of regional parties and other non-BJP and non-Congress parties which came together under the banner of the United Front. Obviously, the gainers were the regional parties. This fact was highlighted by having, for the first time, a regional leader as the Prime Minister of the country. In fact, after the 1996 elections, the regional parties had started playing an important role in Central level politics. This spectacular rise of regional parties had many important messages. One, it can be said that growth in democratic consciousness meant that people in remote corners of the country started to judge parties by their performances. This resulted in even national policies being viewed in terms of their local impact. Not surprisingly, voters today prefer local politicians who are in a better position to understand and respond to issues in the local context. Two, there was no single political party which could claim absolute majority to form the government. Three, this also meant that federalism was placed on the national agenda. Prior to this, it was generally held that although constitutionally and politically, India had a federal system, it had been degraded and distorted in practice. However, after the rise of the regional forces, the substantial chunk of votes was now being shared by regional parties and therefore, suggested the above-mentioned points. The 1996 elections and presence of a variety of parties had given people the chance to exert their preferences, to choose and change their rulers in their own wisdom; this is an interpretation of such a fragmented verdict.[16]

Deve Gowda became the head of United Front government in June 1996, after VP Singh declined the offer for the Prime Minister's office and Jyoti Basu, Chief Minister of West Bengal, was restrained by his party, the CPI (M) from accepting the position. Out of 13 United Front (UF) government partners, nine partners participated in the government, four parties – though formally part of the UF coalition – did not accept ministry positions. The Indian National Congress provided outside support to the UF, because the main aim of the Congress Party was to prevent the BJP from coming to power. In April 1997, less than a year later, the Congress withdrew support from the Gowda government on the ground that the Union Cabinet had failed to check the communal forces and had also tried to marginalise the Congress. Meanwhile, Sitaram Kesri, president, AICC, continued to back the Central government when United Front changed leader and Inder Kumar Gujral became the new Prime Minister of the UF, with support from outside partner (the Congress party). Eventually, the Congress party again withdrew support to the UF after a short period, in November 1997, precipitating fresh elections next year.

It is interesting to note that the United Front became the first Union Cabinet in which a Left Party, the CPI, participated in the decision-making process and the Left leader, Indrajit made Union Home Minister. It was also for the first time that a coalition government formally adopted a Common Minimum Programme (CMP), acceptable to all constituents. Later, the CMP model was also adopted by the NDA and the UPA governments. The results of the 1996 parliamentary elections pointed towards transition towards a new party system and three major changes had taken place since the mid-1980.

*Firstly, the BJP, the Congress and the UF, reformulated their respective ideologies on fundamental issues such as secularism, state intervention in economic reforms, nationalism and social Justice.

*Secondly, the realignments among parties at the State as well as national level, took place. The Congress Party and the BJP tried to form alliances with regional/State parties. The BJP tied up with SAD (B), Haryana Vikas Manch of Bansi Lal and Shiv Sena etc, while INC attempted to make an unsuccessful agreement with BSP in Uttar Pradesh.

The United Front/Left Front was a divided bunch of parties, it could not constitute a cohesive force in absence of a strong leadership, who could unite its disparate members. However, a number of strong regional parties did not align with any of the three major contenders.[17]

*Thirdly, a noticeable change occurred in the social and regional base of the political parties, that is, the BJP improved its position in the Lok Sabha from two seats in 1984 to 161 in 1996. The Janata Dal/National Front won only forty-six in 1996 but enhanced its position in Karnataka.

The Congress suffered the most. It clearly felt the impact of the process of regionalisation. Thus, one can draw a conclusion that the multi-party system at the national level was moving towards federalisation, a process visible in the 1989, 1991, and particularly in the 1996 Lok Sabha elections. The balance of power now tilted towards regional and smaller players with 144 seats and 28.62 percentage of votes, while, five major national parties shared and won only 391 seats with 65.26 percentage of votes.[18]

Since 1967, a distinct State party system at the regional level already existed in some States. Now there was further shift in this position. After 1996, there was a distinct State party system at the regional level, separated but closely linked to the national party system. The regional parties were not only dominant players at the State level, national and State parties now began competing for power. By and large, with the breakdown of the dominant party system, Indian polity entered into a transitional phase, characterised by fluid, fragmented political formations and unstable coalition governments. At the same time, the multi-party system at the national level moved towards greater federalisation.[19]

The results from the 12th Lok Sabha elections in 1998 confirmed the overall tendency towards 'regionalisation of politics', and fecilitated Vajpayee's thirteen-parties coalition government in late March 1998. This election demonstrated that an Indian Prime Minister can be made and unmade in

State capitals, rather than in Delhi. Most of the political parties recognised the importance of pragmatic electoral alliance, except the INC, which subsequently strengthened the range of regional political formations.

The parliamentary elections of 1996 produced a fragmented and polarised picture, as much polarised as the previous elections in the party system had done. The complex pattern of inter-party alliance continued as a patchwork quilt at the Centre as well as at State levels. Three major contenders – the Congress, the BJP, and the UF – were in the electoral fray in 1998 national elections. The UF lacked cohesive leadership as its leaders, such as Jyoti Basu, Mulayam Singh Yadav, Deve Gowda and GK Moopnar were busy strengthening their own regional support base, rather than work for the unity and integrity of the United Front. None of them came forward to save the sinking boat of the United Front in the 1998 mid-term elections. The BJP vigorously searched for new friends because the party had learnt its lesson and now tried to avoid humiliations which had been occasioned in earlier times, as no one had extended support to the Vajpayee government in 1996, except pre-poll partners. The Congress remained as short-sighted as before.

Coalition under BJP-led National Democratic Alliance

BJP forms Government, but for 18 Months only

THE 12TH LOK SABHA elections (1998) provided opportunities to the largest political confederation, the BJP-led coalition, to form government at the Centre. A relatively more stable coalition pattern was witnessed in the case of the 1998 elections. There was the BJP with 19 coalition partners, the Congress with six allies and the UF with eight partners. The crown was thus on the BJP's head, which had captured the maximum number of partners and had reached the magic number of 270 seats in Parliament (depicted in Table 4).

Table: 4 BJP-led National Democratic Alliance in 1998

BJP-led National Democratic Alliance in 1998 with Re-elected Allies	Seates Won	Votes in Percent
BJP	182	25.59
AIADMK	18	1.83
Samta Party	12	1.77
BJD	09	1.25
SAD	08	0.81
AITC	07	2.42
SHS	06	1.77
PMK	04	1.42
MDMK	03	0.44
Lok Shakti	03	0.69
HVP	01	0.24
Tamizhaga Rajiv Cong (O)	01	NA
Independents		
Maneka Gandhi	01	0.10
Buta Singh	01	0.09
Satnam S Kanth	01	0.09
Sub-Total A	**256**	
Post-election Allies	**Seates Won**	**Votes in Percent**
HLD (R)	04	0.53
AC	02	0.05
SDF	01	0.03
MSCP	01	0.05
Citizens Common Front	01	0.02
BSMC	01	0.05
TDP	11	2.77
JKNC	03	0.21
Anglo Indians@	02	NA
RJP (Anand Mohan)++	01	0.07
Sub-Total B	**27**	
Total (A+B)	**283**	**41.07**

Source: Balveer Arora, Negotiating Differences: Federal Coalitions and National Cohesion, in Zoya Hasan (ed.) *Transforming India: Social and Political Dynamics of Democracy,* New Delhi, Oxford University Press, 2000, p. 194.

Notes: @ nominated members ++ Anand Mohan defected from RJP to support the NDA.

The BJP had truly emerged as an all-India party like the Congress and there was addition of 18 seats to the BJP's 1996 tally. It was able to establish a strong presence in the south and in the east areas and was no longer a party solely of the Hindi, Gujarati, and Marathi-speaking areas. At the same time, the improved status of the BJP in the 12th Lok Sabha election results and the BJP's conciliatory approach to regional parties further strengthened ties between the BJP and many regional parties. This relationship was based on two emerging political realities:

First, the BJP learnt that regional parties and assertion of socio-cultural realities were unavoidable forces whose support and cooperation was fundamentally required for government formation. Therefore, it was essential for the BJP to show both a moderate attitude and to get prepared for a common agenda for governance.

Second, it also remained silent on three controversial issues – Ram Mandir, Article 370 and Uniform Civil Code, not as any retreat from its ideological commitment but as a functional necessity to temporarily smoothen the means of achieving power. Compulsions of electoral politics and the prospects of victory in the elections had prompted the BJP to adopt a much more moderate posture.

This, coupled with the strategic alliances, have contributed to the end of its political untouchability and enhanced its credibility to stake a claim to power-sharing in New Delhi.

After the election results of the 12th Lok Sabha elections (1998), about 95 MPs of regional parties extended support to the BJP. This political support was again based on polarisation of regional parties. This clearly shows that smaller and regional parties have significant presence in several States. In the north-east, regional parties have been dominant forces. In the East, they have emerged powerful. In the south, they have expanded their area of influence from Tamil Nadu to Andhra Pradesh. north India shows the balanced strength of regional parties. In the West, regional parties have doubled their strength.

For the first time, the BJP accepted the reality of growing regionalism in politics. Thus, in the 12th Lok Sabha of 1998, the BJP and its allies formed a coalition government of total 18 political parties. It remained in power for approximately 18 months, which also included five months as a BJP-led caretaker coalition government at the Centre.

The BJP forged a number of pre-poll arrangements with various regional parties, such as Samta Party, Lok Shakti Party, AIADMK, Trinamool Congress, Biju Janata Dal etc. and also matured post-poll alignments with the TDP. Three regional parties and few independents added twenty-two seats to the NDA kitty, which led to narrow parliamentary majority for the BJP. The BJP moderated its own ideology and tried to accommodate the demands of its allies during and after the elections. In contrast, the Congress failed to learn the importance of alliance politics early in the electoral campaign.

The Indian Union Muslim League (IUML), Kerala Congress (Mani) and few smaller groups allied with the INC, as they had in the 1996 polls. (See Table 3.2).

Paul Wallace summerises the alliance system as a 'bi-model system', by which, two major or national parties maneuver within a larger vortex of smaller parties. According to the scholar, the 'bi-model' term is accurate, because both the BJP and the Congress are capable of forging a majority coalition or are in a position to bring down the government, given favourable circumstances.[1]

In 1998, the BJP went to the voters with the slogans of *'majboot'*, *'swachha'* and *'sthir Sarkar'* (strong, clean and stable government) – that is strong and good governance. The BJP nominated Atal Behari Vajpayee as prime ministerial candidate, presumably to capitalise on his liberal outlook and national image. The Congress party appeared to be weak under the leadership of Sitaram Kesri, president, AICC in the 1998 national elections.

It was at that time that Sonia Gandhi plunged herself into active politics, agreed to campaign for the party, boosted the morale of party workers and tried her best to restore the fighting spirit in the party to face the elections. Instead of asking for votes on the basis of the Congress manifesto or performance, she played the sympathy card, which appeared to be of paramount importance. Factually, the presence of Sonia Gandhi at the election rallies attracted the crowd but failed to translate into votes. However, her campaign succeeded in checking further erosion of the INC support base, halting the momentum of the BJP and contributing to the collapse of the UF.

The results of the 12th general elections (1998) revealed that the Bhartiya Janata Party and its allies captured 255 seats in the Lok Sabha, which reflected its extended turf beyond the cow belt (Hindu belt), bringing the party into the centre of power. The Congress and its partners got 170 seats only. The United Front (UF) was totally washed away in the elections and was reduced to just eighty three seats (see Table 5).

Table 5: Tally of Seats of Political Parties and Alliances in 1998 General Elections

BJP+	Seats	Congress	Seats	UF and others	Seats
BJP	182	Congress	141	CPI	09
Samta party	12	RJD	17	CPI (M)	32
SAD (B)	08	RPI (M)	04	SP	20
TC	07	IUML	02	DMK	06
Lok Shakti	03	RJP (Gujarat)	01	JD	06
AIADMK	18	KC	01	RSP	05
HVP	01	Others	04	FB	02
Shiv Sena	06			TMC	03
BJD	08				
PMK	04				
Independents	04				
TOTAL	**255**		**170**		**83**

Source: Statistical Report on General Elections, 1998 to 12th Lok Sabha Elections, Vol. I, *http://eci.nic.in/eci_main/statisticalreports/SE_1998/StatisticalReport-DEL 98.pdf.*

By 1998, the major components of the Janata Dal/UF had broken away. Lalu Prasad Yadav had formed the Rashtriya Janata Dal (RJD) in Bihar, Naveen Patnaik had left his parent party and formed the BJD in Odisha, resentment against Deve Gowda encouraged Ramakrishna Hedge to form the Lok Shakti Party. The TDP refused to get into any adjustments with the National Front in Andhra Pradesh.[2] later on, it extended the hand of friendship towards the BJP.

Atal Behari Vajpayee emerged as a leader of the largest party/coalition in the Lok Sabha and was invited by KR Narayanan, President of India, to form the government and win a 'vote of confidence' on the floor of the House. Vajpayee government did it, friend TDP accepted the post of the Speaker in the Lok Sabha and GMC Balayogi was elected to the office on 24 March 1998. The BJP worked hard and succeeded in putting together an eighteen parties' coalition, known as the NDA since then.

After coming to power, the Vajpayee government conducted the Pokhran-II nuclear tests in May 1998, which brought unity to the fractious coalition and enabled the BJP to avoid substantive debate within the government on economic and political issues that were more divisive and potentially dangerous to the survival of the NDA.[3]

But Pokhran provided just a short-term respite. This coalition failed to win the vote of confidence in February 1999, due to the opposition of the Congress and other parties like the BSP and AIADMK.

Right from the beginning, the NDA ministry was weak, and it faced various constraints. The demands of the NDA alliance such as Trinamool Congress, Samta Party and

AIADMK wanting dismissal of West Bengal, Bihar and Tamil Nadu State governments respectively soon grew strident. The SAD (B) and INLD demanded roll back of oil prices and prices of certain essential commodities. These demands increased the vulnerability of the Central government. Under pressure from its allies, the BJP tried to impose President's Rule in Bihar, and partially rolled back the prices of petroleum products to appease Samta Party, INLD and SAD (B) to ensure their continued support to the government.

AIADMK leader Jayalalithaa wanted dismissal of the DMK ministry in Tamil Nadu (on the issues of the Sethsamudram canal and alleged DMK support to LTTE) and also wanted corruption cases against her dropped. When her demands were not accommodated by the NDA, she withdrew her support from the ruling coalition. Even then, the NDA leadership firmly believed it could survive, but the story changed with a last minute withdrawal of support by the BSP – in apparent revenge for BJP's machinations in bringing down the Mayawati government in Uttar Pradesh when she was the Chief Minister in 1995.

In 1998, the most important factor that brought the BJP and its allies to the Lok Sabha in such a large number was because of the alliance that BJP had struck in different parts of India. Although it was anticipated that such a coalition might provide stability to Indian politics, this did not happen. The poles within the BJP-led coalition took their toll and finally the government fell after 13th months of rule. The Vajpayee government lost the vote of confidence by one vote, ie. 269-270. It was Saifuddin Soz of the National Conference (J&K) who defied his party fiat and voted against the government. Odisha Chief Minister Giridhar Gamang – an MP who neither resigned from the Lok Sabha, nor became a member of the State assembly but was CM – and Ramsheth Thakur of PWP (Maharashtra) also said 'no' to the government.

In a way, the NDA government fell by the rarest of margins of a single vote, 269 votes in favour of the NDA government and 270 votes against it. It was a narrow victory for the Congress and the Left parties, who were preparing to bring down the NDA government, but they failed to fulfill and complete the modalities for forming the next government.

The 12th Lok Sabha had special features to its credit:

1. The BJP tried to transform itself into a responsible national party, that is, seen as less untouchable or anti-secular.
2. There was emergence of bi-polar tendency which created a fragile and transitory coalitional government.
3. The changes also occurred in the State-level party system – the regional parties allied either with the BJP or the INC, tried improving their political position in their respective States and increased their bargaining power.

   However, the 1998 alliances were neither ideological nor did they have common objective to cement them together. These were merely short-term tactical arrangements developed by ambitious politicians that were rooted in the exchange of mutual benefits and the compulsions of power. But the gradual, regionalisation of politics at the

State-level was important and a continuing factor in shaping the present national party system.

4. It was for the first time that a government was based on pre-poll adjustments and headed by a larger political party such as the BJP.
5. Almost all partners shared power with the BJP, unlike previous governments, except Mamata Banerjee's Trinamool Congress.

The Indian polity thus jumped into the 'post-Congress era'. It did not mean that the Congress had ceased to be a major player; in fact, it continued to be a major player in all but in a few States like Tamil Nadu. In simple words, the era of a 'post-Congress polity' had begun, in the sense that the party ceased to be the pole around which the political competition had to be structured.[4]

BJP's Catch-All Strategy

The 1999 mid-term elections marked the continuity of federal-coalition governance within the framework of a multi-party system. It was held in the backdrop of perceptions in the wake of Pokhran-II, Bus Diplomacy to Lahore and the Kargil war. A new structural development took place in the Indian party system, when a combination of more than twenty parties decided to jointly contest elections under the umbrella of the NDA, which was based on the formula of seat-sharing arrangements to avoid confrontation and had Common Minimum Programme (CMP). Above all, the partners agreed to again project Vajpayee as the prime ministerial candidate during election campaigns in 1999.

The NDA headed by Vajpayee was a broad 'catch-all spectrum' of parties.* It included major regional parties based on different spectrums, such as TDP in Andhra Pradesh (based on language), SAD in Punjab (non-Hindu), National conference in Jammu and Kashmir (Muslim), Trinamool Congress from West Bengal (fiery secular) and INLD (non-ideological) etc. (See Table 6.)

Of course, the NDA government's demise by one vote in April 1999 had resulted in the BJP re-strategising to design a coalition formulation that was likely to provide higher degree of political stability for the asking price, which entailed a broad accommodation of various parties.

The composition of the NDA was much more diverse in regional and cultural terms than that of the Janata Party, which was essentially a north-Indian phenomenon. Now, the NDA became an all-India affair.

At the same time, the Congress, unlike the BJP, did not commit itself to alliance politics and searched for majority from its own resources. The INC leadership believed that Indian electorates had limited faith in coalition owing to their repeated failures to continue in power. However, the Congress

---

* Catch-All-Party is a term used for structural changes in post-second world war political parties in Europe. These changes were transformational – from old style of bourgeois party of individual representation and mass integration party into a 'catch all people party'.

Table 6: Tally of Seats of Political Parties and Alliances in 1999 General Elections

NDA (BJP-led)	Seats	Congress Alliance	Seats	Third Front & Others	Seats
BJP	182	Congress	114	CPI (M)	33
Shiv Sena	15	RJD	07	CPI	04
JD (U)	21	AIADMK	10	AIFB	02
SAD (B)	02	JMM	00	RSP	03
TDP	27	KC	01	CPIML (L)	01
TC	08	ML	02	NCP	08
BJD	10	RPI (P)	00	RPI (A)	01
NC	04	UMFA	00	JD (S)	01
PMK	05	Others	04	BSP	14
DMK	12			HVC	01
MDMK	04			AGP	00
HVP	01			MNF	00
Lok Dal	05			SJP	01
Loktantric Congress	01			JP	00
Janatantric BSP	01			SDF	00
AC	00			SP	26
Others	04			TMC	00
				TUJS	00
				UDP	00
				Independents	05
				Others	04
TOTAL	**301**		**138**		**104**

Source: Statistical Report on General Elections, 1999 to 13th Lok Sabha Elections, Vol. I, *http://eci.nic.in/eci_main/statisticalreports/SE_1999/StatisticalReport-DEL 99.pdf.*

party offered a few State-specific electoral adjustments with old friends (see Table 3.3). The United Front disintegrated, being reduced to be the tail end of the Janata Dal (Secular) of Deve Gowda. A belated attempt to unite the 'Third Force' was made by Sharad Pawar of NCP, Mulayam Singh Yadav of Samajwadi Party, but this idea did not succeed.

The NDA common manifesto (all constituents of NDA agreed to contest elections on a single manifesto, but retained their original as well as separate identity) pointed out that the 1999 general elections was an unnecessary imposition… by the motely combination of the Congress plus Left parties which promoted political negation, narrow personal interest and greed for power, over the national interests. The BJP's main charge against Sonia Gandhi was on her foreign origin, her property and trusts carved from tax payer's money and her inexperience in politics.[5] The slogan coined by BJP was: *Sarhad par Ghusankar Nahi, Sansad me Videshi Nahi* (we will not tolerate infiltrators at the border and a foreigner in Parliament).

The Congress' main charge against the ruling BJP were abetting criminals and corruption, making convenient deals at the cost of national interest and lack of vigilance on borders. The Congress party appealed to all the secular forces to unite in order to defeat a communal party and save Indian democracy. The CPI (M) manifesto alleged that BJP and its allies were the *Swadeshi agents* (local) of MNCs, whose policies were taking over Indian companies and buying up the Indian partners' share in joint ventures. The Left parties promised land reforms and a better deal to the workers, unemployed, dalits and adivasis, women, youth and children.

The issues spelt out in the manifestos did not catch the fancy of campaigners, leaders and voters. Generally, the electorates were interested in local issues like water, electricity and roads. In addition to this, factors such as poor governance, anti-incumbency, personality, regional parties, State politics and local issues dominated the 13th Lok Sabha polls as never before. The Jat reservation issue became focal point in Rajasthan, Shiv Sena's lack luster performance in Maharashtra, DMK versus Jayalalithaa issue in Tamil Nadu, on Lalu Prasad Yadav, the husband of the incumbent Chief Minister Rabri Devi in Bihar, were the focus of the entire elections scenario. Neither did the personality of Vajpayee, nor did the government's performance matter in the 1999 elections. However, downfall of the Vajpayee government by one vote had evoked sympathy for him in some quarters.

First Stable Coalition Government in History of India

The 1999 national elections gave a clear mandate for the BJP-led NDA with 301 seats. The BJP once again won 182 Lok Sabha seats on the basis of twenty four percentage of votes, while the Congress got twenty eight percentage of votes but crashed to an all time low of 114 seats in the popular House. The CPI (M) was able to maintain its turf by securing thirty-three seats in the House (see Table 3.3). The NDA gained a comfortable majority for a stable coalition government for the first time in India. It is because, the coalition partners provided thirty-four surplus seats in the Lok Sabha.[6]

The BJP's electoral performance in 1999 polls can either be described as a 'repeat performance' or as a 'renewal of the 1998 mandate'. Such descriptions can be disputed mainly on two counts:

*Firstly, several such parties which were not part of the NDA coalition in 1998 (some of them outside supporters), now allied with BJP in the 1999 elections. They were the TDP, DMK, JD (U), INLD, Himachal Vikas Congress and four other smaller parties.

*Secondly, the BJP repeated its 1998 performance in 1999 polls by winning almost the same number of seats and renewed the mandate for the Vajpayee government. So, what happened was that Vajpayee and the NDA won, but the BJP lost as a party.

No doubt, the party (BJP) retained the same number of seats (182) in the Lower House, but its popular base shrank from 25.9 percentage in 1998 to 23.7 percentage in 1999, which was mainly due to the dilution of its agenda, that is, Hindutva which was put on the back burner.[7] The BJP-led NDA government that took office in the end of 1999 also faced negative speculation about the capability of such a large coalition holding together for the full term. However, the Vajpayee cabinet completed more than four years and successfully met various internal and external challenges.

This was the first coalition in the history of India's party system with an optimistice view on regaining power on the issues of development and stability. So confident was the Vajpayee-led government about its success that the Union Cabinet recommended to dissolve the 13th Lok Sabha before its actual tenure ended in November 2004 and decided to contest national elections on the issues/slogans of 'Shining India' and 'Feel good factor' in May 2004.

The November 1999 parliamentary elections demonstrated that a rival of the Congress, which had become a national party like the GOP, the BJP was prepared to negotiate with other parties and was able to offer the nation a viable alternative to the Congress.

The BJP/NDA's success and Congress' failure rested on two critical factors: leadership and alliance. The BJP's foresightedness in formulating broad coalition/alliance proved crucial to attain majority in the Lok Sabha. Secondly, the differences between winning and losing were hinged to an understanding of a greater acceptability of Vajpayee as well as the rejection of Sonia Gandhi.

One can therefore move forward on the premise that leadership rather than institutionalisation of parties appears to be important: the alliance cohesion depends on the ability of the leadership to reach out in a non-ideological manner to its members as well as to maintain its core party support. There is no ignoring the fact that regional parties hold balance of power, now necessary for the formulation of ruling alliances. Consideration of staying in power rather than ideological or specific issues tend to dominate alliance choices. In 1999, the Lok Jan Shakti Party, Bhartiya Lok Dal, INLD, TDP, DMK or AIADMK brought a classic touch to the balance of power system and functioned as a check on national parties preventing them from adopting majority dictatorship.

Ten Years of Party Politics

The outcome of the five general elections, held between 1989 to 1999, demonstrated four facts concerned with party politics.

*Firstly, the Indian National Congress was unable to return to the position it had held before 1989.

*Secondly, negation of the idea that there was no viable alternative to replace the Congress party. By 1999, the Janata Dal (JD) had turned into a small number of region-based parties, with various JD offshoots willing to join BJP coalition governments.

*Thirdly, the BJP was successful in establishing a broader base in the Hindi heartland and then extend it to other parts of the country.

*Fourthly, the results of elections suggested that a national party could only form a government at the Central level, if it made alliance arrangements with several State or regional parties, that is coalition/alliance.

Thus, with the political scenario in India changing rapidly, the politics of alliance has become inevitable in Indian politics. The motive behind coalition strategies of both national and State parties are the prime movers in India's first-past-the-post system** that can bring in the votes and ensure majority seats.

** A first-past-the post (FPTP) voting method is one in which voters indicate on ballot the candidate of their choice and who receives the maximum votes wins. This system is practiced in various countries including Canada, India, Pakistan, UK, as well as in most of the current or former colonies and protectorates. The USA has a different system.

CENTRE-STATE RELATIONS IN INDIA

Constitutional Provisions for Centre-State Relations

Union of States, not of Federations

THE TERM FEDERALISM is derived from the Latin word 'foedus' which means treaty or agreement, which is made by different States intending to federate. They all agree by a written treaty or instrument, to form a dual polity, each having a clear constitutional field of its own. A federation is an association of States formed by written Constitution. Several States having common aims and objectives may form an association on constitutional, legal and permanent basis.[1]

The Sovereign Democratic Republic of India is a 'Union of States'. The term 'Union' instead of federation was intended to connote a higher degree of integration. Various federal

Constitutions were looked into. Federalism as contemplated under the Government of India Act 1935 was also kept in view. After long deliberation, the foundations of the federation as envisaged under the Constitution Act of 1935, structured after the Canadian pattern, was erected and deemed to be the best suited to the genius of the Indian masses. The experiences of the American and Australian federations were also given consideration. Their good points were embodied in the Indian federation and their pitfalls avoided.[2]

The basic principle of federalism is that the legislative, executive and financial authority is divided between the Union and States not by any law passed by the Centre but by the Constitution itself.

The nature of distribution of power varies according to the local and political background in each country. In America, the sovereign States which were keen to federate, did not like complete subordination to the central government, hence they believed in entrusting subjects of common interest to the central government, while retaining the rest with themselves. Thus, the American Constitution only enumerates the powers of the Central/Federal government and leaves the residuary powers to the States.

Australia follows the American pattern of only one enumeration of powers, ie. of the central government, leaving the residuary powers to the State because their problems were similar to the Americans.

The Canadians were conscious of the unfortunate happenings in the USA, culminating in the Civil War of 1861. They were aware of the shortcomings of a weak Centre. Hence, they wanted to opt for a strong Centre.

Indian Constitution-makers followed the Canadian scheme, obviously opting for a strong Centre. However, they added one more list – the Concurrent List. The Government of India Act 1935 introduced a scheme of threefold enumeration, ie. Federal, Provincial and Concurrent. The present Constitution adopts the method followed by the Government of India Act 1935.[3]

Ambedkar, while moving the different parts of the Constitution for adoption in the Constituent Assembly, had repeatedly emphasised upon the centralised character of Indian federalism and went to the extent of remarking that the 'Indian Union' had been deliberately used in preference to the 'Indian federation' which was the name used in the Government of India Act 1935.[4]

Jawaharlal Nehru, chairman of the Union Powers Committee, had taken the first step in this direction when he said that even though going back to the unitary state would be a retrograde step, the Centre should be armed with adequate powers to be able to maintain internal peace, solve economic problems and project a unified image of the country in foreign affairs.[5]

If the Indian federation is centralised, it is not because of recent developments in science and technology, modalities of warfare, emergence of international institutions or necessity for central planning but because *the architects of the Constitution of India have deliberately erected a centralised federal polity and named it as Indian Union.* The different organs of the state, in their composition and functions, are intended to subserve this end, and *division of power between the Centre and the States puts a premium on the leadership, strength and solidarity of the Government of India.*

The essential feature of our Constitution is that legislative, executive and financial authority – all three vital functions – is divided between the Centre and the States. Union executive authority normally extends only to subjects on the Union List, yet according to Article 73, Parliament may extend its authority to the Concurrent List. Article 256 and 257 provide that executive power of a province must be exercised so as to comply with Union laws and so as not to impede or prejudice the exercise of Union executive authority.[6] To ensure that both these stipulations are obeyed, the Union executive may give directions to a provincial government as to the manner in which it should act, and if a provincial government does not comply with these directions, the Union, under the Emergency Provisions, may take over the running of the State government (Article 365).[6] The Union executive may also devolve upon a provincial government, with that government's consent, exercise of any of its powers. Finally, Article 249 provides that the Council of States may empower Parliament to legislate on any matter included in the State Legislature List, thus, allowing the government to become nearly as unitary as under the Emergency provision.[7]

The Union, State and Concurrent Lists of power are enumerated in the Indian Constitution in the Seventh Schedule. The residuary powers or those not specifically indicated in any of the Lists are vested in the Central government as per Article 248. Conflicts of jurisdiction regarding this constitutional demarcation are subject to adjudication by the Judiciary.[8]

In order to modernise the Indian polity and society, the framers of Indian Constitution contrived an advanced pattern of democracy and provided it with a strong Centre to operate it. The Centre has more important, effective and wide-ranging subjects than the States have. Apart from the enormous powers of the Centre in legal, financial and administrative fields, there are bodies like the Supreme Court, Union Public Service Commission, All India Services, Central Services, Election Commission etc. which make the political system more unitary.

Legislative Relations

The basic provisions regarding the distribution of powers between the Central and provincial governments are in Part XI of the Constitution. This part is divided into two chapters, legislative relations and administrative relations. Part IX (Article 245-255) and Seventh Schedule spell out the equation between the Centre and the States in terms of the distribution of powers, enumerated in the Seventh Schedule of the Constitution in the

Union List, State List and Concurrent List.

The Union List includes subjects, over which Union shall have exclusive powers of legislation, including 99 subjects. This includes defence, foreign affairs, banks, currency and coinage, Union duties and taxes and the like.

The State List comprises 61 items over which the State legislature shall have exclusive powers of legislation, such as public order and police, local government, public health and sanitation, agriculture, forests, fisheries, State taxes and duties.

The Concurrent List gives powers to the Union and State legislatures over 52 subjects or items such as criminal law procedure, civil procedure, marriage, contracts, torts, trusts, welfare of labour and insurance, economic and social planning and education. In case of overlapping of a matter in the three lists, predominance has been given to the Union legislature as under the Government of India Act, 1935. In the Concurrent sphere, in case of a repugnancy between a Union and a State law relating to the same subject, the former prevails. If, however, the State law was reserved for the assent of the President and has received such assent, the State law may prevail not withstanding such repugnancy, but it would still be competent for Parliament to override such State law by subsequent legislation (Article 254 (2).[9] The history of river water disputes among Indian States tell us there is justification for moving 'water' from the State list to the Concurrent list. So is the case with real estate – buying land is prohibited to

Indian citizens in States like Kashmir but in States like Asssam, immigrants from neighbouring countries are allowed property and are considered settlers.

The residuary powers, the touchstone of determining the federal balance including taxation are vested in the Union Parliament. The Constitution lists in a fairly exhaustive manner the subjects of legislative competence. Besides, it was also anticipated that situation might occur when Parliament would have to introduce legislation on a matter not found in the Union List or Concurrent List. In such situation, the Union Parliament can resort to its residuary powers under Article 248.[10]

The special feature of Union/Centre-State legislative relation in India is the fact that in certain circumstances, the legislative powers of the Union can be expanded to the State sphere, an expansion which is not possible in federations like the USA and Australia.

Under Article 249, if the Council of States has decided by a resolution, supported by not less than two thirds of the members present and voting, that it is 'necessary or expedient in national interests' that Parliament should make laws with regard to any matter enumerated in the State List, and has so declared and specified in the resolution, then Parliament enjoys Concurrent jurisdiction with State legislatures on this subject. This power lasts for a period not exceeding one year; thereafter, as often as the resolution is renewed by the Council.

Under Article 250, Parliament is empowered to make laws on any item included in the State List for the whole or any part of India while Proclamation of Emergency is in operation. Since 1951, this provision had not been used. This is perhaps because of the reason that the Union and almost all States governments had the same political party in power. As a result, the Union could influence the State governments by informal channels such as Chief Minister's Conferences, Governors' Conferences, bilateral meetings between union and State officials etc. Party whips also acted as controls. But after the fourth general elections in February 1967, the political complexion of the country changed considerably, with parties other than the Congress forming governments in many States. This change affected the composition of Rajya Sabha, with the result, the Union Parliament today finds it extremely difficult to get any such resolution transferring State subjects to itself passed by two-thirds majority in the Rajya Sabha.[11]

Article 252 is another bone of contention which empowers Parliament to legislate on matters in the State List. Under this Article, if the legislatures of two or more States desire that any of the matters with respect to which Parliament has no power to make laws for the States, be regulated in such States by Parliament, and if resolutions to the effect are passed by all the Houses of the legislatures of these States, it is lawful for Parliament to act accordingly. Such a law applies only to States whose legislatures make the request or which subsequently adopt a law. Any Act so passed cannot be amended or repealed by the legislature of the State to which the law applies.[12] This Article actually provides for the enlargement of the legislative power of Parliament by the consent of the States. The main objective of incorporating this provision under the Indian Constitution was to promote uniform legislation passed by the Parliament for the benefit of contiguous States in matter of common and general interests.

For example, wild life was a State subject of legislation. As the Constitution says, government can declare any area to be a sanctuary for birds or animals and their killing has been made unlawful. In the year 1972, several States adopted resolutions in terms of Article 252 of the Constitution of India empowering Parliament to pass the necessary legislation.

Another relevant example is when a legislation for inaction on the part of the State in securing implementation of such national law amounts to denial of the right to live with human dignity enshrined in Article 21, more so in the context of Article 256 which provides that the executive power of every State be so exercised as to ensure compliance with the laws made by Parliament and any such laws which apply in that State.

The predominance of Parliament has been further established by Article 356 and 357 of the Constitution. Article 356 stipulates that if the President is satisfied that a situation has arisen in which the government of a State cannot be carried on in accordance with the provisions of the Constitution, s/he might declare that the powers of the legislature of that State has been exercised by or under the authority of Parliament. The effect of Article 356 is that the legislature of the State in question stands dissolved or suspended and the law-making power now rests in Parliament during the period the Proclamation of Emergency in the State is in force. Not only does Parliament enjoy the predominance over law-making in the States, the union executive also exercises control.[13] The case here is for a straightforward President's Rule.

The Constitution provides certain discretionary power to the Governor through which he can reserve a bill and refer it to the President of India for his acceptance under Article 200. Thus, the State Governor is constitutionally competent to reserve a bill passed by a State legislature for the consideration of the President. The reservation of a bill on the part of the Governor for reference to the President is an important field of irritant in the Centre-State relations. Any bill, other than those related to the high court, may also be reserved by the Governor for the consideration of the President under Article 201. This power of reservation extends to money bills also and there is no provision in the Constitution for State legislation to override the President's veto. Some political parties have been resenting this power of the Governor and in their opinion, such scheme of distribution of legislative powers between the Centre and the State has resulted in a high degree of centralisation.

Administrative Relations

The administrative relations between the Union/Centre and the States have been conditioned by the experiences in the administrative sphere during the British period of operation of the Government of India Act 1935. Therefore, the relations between the Centre and States in India varies from that in other federations. In federal States like the USA, there is a clear demarcation of administrative functions and personnel between the States and the federal government. Personnel manning the federal services have no connection with the States and the States and the federal governments have their respective personnel to implement their programmes.

The administrative relation between the Union/Central and State governments in India is on different footings.[14] In India, the position of the Union/Centre is very strong. Thc Union is so strong that the State governments have virtually become agents of the Centre. The area of jurisdiction is no doubt marked out, but the power of superintendence, direction and control have been kept as subordinate. The control of the Union on the States in areas of administration is manifest not only in the existence and power of the unified All-India Services, but also in the authority given to them to give directions to the States and provide grants to the States.[15]

Under Article 256, the executive power of every State is to be exercised in such a way as to ensure compliance with the laws made by Parliament. Further, the Union executive is empowered to give such directions to a State as may appear to the Government of India to be necessary for the purpose. If the Centre did not have such power, it would have been impossible to secure proper execution of the laws which Parliament is obliged to enact. Similarly, in Article 257, the Constitution calls upon every State not to impede or prejudice the executive power of the Union in the State. If any union agency finds it difficult to function within a State, the Union Executive is empowered to issue appropriate directions to the State government to remove all obstacles. Article 256 and 257 lay down a system of comprehensive administrative control and direction of the State. This aspect of administrative relation has come for scathing criticism.

President's Rule

Emergency Provisions in the Constitution as provided in Part XVIII – Articles 352, 356, and 360 – constitute the most explicit statement of the overwhelming power of the Centre, not only to transform the normal federal arrangements in three circumstances, ie. National Emergency (Article 352), failure of constitutional machinery in States (Article 356) and financial emergency (Article 360) into abnormal unitary functioning, but also to suspend and abridge the authority of States and impose Central rule for certain period of time (Article 356 and 365). The Constitution has also provided a section against non-compliance by the State. Article 365 provides that in case of non-compliance, the President shall be competent to make a Proclamation under Article 356 that the constitutional machinery of that State has failed and therefore, declare a state of Emergency there.[16] The Constitution prescribing a coercive section for the governance of the State by the President, under Article 356, is no doubt, a very drastic step. This has given rise to a new area of tension between the Centre and the States relating to law, order and maintenance of Central government property.

Since Independence, President's Rule has been imposed 124 times to dismiss elected governments. Article 356 was first invoked in March 1953 to dismiss the Gian Singh Rarewala-led United Front government of Patiala and East Punjab States Union, a union of eight princely States (PEPSU). Then it was used in Uttar Pradesh 1954. After that, it was used against the Communists, during the *Vimochana Samaram* to dismiss the democratically elected Communist State government of Kerala, led by EMS Namboodiripad, on 31 July 1959. So far, Chhattisgarh and Telangana are the only two States where President's Rule has never been imposed. Following its landmark judgment in the 1994 Bommai case, the Supreme Court of India has restricted arbitrary impositions of President's Rule.

A significant illustration of the Centre's 'direction issuing power' to the States is the measures taken by the Central government to combat the threatened strike by Union government employees in September 1968. To meet this threat, the Central government had promulgated an ordinance and issued directions to all the State governments to take action under it. Kerala was the first State to publicly declare that it would not implement Central directives but follow its own policies in this matter. The then Chief Minister, EMS Namboodiripad, reserved his right to interpret the ordinance and to give directions to its police officials accordingly. EMS considered the Centre's action as an encroachment upon the State's jurisdiction. He denied the allegation that he deliberately chose to ignore the ordinance.[17] It was considered by the Centre as a clear violation of constitutional obligations of the State towards the Centre. And for a time, there was much talk that the Centre would again invoke the drastic step of Presidential intervention to cow down defiant Kerala.

An acute controversy also arises on the use and role of the Central Reserve Police Force's presence in States.[18] Serious Centre-State confrontation occurred when on 24 March 1969, the Central Reserve Police (CRP) fired at a mob in the administrative building of the Durgapur Steel Plant, as a result of which sixty people were injured. The then West Bengal Home Minister, Jyoti Basu, urging the withdrawal of all CRP units from the State offered strong argument that maintenance of law and order including the protection of all types of property – Central, State and private – was within the constitutionally delimited jurisdiction of the State government.[19] Keeping in view the administrative structure of Indian federalism, it can be said that a State government has the exclusive right relating to the protection of law and order, including safeguarding of property, and the Central government is empowered to issue the necessary directives to the States. These directives are binding upon the States since their violation by the State would empower the Central government to call into operation, the coercive measures contained in Article 356. *The working of the Constitution of India has shown that these Articles have been misused to established Central hegemony to disallow such a legislation which does not conform to the ideology of the ruling party at the Centre and sometime to discredit the opponent party ruling in the State.*

The trend of centralisation in this sphere reached its climax during the Emergency when the 42nd Amendment of the Constitution, 1976, incorporated Article 257A to the Constitution, empowering the Central government to deploy any armed force of the Union or any other force subject to the control of the Union for dealing with grave situations of law and order in the States. These forces were to act in accordance with the directions of the Central government and were not to be under the superintendence or control of the State governments. The States resented this provision vehemently which, inter alia, found expression in the memorandum put forth by the West Bengal Government in 1977, during the Janata rule at the Centre. The memorandum advocated the scrapping of Article 257A. Consequently, the Constitution 44th Amendment Act,

1978 enacted during the Janata rule, deleted this provision with effect from 20 June 1979. With the scrapping of Article 257A, the *status quo ante* has been restored as regards the use of paramilitary forces. The Centre may have the right to send the CRPF without consultation and concurrence of the State but for the purposes of Centre-State amity and coordination, for the success of the Centre's effort, voluntary consultation and cooperation are to be preferred over unilateral action.[20]

Like all other federations, there is an additional provision in the Indian Constitution for All-India Services which are common to both, the union and the States. The existence of such All-India Services is one of the special features of the administrative relationship between the Centre and the State in India and has been a force in improving the quality of administration in the States and at the Centre and also a force for integrating the Central and State governments in the administrative sphere. For example, the Central government has practically no staff of its own to implement programmes drawn up by it in areas such as agricultural production, rural development, social welfare etc, and while it draws up programmes of nationwide application, it has to depend on the States for the implementation of these programmes. Use of All-India Services by the Centre over and above the heads of the State government has been a cause of Centre-State tension. The main reason for opposition from the States against All-India Services is that they do not have full control over these services and there is a feeling among them that the All-India officers are the agents of the Centre.

The Governor

The Indian Constitution provides for a federal government having separate system of administration of the Union and its units ie. States. In addition to its federal structure, the Constitution provides for establishing the Parliamentary form of government both at the Union and State level. In the context of the State, Article 154 (1) and 163 (1) of the Indian Constitution provides that the executive power of the State shall be vested in the Governor and that there shall be Council of Ministers with the Chief Minister, as the head, to aid and advice the Governor in the exercise of his functions.

The role of Governors of the States continues to be a controversial issue in Centre-State relations, not only in the context of imposition of President's Rule. The Governor has to play a dual role as the representative of the President and also as the agent of the Centre. As the head of the State government, the Governor has to exercise discretionary powers in the appointment of Chief Ministers, dismissal of the ministry and dissolution of the legislature besides exercising general supervision over the State administration.

In fact, the Constitution makers never intended the Governor to be only a component of the apparatus of governance of the State level. They meant him to be an important link with the Centre. These efforts were to provide a cooperative federalism leaning towards unitarianism, which could balance the fissiparous tendencies prevalent at that time. For this purpose, Article 356 has been enacted in the Constitution. Normally the first and foremost requirement of any action under the Article is submission of report by the Governor. As far as the advice of the Council of Ministers is concerned, jurist DD Basu, justifying the situation says: 'As a result of such report, if advised, the State government itself would be suspended. So, the Governor's Council of Ministers cannot be expected to sign their own death warrant.'[21] This observation indicates that the Governor has to act as per his discretion in this regard.

In 1952, no political party was able to secure absolute majority in Madras. In the legislative assembly of 375, the Congress won 155 seats, and the opposition parties formed a coalition under T Prakasam, with the title, United Democratic Front (UDF) and submitted a list of 167 members to the Governor. But the Governor invited the leader of the Congress party to form the government. Similarly, in November 1967, the West Bengal government, headed by Ajoy Mukherjee, was dismissed by the UF government at the Centre without giving the Chief Minister a chance to prove his majority on the floor of the House. After the 1967 general elections, the Congress party retained its control over the Central government, but it could not secure absolute majority in a number of States. But even in such cases, Governors, in general, showed their preference for the Congress party and this made them suspect in the eyes of opposition parties and led to the conclusion that a Governor is essentially an agent of the Central government rather than the Head of the State over whose destiny he presides.

Planning Commission: A Bone of Contention

The role of the Planning Commission has also been a bone of contention between the Centre and the States ever since its inception by the Cabinet Resolution in 1950. From an advisory body, over the years it assumed the stature of a parallel government (until its dissolution). It prepared plans for whole of the country under the instructions of the Union government and the views of the States were often ignored. KM Munshi pointed out in 1959: 'The Parliament, in fact, does not govern the country ... the nominated Super Cabinet, the Planning Commission does the supervision, control and direction of the Government of India and owes no responsibility to Parliament.'[22]

The Planning Commission was required to make recommendations to the Cabinet. It was expected to work in close understanding and consultation with the Finance Ministers of the Union and State governments. The decisions for implementation were supposed to be taken together by the Central and State governments.

The federal system of India's polity presents certain problems of coordination between the Centre and the States.

The Constitution includes 'Economic and Social Planning' as per Entry 20 in the Concurrent List in the Seventh Schedule of the Constitution. Hence, after the Planning Commission prepared its draft for the Five-Year plans and annual plans, it was supposed to coordinate them with the general plan.

The highest deciding body for planning is the National Development Council (NDC), which meets under the chairmanship of the Prime Minister, and includes all the Chief Ministers of the States and the Union Territories, concerned Union Cabinet Ministers including specially those in charge of Finance and members of the Planning Commission. The Secretary of the Planning Commission used to be its secretary. The NDC discusses, and if necessary, modifies the draft plan and approves it, after which it goes to the Parliament for the final approval.[23]

The Planning Commission's working has been severely criticised for exceeding its function and failure to enlist the cooperation of local government units and officials and of the people in general. In 1967, the Administrative Reforms Commission (ARC) reported: 'Unfortunately, over the past seventeen years, the Planning Commission has, in some measure, earned the reputation of being a parallel Cabinet and sometime a Super Cabinet.'[24] However, with regard to the utility of Planning Commission, Jawaharlal Nehru remarked in the Lok Sabha, in December 1963, that the Planning Commission 'has performed an essential task; without it we could not have progressed... we are a federal structure and it has served to bring the various States together and have an integral planning. If it had not been there, the Central government could not have done their job because immediately, difficulties would have arisen that the Central government was encroaching on the rights of the States.'[25]

In practice, it had, no doubt, become a very important body and its decisions were generally accepted, but this is due to its composition and influential membership. It was 'the highest national forum for planning which has in practice embodied and given informal sanction to the underlying concept of partnership and cooperation between the Centre and the States over the whole range of development and which brings State governments into an organic relationship with the organisation of planning at the national level.'[26]

The administrative relation between the Union and the States shows that the federal system established under the Constitution, like other similar systems, aims to achieve the fundamental objectives of unity in diversity. The framers of the Indian Constitution intentionally bestowed a somewhat dominant role upon the Centre in order to avoid the inherent dangers of a federal system, which as Dicey* pointed out, provides for predominance and legalism. They were very

---

* AV Dicey, *An Introduction to the Study of the Law of the Constitution* (1855), London, 1959, 175.

sensitive to safeguarding the century-old effort at national unity. At the same time, they showed sufficient political insight and realised the practical necessity of establishing a federal unity.

The Constitution of India recognises the autonomy of the federating units and also establishes an effective administrative nexus between the Union and the States. This nexus exists both for the security and safety of the Union and the States, and for securing uniformity and coordination in matters of common interest. But, the provisions of the Constitution have a bias in favour of the Centre.

NITI (National Institution for Transforming India) Aayog

With a view to easing Centre-State relations, particularly with regard to the whole range of development which brings State governments into an organic relationship with the organisation of planning at the national level, the NDA government established the NITI Aayog on 1 January 2015. It was established as replacement of the controversial Planning Commission. This came about after extensive consultation across the spectrum of stakeholders, including State governments, experts and relevant institutions.

NITI Aayog has been set up 'to provide a critical directional and strategic input into the development process'. It is supposed to act as a 'think tank' and advise the Centre and States on policy matters. The Aayog says it seeks to end 'slow and tardy implementation of policy', by fostering better Inter-Ministry Coordination and better Centre-State Coordination (cooperative federalism). The Prime Minister is its ex officio chairman and Arvind Panagariya its vice chairman while Chief Executive is Amitabh Kant.

Functions of NITI Aayog

1) To evolve a shared vision of national development priorities sectors and strategies, with the active involvement of States in the light of national objectives.
2) To foster cooperative federalism through structured support initiatives and mechanisms with the States on a continuous basis, recognising that strong States make a strong nation.
3) To develop mechanisms to formulate credible plans at village level and aggregate these progressively at higher levels of government.
4) To ensure, in areas that are specifically referred to it, that the interests of national security are incorporated in economic strategy and policy.
5) To pay special attention to the sections of Indian society that may be at risk of not benefiting adequately from economic progress.
6) To design strategic and long-term policy and programme frameworks and initiatives and monitor their progress and efficacy. The lessons learnt through monitoring and feedback will be used for making innovative improvements, including necessary mid-course corrections.

NITI Aayog is Different from Planning Commission

1) As advocated by its supporters, the new National Institution for Transforming India (NITI Aayog) will act more like a think tank or forum, in contrast with the Commission which imposed five-year plans and allocated resources to hit set targets.
2) NITI Aayog will include leaders of India's 29 States and seven union territories. But its full time staff – Vice Chairman, Chief Executive Officer and Experts – will answer directly to its chairman, the Prime Minister. It is different from the Planning Commission, which used to report to the National Development Council.
3) The major difference in approach to planning, between NITI Aayog and Planning Commission, is that the former will invite greater involvement of the States, while the latter took a top down approach with a one-size-fits-all plan.
4) The Planning Commission's role was formulation of broad policy and its capacity was more advisory. NITI Aayog shall have powers for resource allocation to States, based on their respective needs.
5) All these years, the States had little direct say in policy planning, which was the purview of the Planning Commission. Involvement of the States was indirect through the National Development Council; but now the State governments are expected to play a more significant role.

Financial Relations

No other federal constitution makes such elaborate provisions as the Constitution of India in respect of relationship between the Union and the States in the financial field. In fact, by making provision for the establishment of a Finance Commission for the purpose of allocating and adjusting the receipt from certain sources, the Constitution has made an original contribution in this extremely complicated aspect of federal relationship.

Financial relationship between the Centre and the States in India constitute the most contentious and most difficult issue of federal balance. The Constitution of India has tried to demarcate the area of taxation as completely as possible. Every possible tax has been allocated either to the Centre or to the States and any unspecified tax goes to the Centre. Financial relations between Centre and the States are specifically defined in Part XII of the Constitution (Article 262-300). Items of taxation of Centre and States are provided in the Seventh Schedule.[27]

Unlike other powers of the federal and State governments, the financial powers are divided into two Lists: the Federal and State Lists and residual powers rest with the Centre. The Union List contains twelve items of taxation and these taxes fall under five categories:

1) Taxes levied by the Union but collected and appropriated by the States, viz. stamp duties and duties of excise on medical and toiletries (cosmetics) preparations etc.

2) Taxes levied and collected by the Centre but assigned to the States, viz. succession and estate duties, terminal taxes on passenger and goods carried by railway, sea or air, taxes on railway fares and freight etc.
3) Taxes levied and collected by the Centre and compulsorily distributed between the Union and States, viz. taxes on income other than agriculture.
4) Taxes levied and collected by the Centre that may be distributed between the Union and the States, if Parliament by law so provides, viz. Union excise duties, excise on medical and toiletries preparations.
5) Taxes levied and collected and retained by the Centre, viz. custom, corporation tax and surcharge on income tax.

The State List contains 19 items of revenue. There is, therefore, no Concurrent sphere in the distribution of financial powers and income tax levied by the federal and State government.[28] Being aware of the inadequacies of the resources of the States under the existing Constitutional Provisions regarding taxation and revenue, the founding fathers tried to mitigate imbalance between resources and obligations of the States through certain other measures. These include obligatory sharing of Union taxes on income, permissive sharing of Union excise duties, assignment of certain Union duties and taxes wholly to the States, and provision for giving financial assistance to the States in the form of grants and loans.

The main sources of revenue for the States are the sales

tax, motor vehicle tax, excise duty on liquor. For the Centre, custom duties, corporation tax, excise and income tax are the main sources of revenues.

There are some restrictions on the power of taxation of the State in respect of tax on sales which have to be mentioned in the context of inter-State relations in the federation. Under Article 286, no State can levy a tax on a sale or purchase which takes place outside the State or in the course of import or export of goods to or from India. Inter-State taxes are taxable by the Union and these taxes are returned to the State of origin. Thus, Central government levies Central sales tax on such transactions and this tax is collected by the originating State and retained by it. Certain goods of steel, cotton yarn etc. can be taxed by the State only at a maximum rate to be fixed by the Government of India. In respect of declared goods, the tax levied under the State sales tax, legislation cannot exceed maximum level laid down by the Government of India.[29]

These constitutional divisions and provisions had mired the country in a plethora of taxes/double taxation etc. It made inter-State goods transport captive to license raj and paved the way for huge country-wide corruption at every crossing and naka. This was detrimental to the concept of One India-One Tax structure nation-wide. It not only took economic liberalisation of the 1990s but also several Finance Bills and amendments to the various financial clauses in the Constitution to finally arrive at the one tax structure, the GST (general goods and services tax) that we see in the country in 2019.

Apart from the division of tax power between the Centre and States, powers of borrowing have also been set out in the Constitution. Article 292 empowers the Centre to borrow funds within and outside the country as per the limits imposed by the Parliament. Article 293 (3) empowers the States to borrow funds within India; while Article 293(2) empowers the Centre to give loans to any State, subject to the conditions as laid down by the Parliament. However, in practice, a State cannot raise any loan without the prior permission of the Centre or if there is an outstanding loan from the Centre to the State or an outstanding loan for which the Centre has given a guarantee.[30]

Some State governments are not financially self-sufficient. They often depend upon the Union government for financial help in the form of grant-in-aid. Provisions have also been made in the Constitution for giving assistance to States in the form of grants and loans. Article 275 provides for this by empowering Parliament to pay out from the consolidated fund of India, certain sums every year as grant-in-aid of revenues to such States to the extent that such assistance is necessarily adjudged. The grants so fixed are based upon the recommendation of the Finance Commission. It is not necessary that every State should get grant-in-aid every year. If, in the opinion of the Finance Commission, a particular State does not need such assistance, Parliament may leave it out for allocation of such grants.

In terms of efficiency, in a made-up-of States system –

this should be a function of the Union Finance Ministry – with an arm/division for grants-in-aid or a States division handling all transactions with States. The methodology as a result of Constitutional provisions now is again top-down and devious, with huge costs in implementation/disbursal and the bureaucracy itself.

The division of resources and functions leads to a vertical federal imbalance, while the differences in the endowment position of economic resources cause a horizontal federal imbalance. The Constitution, however, attempted to anticipate this. It incorporated a mechanism of fiscal adjustment by way of federal fiscal transfers.

Provisions were made in the Constitution under Article (3) for setting up of a Finance Commission. It is reconstituted every five years. The Finance Commission has some obligatory duties and it also has some optional responsibilities. There are two obligatory duties. It has to make recommendations to the President regarding the shares to be assigned of duties which ought to be or may be shared, that is, income tax and excise, and also the method of distribution of the shares among the States. Then the Finance Commission has also a duty to recommend the principles governing the issue of grant under Article 275. Beyond the two obligatory duties, it is open to the President to refer to the Commission any matter on which he considers it desirable to get the views of the Commission in the interest of sound Finance.[31]

The constitutional provision actually resulted in more bureaucratic rigmarole – what should ideally be the job of the Union finance ministry cooperating with a/the respective State finance ministry when the need arises. Routinely, every State ministry structure – in its State finance ministry – should have a liasoning structure with the Union Finance Ministry. This would improve Centre-State relations much more and create greater transparency than the roundabout method now adopted by constitutional provision.

The establishment of the Planning Commission and the beginning of the planning process has affected Centre-State relationship. Originally established to look after the formulation and evaluation of Five-Year Plans, the Planning Commission entered into every fiscal aspect of the country. Using Article 282 of the Constitution, it recommended grants for States' financial plans, Central sector schemes and centrally-sponsored schemes, in addition to loans. In due course of time, it overtook the statutory body (the Finance Commission) in recommending fiscal resources in bulk amounts. The overwhelming influence of the Planning Commission in the sphere of Centre-State financial relations downgraded the Finance Commission's role in the process of fiscal adjustment. Thus, the functioning of the Planning Commission had an important bearing on the States' fiscal position.

This development not only affected the pattern of financial relations between the Centre and the States, as envisaged by the framers, but also gave rise to a pertinent problem of proper relationship between the Finance Commission, as a constitutional body, which deals with fiscal need and expenditure, and the Planning Commission which deals with plan expenditure. But such a distinction was no longer justifiable in practice as budgets of States were determined after a discussion with Planning Commission. The growing importance of Planning Commission had devalued the role of the Finance Commission in allocation of resources.

Besides these, it has been a constant complaint of the opposition-ruled States that the Centre was discriminating heavily against them in allocation of funds. So far, the Centre has, once too often, used the mechanism of resource transfers to reward States which have provided strong political support to the party in power and to punish those that have been controlled by opposition parties – as chief ministers NT Rama Rao and Jyoti Basu had often complained, of the mendicant status of their States and the Centre's step-motherly treatment of their States.

For a healthy Centre-State relationship, federal finance needs a sound structure. Without autonomy in financial resources, there cannot be State autonomy in real sense of the term. As a matter of fact, the States are not in a comfortable position vis-a-vis the Union in respect of how the finances of the nation are managed. They have a feeling that the Centre discriminates while giving grants-in-aid and other financial assistance. Hence, the causes for the demand of State autonomy will continue to linger so long as grievances are not removed. It is desirable for the Central government to accept some of the legitimate demands for an equitable distribution of financial resources between the Centre and the States. NITI Aayog is just one part of the financial wheel, the other spokes need to be also reset for a sound economy. Poor financial management in States/poor States does not make for a robust national economy.

Centre-State Relations During Nehruvian Era

Centre-State relations in India today is the direct inheritor of the Government of India Act 1935 that had been enacted by the British Parliament long before India became an independent nation. The post-independent era has further strengthened this position and led to a state of Centre-State relations resembling and somewhat comparable to that exercised by the Centralising role of the British rule in this country. Post-independence, long periods of dominance of one political party, both at the Centre and the States, has further added to Central dominance and inequitable treatment of States.

The constitutional framework of Union-State relationship worked reasonably well during the seventeen-year period from 1950-1967. This period is characterised by the dominance of a single political party, the Indian National Congress (INC), in India's political system and the dominance of a single individual, Jawaharlal Nehru, who held the posts of both the party president and the Prime Minister of India.

Thus, politically, the Centralisation of political power in the Union government and within the government in one individual was inevitable. However, Nehru stood for democracy, socialism, planning and broad humanism and under his leadership the Congress adopted, first, the 'Socialistic Pattern of Society' and subsequently, 'Democratic Socialism', as the goal to be pursued. On these issues Nehru represented a wide consensus within the party and across the nation and therefore, he came to be acknowledged as not only the leader of the Congress party and government but of the people as a whole. *The interesting characteristic of the one-party dominance system in the Nehru period was the large degree of autonomy that the provincial party units were able to assert in relation to the Central party leadership.*

The Pradesh Congress Committees (PCCs) largely became financially independent, raising their own party funds for running the organisations or contesting elections. Their recommendations for candidate for parliamentary or assembly seats were almost always accepted without modification by the central leadership, except when the State party was deeply divided. This dissent paved the way for the dominance of Central leadership over the State leadership in different parts of the country. Yet, Congress politics in the States was dominated during the Nehru period by powerful Chief Ministers like N Sanjiva Reddy (Andhra Pradesh), BP Chaliha (Assam),

Sri Krishna Sinha (Bihar), YS Parmar (Himachal Pradesh), S Nijalingappa (Mysore/Karnataka), YB Chavan (Maharashtra), HK Mahtab (Odisha), Pratap Singh Kairon (Punjab), Mohan Lal Sukhadia (Rajashthan), K Kamaraj (Madras/Tamil Nadu), Sampoornanand, CB Gupta (Uttar Pradesh) and BC Roy (West Bengal) or occasionally by party bosses such as SK Patil in Bombay or Atulya Ghosh in West Bengal who worked in close association with their respective Chief Ministers. The influence and autonomy of the State units in the Congress party structure were seen most clearly in 1964 – when the successor to Jawaharlal Nehru as Prime Minister (Lal Bahadur Shastri) was effectively chosen by Kamaraj as Congress president, in association with the Chief Ministers and party presidents of major States. In that respect, it was a democratic choice.

Under Nehru, government-to-government relations were developed to a considerable degree and to a great extent, it was formalised. A political party operating as a two-way communication and command channel in parallel to constitutional federalism became an established pattern. This was derived from the relationship between the Congress Working Committee and Congress-led provincial governments after the 1937 elections.[32]

The powerful Chief Ministers shared Nehru's national outlook and constituted counter weights to Central power, acting as partial brakes on Central authority in many administrative matters. They, in fact, acted as buffer between the first and second Prime Minister in succession. The Chief Ministers were so often successfully defined as the 'Congress High Command' that the party general secretary in the sixties expressed the fear that a situation may arise 'when State party Chiefs would rule Parliament'.[33] Also, Nehru showed himself sensitive to State sensibilities. He apologised for a Central minister visiting a State on official business without first informing that government and said that this should not be done. When TT Krishnamachari spoke critically in Madras of the State government, Nehru admonished him: 'We have been trying to avoid public arguments and criticism between ministers of the Central government and the State governments because… (they) only create conflict and ill will.'

Nehru also initiated the Community Development and Panchayati Raj programmes, which could have led to a degree of political decentralisation and empowerment in the villages. However, none of the programme succeeded, but they were the progenitors of the movement toward a 'third tier' of government that gained momentum during the 1990s.[34]

During these years, constitutional and sub-constitutional institutions began to play their part in Centre-State relations. The Finance Commission began allocating Centrally collected revenues to the States and, in response to State pressures, increased these allocations. The Planning Commission commenced disbursing capital development grants to the States, reinforcing New Delhi's political reach. Zonal Councils were established.

Three Constitutional Amendments – The Third, Sixth and Seventh, increased Central authority by extending Parliament's taxing power and New Delhi's authority over the production of and trade in foodstuffs and certain commodities.[35]

There were occasions during this period when strains were witnessed, particularly when the Union government set aside the constitutional machinery in a State and imposed President's Rule under Article 356. This was done in East Punjab on 20 June 1951, in Patiala and East Punjab States Union on 5 March 1953, in Andhra on 15 November 1954, and in Travancore-Cochin on 23 March 1956. In all those cases, the opposition parties criticised the Congress government at the Centre for not giving them the opportunity of forming an alternative government. They alleged that the Congress party was not willing to tolerate a non-Congress government in any State.

Allegations during this period were also made that the Governors were not impartial in the discharge of their duties. There was, however, no open confrontation between the Union and the aggrieved State, especially due to Nehru's stature, and matters were somehow or the other sorted out after the event passed off. The enormous size of its regional spread and the ideological diversity of its membership turned the Congress party into a loose organisation with groups ideologically stretched across a spectrum from extreme right to mild radicalism. Opposition groups were so disproportionally small, compared to the Congress, that their success depended mainly on the severity of the Congress' internal ideological conflicts which became evident soon after independence.

A look into the political dynamics during the period between 1947 to 1966 indicates that because of the commanding position of the Congress party, the Indian federal governance did not encounter any serious challenges both from the structural and functional point of view. During this period, important economic policy declarations were made and steps were taken for rapid industrialisation. It was thought that what was needed during this period was a steady growth of Indian economy and creation of opportunities for providing employment to the youth. Thus, the Nehruvian era from 1947 to 1966 is known for integration, security and rapid industrialisation of the country even as the newly-independent nation was passing through an intense phase of inherent under-developed economy, poverty, hunger and socio-political upheavals at the Centre and at the States level as well.

Centre-State Relations in Post-Nehru Era

Decline of the Congress party-dominance era of the Union-State cooperation started partially after the death of Nehru on 27 May 1964 and largely after the fourth general election held in February 1967. After Nehru, no one within the ranks of the Congress party could command that much respect and awe, and the affairs of the party and the government at the Centre and the States passed into the hands of group leaders (coterie heads) and in later years, these became known as 'Syndicates'. The party dominance at the Centre and in some States declined considerably. It's majority in the Lok Sabha was reduced from 361 in 1962 to 282 seats and in six States non-Congress parties formed United Front or coalition governments in 1967. The State bosses of these parties began to speak the language of conflicts, threats, warnings and complaints.

The proverbial phase of one-party dominance gave way to a new phase of coalition government and politics. The political system, for the first time, ceased to conform to the constitutional form of centralised federalism. In 1967, India presented a picture in which the main components were considerably more powerful States, capable of exercising coercive power on the mass of the population more or less at will. It had an economy dominated at the national level by the States, acting mainly in the interests of the national bourgeoisie and a rising class of rich and middle peasantry. It had a polity in which the intra-party differences of the Congress – revolving so long around the question of relative autonomy of the States within the federal framework of the Indian Constitution – were rapidly yielding place to conflicts of substantial nature between the Congress party on the one hand, the national and regional opposition parties belonging to the entire political spectrum from the left to the right on the other.[36]

The fourth general elections resulted in giving the Congress a bare majority in Parliament and unseating the Congress from power in a number of States, and the result was that the States began to assert their constitutional rights and to call in question the Central dominantion and to demand revision of financial allocation.

The Communists in Kerala claimed that the State should be allowed a share of its foreign exchange earnings to enable it to purchase rice from China. Tamil Nadu Chief Minister, C Annadurai, demanded that Madras should be allowed to obtain rice from Burma as compensation for loss suffered by repatriates belonging to the State. Even the Bihar Chief Minister, MP Sinha, appealed to the USSR to come to the State's aid to meet the famine situation in the State. Food shortage was acute though the technological intervention of the Green Revolution had begun in the late 1950s and was in operation in full force in the 1960s. From the State demands, it is apparent that emphasis on wheat cultivation in the GR projects gave rise to dissatisfaction in rice-eating States. Also to be kept in mind is that from 1961 to 1969, from the time of Kennedy, American food aid, PL 480 provided the Nehru-Shastri-Indira Union governments food grains.

Although this period was marked by apparent chaos, instability and increased personal opportunism and corruption, it proved to be a prelude to fundamental changes in the nature of Indian politics, and of which two factors have been especially important:

*The first is that chaos and instability were followed by

the establishment in several States of either stable regimes dominated by regional parties, or parties whose strengths were confined to one or two States. These included most notably the entrenchment of the DMK, and later the AIADMK, as the dominant party in Tamil Nadu, the CPI(M) in West Bengal and alternative coalitions in Kerala.

* The second important development of this period was the rise of parties based on the middle peasantry and backward castes and the beginning of the entry of backward caste politicians into positions of political power in several States, particularly in the north.

The Janata Party Period and Indira's Ascent

After the 1967 elections, multi-party politics began to manifest itself on the Indian political stage. Fragmentation and split in political parties also occurred during this period, resulting among other things, in the emergence of powerful regional parties and coalition governments in the States. No party was able to command absolute majority in the non-Congress ruled States and this resulted in a formation of hotch-potch of coalitions. In some States as many as a dozen parties entered into electoral/post-electoral alliance to seize power. The drama of splits and counter-splits, alignments and realignments and defections and counter-defections became common phenomenon. Vox populi described it as the 'Aaya Ram, Gaya Ram' game.

The uncertainty prevailing in some of the States gave the Centre, through its agent (Governor), occasion and opportunities to use Article 356. In about a decade from 1967 to 1976, the Central takeover, under Article 356, took place in thirteen States for as many as 26 times. The 'safety valve' under this Article was increasingly and unscrupulously used as a weapon of political management and as an effective tool of power politics.

In certain cases, President's Rule was imposed primarily to enable the legislature party of the ruling group to tide over the crises of internal dissensions which might take the form of dislike of the ruling Chief Minister by the party high command. This was a disturbing precedent, as it definitely amounted to the violation of the spirit of the Constitution. The Proclamation of President's Rule in Punjab (1951 and 1966), in Uttar Pradesh (1973 and 1975), in Andhra Pradesh (1973), in Gujarat (1974) are instances for misuse of Article 356 for sorting out intra-party disputes. In all these cases, the surprising aspect was that there were Congress ministries with majorities in the legislatures which were temporarily put to sleep whenever its factional fight crossed the 'reasonable limit', according to New Delhi, of party discipline and they revived after political differences were resolved under the threat of continuance of the President's Rule.

So far as the Congress practice of imposing Article 356 is concerned, three broad features can be delineated:

*Firstly, the Union government, which had a Congress majority at the Centre as well as in most of the States, acted in accordance with political expediency of intra-party dynamics in imposing President's Rule;

*Secondly, it exercised extraordinary power in maintaining the State administration under the direct supervision of the Centre when no alternative ministry could be formed;

*And finally, on a good number of occasions, the Central government led by the Congress gave the impression that the Emergency provisions under Article 356 have been exercised to restore democracy in the States.

After the 1967 elections, presidential takeover of the States under Article 356 became a frequent affair. Up to 1966, President's Rule was proclaimed only twelve times in about seven States. From 1967 to 1970, Article 356 was imposed eleven times in eight States. In 1971, this Article was invoked eight times in six States. In 1977, the figure increased to fourteen times in fourteen States. And in 1980, it was applied eleven times in eleven States. Therefore, compared to the first sixteen years (1950-66), there was almost five-fold increase in application of Article 356 in the subsequent twenty nine years (1967-95).

It may be stated that on most of the occasions, there was no justification for invoking Article 356 and imposing President's Rule. It is seen that the ruling party at the Centre has wantonly misused the Article for its petty political ends. It is true that with few exceptions, the Article maintained its genuine spirit till 1967, after which political pluralism began to dominate the scene. In the changed political scenario, the position shifted from 'as the last resort of President' to the 'first resort of the ruling party at the Centre'. On 31 January 1976, the Karunanidhi-led DMK government was dismissed by the Centre (under Prime Minister Indira Gandhi) citing corruption charges against Karunanidhi and President's Rule was imposed on the State. In 1977, the first non-Congress government headed by Morarji Desai came to power at the Centre on the basis of a mandate against the excesses committed during Emergency. It wasted no time in toppling down Congress governments in all States where the party had been routed in the parliamentary polls. This provision had been misused to promote the political interest of the party in power. The Congress was to repay the Janata Party in the same coin when it returned to power again in 1980 and issued the Presidential proclamation under Article 356, dissolving the nine assemblies under Janata rule.

During Indira Gandhi's rule, the main reason for the Central intervention was to maintain her supreme authority and her control over the entire country. It also involved increasing use of Central government funds for patronage purpose in the States and to establish an independent base for her in the countryside through such measures as anti-poverty programmes. Between 1967 and 1971, Indira Gandhi rose into prominence like a shooting star. Her drive to eradicate poverty and to ensure social equality was translated into practice through the policies of bank nationalisation, abolition of privy purse and other measures aiming to improve the conditions of the poor. Her position appeared invincible after India's victory in the 1971 war against Pakistan which led to the emergence of Bangladesh as an independent nation. Capitalising on her image as a radical and a patriot, she won a double victory; first against her enemies within the party and secondly, against the opposition.

Indira took centralisation in more radical directions. Under her leadership, Parliament, in the 24th Amendment, empowered itself to amend or repeal any provision of the Constitution. And it sacrificed in the Twenty Fifth Amendment, the fundamental freedom of Article 19 and also the major provisions of the Directive Principles. Civil liberties and the character of Centre-State relations were placed in the care of Parliament and persons dependent upon Mrs Gandhi's favour. Equally audacious was the attempt in 1973, in the supersession of Judges, to reduce the Constitution's three branches of government to two by mutilating the Supreme Court, again with great potential for affecting Centre-State relation.[37]

Rajamannar Committee Sponsored by Tamil Nadu CM

The centralisation of authority and Indira Gandhi's contribution to it evoked critical reactions early in her Prime Ministership. In 1969, a three-member expert committee was formed to examine the working of India's Constitution and to recommend the reallocation of powers between the Union government and the States. Justice PV Rajamannar chaired the committee sponsored by the Chief Minister of Tamil Nadu, M Karunanidhi. The Rajamannar Committee issued its recommendations based on the questionnaire that was sent to all Chief Ministers, party leaders and Tamil Nadu representatives in both Houses of Parliament, and to all members of the Tamil Nadu State assembly.[38]

The Committee assumed that the Indian Constitution was neither explicitly unitary nor explicitly federal. But, its working had made it more unitary than what was originally intended. The Committee did not want to disturb the essential framework of the Constitution so as to affect adversely the integrity of the country. It stood for an ideal form of government by recording the components; State autonomy was conceptualised in terms of minimal Centre and maximum State. The Committee recommended that an Inter-State Council comprising Chief Ministers of all States or their nominees with Prime Minister as chairman should be the statutory body consisting of scientific, technical, agricultural and economic experts to advise the States which should have their own planning boards. The Governor should be appointed by the President in consultation with the State cabinet or some other high powerful body to be set up for that purpose. The provision that the ministers hold office during the pleasure of the Governor, Article 164 (I), should be deleted.[39]

The Rajamannar Committee called for the abolition of Articles 249, 356 and 357 in the Constitution which give the Parliament the power to legislate a matter with respect to the State List and which give power to the Central government to determine and act on failure of the constitutional machinery due to Emergencies. The Committee also pleaded for setting up of a Finance Commission on a permanent basis, larger devolution of taxes in favour of the States and transfer of some subjects included in the Union and Concurrent List to the State List.[40]

The Central government refused to take cognisance of the appointment of a committee by a State government. But, as a matter of fact, the State government did not refrain from making such efforts. Thus, the new political environment injected a good deal of strength to the theory of State rights and new dimension was added to it by the national split of the Congress in the year 1969. Nevertheless, the Congress party took its revenge on the DMK in 1976.

Centre-State Relations During 1969-77 Periods

In the year 1973, the Akali Dal adopted the historic Anandpur Sahib Resolution which shows how the theory of a State autonomy can be abused to cloak a strategy for cultural chauvinism and in defence of vested interests. However, the end of intra-party democracy in the Congress, Centralisation of all the powers in the hands of Indira Gandhi and the emergence of extra-constitutional authority of her son Sanjay Gandhi, reduction of the Chief Minister's status to that of 'subedars', once again revived the demand for restructuring of the polity.

This amply found expression in the JP-led movement for 'Total Revolution' in 1974. The imposition of Emergency in June 1975 brought with it a host of problems. The strengthening of the one-party rule system and the authoritarian rule of Indira Gandhi resulted in Sanjay Gandhi and his cronies converting India virtually into a unitary system. This trend was institutionalised through the 42nd Amendment in 1976. This controversial Act, enacted on the recommendations of the Swaran Singh Committee, changed the basic structure of the Constitution and strengthened the authority of the Prime Minister in particular and the Centre in general.

After the change of power at the Centre and the end of Congress dominance, the Janata Party emerged as a credible national alternative to the Congress at the Centre. This triggered a fresh debate on restructuring Indian federalism.

The 1977 general election provided the first occasion for the transfer of control of state power from the Congress party to the loose-knit Janata coalition representing a variety of ruling class interests, without putting on an artificial gloss of homogeneity to cover their disparateness and contradictions. Even though the new ruling coalition, unlike the Congress party, was both organisationally and ideologically weak, it did preside over a state which had become immensely strengthened during the previous three decades.

States Start to Get Assertive

After assembly elections of May 1977, the CPI(M) led by Jyoti Basu, the Chief Minister of West Bengal, was actively advocating the case of State autonomy. Consequent upon his efforts, for the whole of 1978, the country was engaged in a national debate on the restructuring of Centre-State relations. The West Bengal memorandum sought to eliminate all such provisions which gave the States a 'medicant status'. A symbolic change was sought so that the Indian Constitution is represented as a 'federation' rather than a Union.

The legislative power of the Centre was sought to be taken away so that the residuary power remained with the States, and Parliament's power to legislate in the national interest after the consent of the Rajya Sabha was sought to be removed.

It was felt that there should be major modifications with respect to industrial licensing and the State's power to raise revenue should be strengthened.

The memorandum left no doubt that President's Rule as well as other Emergency provisions which concerned the States should be deleted and that the territorial integrity of the States preserved. However, Prime Minister Morarji Desai made it clear that the Constitution had been framed 'wisely' and said there was 'no need for revision in term of Centre-State relations' and it was not necessary 'at the present time' to hold a national debate on Centre-State relations. However, if any Chief Minister desired to raise the matter again, he was free to do so.[41]

The Janata Party, which had replaced the Congress in New Delhi, was essentially a party of the north and was not at all comparable to what was known as the 'Congress High Command', nor did any of its leaders have the charisma of Jawaharlal Nehru or Indira Gandhi. The party's central leadership was too weak to be able to keep even the Janata-ruled States in tight control. Under these circumstances, the regional political parties in Tamil Nadu, Jammu & Kashmir, Punjab and the CPI(M)-led government of West Bengal and many others began to re-establish their demands for greater autonomy.

A new feature of the post-1977 period was greater competition between political parties and also greater social polarisation in the States with reduced manoeuvring power for the Central government since the control of the Centre itself was beginning to be contested. During this period, the Congress party continued to wield power over a highly Centralised state, but its political authority was greatly reduced in the States. This opened up the space for new alignments to reinforce the growing opposition from the States.

Centre-State Relations Worsen between 1974-84

Central control reached unprecedented level in the context of worsening government-opposition relations between 1974-84. Demands from the States for greater participation in policy processes were met with stiffening controls and continuation of the centralised set up. One effect of excessive centralisation was manifest in the continuously shrinking support base of national parties, and the rise of regional parties to power at the State level – the most dramatic example being the electoral success of Telugu Desam in Andhra Pradesh in the 1982 assembly elections. The rise of Telugu Desam indicated that regionalism could be ignited simply by the understanding of political discrimination of centralised decision-making by the Centre. Against this new development, non-Congress Chief Ministers of Andhra, Karnataka, West Bengal and Jammu and Kashmir organised several conclaves in 1983-84, with the explicit purpose of creating a united anti-Congress front. The front's chief demand was a fundamental renegotiation in Centre-State relations and vesting of greater power in the States.[42] In the 1980s, these demands precipitated the formation of a government commission to study federal relations in India.

Sarkaria Commission

As has been stated, from 1967, the opposition parties started blaming the Centre for all national and State ills, as according to them, the Centre had started violating the constitutional norms. It was alleged that the Centre had been making steady inroads into the States' autonomy. Because of the pressure from all these regional parties, the then Prime Minister, Indira Gandhi appointed a Commission under Justice Sarkaria to look into the Centre's relations with the States. The Sarkaria Commission made a lot of effort to study this crucial issue. It took sufficient time to review the subject of Centre-State relations.

The chairman himself explained the objectives of the Commission in the questionnaire released to the public. The Government of India constituted the Commission vide the Ministry of Home Affairs notification No. W/11017/1/83 CSR, dated the 9 June, 1983 with the following terms of reference:

> The Commission will examine and review the working of the existing arrangements between the Union and States in regard to powers, functions and responsibilities in all spheres and recommend such changes or other measures as they may be appropriate. In examining and reviewing the working of the existing arrangements between the Union and States and making recommendations as to the changes and measures needed, the Commission will keep in view the social and economic developments that have taken place over the years and have due regard to the scheme and framework of the Constitution which the founding fathers have so sedulously designed to protect the independence and ensure the unity and integrity of the country which is of paramount importance for promoting the welfare of the people.[43]

The Commission's chair, Justice RS Sarkaria was a former Supreme Court Judge. His panel included two retired civil servants, B Shivaraman and SR Sen. The Commission submitted its 5,000-page long report in two volumes in 1988. The Commission released the questionnaire in 1984. It had sent 109 questionnaires to all the State governments, political parties, political scientists and members of civil society. The

Commission also toured all the States and collected their views and opinions on Centre-State relations.

It made about 247 recommendations to deal with the concern of the State governments. First, in its discussion of legislative relations, the Sarkaria Commission rejected the argument to reverse legislative supremacy of the Union Parliament. According to the Commission, the 'simultaneous operation side by side of the two inconsistent laws each of equal validity, will be an absurdity. The rule of federal supremacy is a technique to avoid such absurdity, resolve conflicts and ensure harmony between the Union and State laws. This principle ... is indeed the kingpin of the federal system'.[44]

It maintained that the argument that 'the States should have legislative paramountcy over the Union is basically unsound. It involves a negation of the elementary truth that the whole is greater than the part'. Nevertheless, the Sarkaria Commission recommended that an informal convention of consulting the State governments whenever the Union Parliament decides to make legislation on an item in the Concurrent List 'should be strictly adhered to, except in rare and exceptional cases of extreme urgency or emergency'. In the absence of an emergency, the Sarkaria Commission recommended that 'there should be prior consultation not only with the State governments individually, but also collectively, with the inter-governmental council which we have recommended, should be established under Article 263'. The Commission emphasised that the coordination of mutual consultation is 'a pre-requisite of smooth and harmonious working of the dual system' of governance in operation in India.[45]

Regarding the role of the Governor, the Commission recommended that only eminent persons, who are not active in politics, should be appointed as Governors, the selection should be made in consultation with the Vice President of India, Speaker of Lok Sabha, and the Chief Minister of the State concerned. The Governor should test the majority support for a Chief Minister only on the floor of the legislative assembly. While the Sarkaria Commission envisioned a qualitative improvement in the selection of the Governor, it also proposed a more limited role for the Governor's power of dissolution of an assembly under the Emergency provision of Article 356. It recommended that Article 356 should be used only in extreme cases. An 'errant' State should be warned 'in specific terms' that it was not acting according to the Constitution, the State's response should be considered, before the President acted.

The Governor's report to the President – precise, clear – should be given full and wide publicity, said the Commission. The 'material facts' should be made 'an integral part' of the proclamation so that judicial review on the ground of bad faith would be 'a little more meaningful'. The Commission said that to dissolve the legislative assemblies and to impose the President's Rule, the Centre (the Union government) should take the approval of the Parliament.[46]

The Sarkaria Commission did not recommend any major

change to the basic scheme of the Constitution in the field of taxes between the Central government and the States. However, it did recommend a constitutional amendment for the sharing of the corporation tax and other consignment taxes on advertising and broadcasting.

Institutionally, the Sarkaria Commission expressed an interest in setting up an expert committee to recommend desirable reforms in taxation and the distribution of resources from the Centre to the States.

It proposed the establishment of an Inter-State Council as a forum to discuss federal issues of national importance. It also called for a reconstitution of the National Development Council (NDC) so that it would work alongside the newly-established Inter-State Council on issues of economic planning and development. In order to improve the coordination between the Planning Commission and the Finance Commission, the Sarkaria Commission proposed that the Finance Commission should work under the general supervision of the Planning Commission member in-Charge of financial resources.[47]

The Sarkaria Commission, therefore, expectedly did not favour the idea of strengthening the States vis-à-vis the Union. It failed to gauge the intensity of feeling for more autonomy for the States. It recommended essentially in favour of the *status quo* and made no radical recommendation for restructuring the Centre-State relations in India.[48]

Failed Efforts to Restore Centre-State Balance

Indira Gandhi's efforts to restore the balance of influence in Centre-State conflicts in favour of the Centre failed because she was not willing to change her political methods of the early 1970s, even in the changed socio-economic circumstances of the 1980s. The Janata Coalition (1977-79) had an adequate understanding of the tensions brewing in the relations between the national industrial clan and the agricultural clan which could only be resolved by loosening the political grip of the Centre over the States and by establishing a broad consensus between the different opposing segments of the ruling class dominating different spheres of economy.

Despite the Emergency, when general elections were held in 1980, Indira returned to power in free and fair elections.

Talking of Centre-State relations, Darbara Singh of the Congress became Chief Minister of Punjab in 1980 and remained in office for three years. The Golden Temple in Amritsar, however, was under the management of the Shiromani Gurdwara Parbandhak Committee. In July 1983, the Sikh political party Akali Dal's president Harchand Singh Longowal invited a militant religious leader, Jarnail Singh Bhindranwale, to take up residence in the Golden Temple complex to evade arrest. Bhindranwale was sympathetic towards the Sikh separatist movement, the Khalistan movement, which had taken root in 1971 and had gathered momentum in the 1980s.

Longowal was trying to defy the ruling Congress in the

State as well as at the Centre. Bhindranwale soon made the sacred temple complex an armoury and headquarters of his armed followers. President's Rule was imposed in Punjab from October 1983 to September 1985, almost for two years. In the first week of June 1984, Pime Minister Indira Gandhi ordered 'Operation Blue Star', an Indian military operation to remove Bhindranwale and his armed followers from the buildings of the Harmandir Sahib complex by India's armed forces. After Operation Blue Star, Indira was assassinated by her own Sikh bodyguards and Sikh nationalists on 31st October 1984. The Congress too retaliated with the anti-sikh riots.

This is again an example of how local politics can influence national security, as following Indira's killing by Sikhs, the secessionist movement caused large-scale violence among the local population as well as took the lives of many Congress politicians and it included the bombing of an Air India plane killing 328 passengers.

Another case in point is the enactment of the Terrorist and Disruptive Activities (Prevention) Act, commonly known as TADA, which came into force between 1985 and 1995 (modified in 1987) in the background of the Punjab insurgency and was applied to the whole of India.

During Rajiv Gandhi's leadership, the strategies adopted by the Congress to meet the crisis originating from the States under non-Congress governments became counter-productive on many issues. Rajiv did not deviate very much from his mother's style of governance, though he exercised a good deal of political restraint in dealing with the non-Congress State governments. He seemed, at least in the beginning, to be genuinely interested in restricting the policy, but he soon became prisoner of the very existing political order. The preceding administrations, except that of Lal Bahadur Shastri, were under siege within; they bickered and collapsed under their own weight. No doubt, Chief Ministers, or at least some of them, experienced a great sense of autonomy from the Centre but these periods of autonomy did not evolve into more equal and balanced Centre-State relations.

The decline of the Congress system brought a number of issues to surface. One of these issues was to make room for other political parties to play their role in the national as well as local politics. The installation of non-Congress governments at the State level, after the fourth general elections, may be considered as the beginning of the process of erosion of Congress hegemony. In fact, this was the starting point for the emergence of coalition politics in India. Needless to mention that there have been a good number of coalitions of different forces playing at different levels but their manifestation at the political level could not be seen before 1967. The space gained by the regional political parties was fully utilised by them to advance their own interests. For the first time, these parties were able to play important roles in regional as well as national politics. The growth of regional political parties in India is the result of the interplay of many forces and it is difficult to pin point only one factor as solely responsible for it. It has been correctly pointed out that this development should not be viewed merely as a consequence or by-product of regionalism – rather as a phenomenon in its own right.

Growth of Federal Polity in India and Centre-State Relations

Foundation Laid by British Before 1947

THE INDIAN CONSTITUTION provides for a federal framework with powers divided between the Centre and the States. The framers of the Indian Constitution chose a federal polity for the country, taking into consideration the situation prevailing in India at that time. The foundation for the federal structure had been laid by the British before 1947 itself, as per provisions made in the Acts of 1919 and 1935.

The development of federal polity, as a matter of fact, was felt necessary in view of the vast size, regional diversities and social fragmentation of India. Although the British ruled India as a unitary system, certain mechanism of administrative decentralisation were introduced prior to independence. The sixty years between passing of the Indian Council Act 1861 and the inauguration of the Mont-Ford Reforms in 1921 formed a period during which a significant measure of delegation of powers to the provinces took place without, of course, making any fundamental change in the Centre-province relations. The Montague-Chelmsford Reforms, which is known as the Mont-Ford Reforms, were carried out by the British colonial government in India to introduce self-governance to India. Montague was Secretary for the state of India, while Chelmsford was the Viceroy of India between 1916 and 1921.

The new policy of decentralisation was by no means applied with any marked degree of consistency. All the same, the period saw a general, though by no means systematic, broadening of the sphere in which provincial governments could exercise some freedom of initiative and decision, even though formally and constitutionally, the authority of the Central government remained supreme and all-embracing. However, the British attempt to impose a centralised administration on India suffered inevitably under the impact of the natural dynamics of the country's sub-continental size and her varying local conditions and problems. Decentralisation was unavoidable in any case. What hastened it, was the rise of nationalism and policies followed by the British in meeting the challenges posed by it. These policies, which constituted one of the political foundations of Indian federalism, generated other factors in the shape of linguism, Muslim separatism and other problems of the Indian States. The interplay of these factors made inevitable, indeed, a course for the establishment of federal polity in India.[1]

The roots of India's present federal system are found in the Indian Council Act 1861, Morley-Minto Reforms of 1909, Government of India Act 1919 and the Federal scheme of 1935.

The Indian Council Act, 1861 marked a watershed in the constitutional history of India under British rule. It represented a formal recognition of the fact that the policy of increasing centralisation, initiated with the passing in the English Parliament of the Regulation Act in 1773, and the Charter Act of 1833, were not suited to the conditions of India. The creation of an administrative apparatus implying centralisation and uniformity, was basically in disharmony with the imperatives of India's geography and variety.[2]

However, the 1909 Act unquestionably brought constitutional advance to the threshold of representative government in the provinces. Only in 1909, the principle of election was conceded in the Indian Council Act and provision made for a specific number of seats, both in the Central and provincial legislative councils being filled by elections. Although this Act considerably enlarged the size of the Central and provincial legislative councils and added to their powers, nevertheless, the change was one of degree and not of kind. The system of government still remained unitary in principle. The major drawback of the 1909 Act was that the members were not returned by general constituencies of the normal democratic type, but by constituencies formed to represent communities and special interests.[3] Moreover, the control spelled out in the devolution fell short of attaining a federal character because the line of demarcation was not so definite or rigid as in a federation. The 1909 Act was welcomed by responsible political opinion in India as an acceptable step forward. This response received a jolt from a debate in the House of Lords in 1912, when it was made clear on behalf of the British government that the contemplated transfer of larger power to the provinces was only a move towards constitutional autocracy.[4] There was no possibility of India ever attaining self-government.

The government of India Act 1909, however, gave a more or less precise and legal form and a definite direction to the process of devolution, which had been developing over the decades in the shape of informal administrative arrangements. The announcement with regard to diarchy (dual form of government) under the 1919 Act was made by Montague in the British House of Commons on 20 August 1917. 'The policy of his Majesty's government, with which the Government of India are in complete accord, is that of the increasing association of Indians in every branch of the administration and the gradual development of self-governing institutions with a view to the progressive realisation of responsible government in India as an integral part of the British Empire.'[5]

Therefore, the 1919 Act was passed as a part of Britain's commitment to the gradual development of responsible government in India and also to lay the basis of federalism, as a goal of constitutional development. The 1919 Act provided, for the first time, the division of field administration into two spheres, the Central and the provincial. But no provision was made for the establishment of an important tribunal for the settlement of such disputes as might arise between the Centre and the provinces. On the other hand, it was laid down that in case of doubt as to whether a particular matter did or did not relate to a provincial subject, it was for the Governor General in Council, himself a party to the division of functions, to give a decision.

Decentralisation, as a process, had been in operation for quite sometime and it could, in due course, help in the development of a federal relationship between the Centre and the provinces, especially with the 1919 Act. Responsible government in the provinces, even if extended only for a part of the provincial administration, as was introduced by the diarchy under the Government of India Act 1919, meant that a part of the provincial executive must become responsible to the provincial legislature. Naturally, this responsibility could be genuine and effective only in degree. In other words, responsible government in the provinces, partially, had to be accompanied by a corresponding federalisation of the Centre-province relation. The two questions of 'responsible government' in the provinces and provincial autonomy were joined together by the Act and no progress was possible in the former unless there was substantial attainment of the latter.[6]

However, the provisions of the Act of 1909 made a great advance because of the Morley-Minto reforms of 1919; yet no attempt was made to incorporate the Indian States within the new system of administration. And nearly 600 princely units were exempt from this administrative oversight. There was no relaxation of the general process of superintendence and control by the Secretary of State over the administration of India and this subsequently excluded the possibility of relaxing control of the Central government over the provinces. Nevertheless, the most significant contribution of the Government of India Act 1919 to the growth of federalism in India was the creation of a climate favourable to the federal idea and the stimulation of these social and political forces, which set the constitutional evolution of this country definitely in the direction of federation.

Impact of India Act 1935 on 'Federal State' in India

The Government of India Act of 1935 marked a definite milestone in the constitutional history of India. This Act may be regarded as a constitution for a federal state in India. The 1935 Act brought about a qualitative change in the status, power and authority of the provinces. For the first time, in the history of British India, each province acquired an independent position and was invested with a distinct legal position of its own. The truly federal element in the Act of 1935 was the more or less clear and precise division of powers between the Centre and the provinces. Under the Act of 1935, the constitution itself laid down an elaborate distribution of Central and local powers and provided for the establishment of a federal court charged with duty and power to secure the observance of limits placed on the Central and the provincial government.

Thus, the provinces ceased to be mere administrative agents of the Government of India and instead, they became autonomous entities deriving their authority and power from the Act itself. The 1935 Act also brought about a major improvement in the fiscal position of the province by introducing the principles of federal finance.[7] The Act provided for important adjustments in the financial relations between the Centre and the provinces. But the changes made by the 1935 Act can't be said to have given complete financial independence to the latter. The source of revenue was so distributed that provincial prosperity and development were consciously subordinated to Central security and all elastic sources of revenue was kept by the Government of India.

Though the 1935 Act created the façade of a federation, it retained in reality the essentials of a unitary form of government.

The autonomy of Indian province was, in fact, subject to manifold limitations. The division of power, as it finally emerged, created a very powerful central authority in India and placed a significant restriction on the ambit of provincial autonomy. The distribution of legislative powers embodied in the Act of 1935 was such that it tipped the scale distinctly in favour of the Centre. The Centre-province balance of power finally laid down in the Act of 1935 gave evidence of a considerable degree of centralisation.[8]

The 1935 Act, before it came into operation, witnessed a long and fierce battle fought between the autonomists and the centralists. Sir Samuel Hoare pointed out in the House of Commons: opinion were definitely divided between the Hindus, who wish to keep the predominant power in the central authority[9] and the Indian Muslims who stood for the maximum measure of autonomy for the provinces with a view to security, protection for their special interest and maintaining themselves as a distinct political entity in India. The nationalists were concerned with the security and stability of the country as a whole than about the extent of provisional self-government, though the principle of provincial autonomy was universally recognised. As a result, their efforts were directed towards vesting adequate powers in the Centre to safeguard national solidarity. Congress party also opposed the constitution of 1935 Act as it did not bring India anywhere near the cherished goal of their self-government. Jawaharlal Nehru voiced an opinion generally shared by nationalists in India, when he described the Act as 'this new chapter of bondage'.[10] The Indian National Congress rejected the new constitution/Act in its 'entirety' as a constitution designed to facilitate and perpetuate the domination and exploitation of the people of India.[11] The

Muslim League was also no less vehement and forthright in its rejection of the new constitution as the Congress. During the debate on the joint parliamentary report in the Indian legislative assembly, Jinnah declared 'the scheme is wholly unnatural, artificial and unknown to any Constitution.'[12]

Table 7.1: Carving out of the Provinces (First States)

Provinces of British India	Area (in thousands of square miles)	Population (in millions of inhabitants)	Chief Administrative Officer
Burma	170	9	Lieutenant-Governor
Bengal	151	75	Lieutenant-Governor
Madras	142	38	Governor-in-Council
Bombay	123	19	Governor-in-Council
United Provinces	107	48	Lieutenant-Governor
Central Provinces and Berar	104	13	Chief Commissioner
Punjab	97	20	Lieutenant-Governor
Assam	49	6	Chief Commissioner

Open Source Information

At the turn of the 20th century, British India consisted of eight provinces that were administered either by a Governor or a Lieutenant-Governor. The tables in this chapter list their areas and populations (but does not include those of the dependent 'native States' or princly States). During the partition of Bengal (1905–1912), a new Lieutenant-Governor's province of Eastern Bengal and Assam existed. In 1912, the partition was partially reversed, with the eastern and western halves of Bengal re-united and the province of Assam re-established; a new Lieutenant-Governor's province of Bihar and Orissa was also created.

Minor Provinces

In addition, there were a few minor provinces that were administered by a Chief Commissioner:

Table 7.2 Minor provinces in British India

Minor Provinces	Area (in thousands of square miles)	Population (in thousands of inhabitants)	Chief Administrative Officer
North-West Frontier Province	16	2,125	Chief Commissioner
British Baluchistan	46	308	British Political Agent in Baluchistan served as *ex officio* Chief Commissioner
Coorg	1.6	181	British Resident in Mysore served as *ex officio* Chief Commissioner
Ajmer-Merwara	2.7	477	British Political Agent in Rajputana served as *ex officio* Chief Commissioner
Andaman and Nicobar Islands	3	25	Chief Commissioner

Open Source Information

Provincial elections were held in British India in the winter of 1936-37 as mandated by the Government of India Act 1935. Elections were held in eleven provinces – Madras, Central Provinces, Bihar, Odisha, United Provinces, Bombay

Table 7.3: Legislative Assemblies

Province	Congress	Muslim League	Other parties	Independents	Total
Assam	33	10	24 (Muslim Party) 14 (Non-Congress)	27	108
Bengal	54	37	36 (Krishak Praja Party) 10 (Independent Muslims)	113	250
Bihar	92		20 (Muslim Independent Party) 05 (Muslim United Party) 03 (Majlis-e-Ahrar-e-Islam)	32	152
Bombay	86	18	14 (Ambedkarites) 9 (Non-Brahmin) 6 (Other)	42	175
Central Provinces	70	5	8 (Muslim Parliamentary Board) 8 (Other)	21	112
Madras	159	9	21 (Justice Party)	26	215
North West Frontier Province	19		7 (Hindu-Sikh Nationalists)	24	50
Odisha	36		14	10	60
Punjab	18	1	95 (Unionist Party) 14 (Khalsa National Board) 11 (Hindu Election Board) 10 (Akalis) 4 (Majlis-e-Ahrar-e-Islam)	22	175
Sind	7		17 (United Party) 16 (Ghulam Husain's) 12 (Hindu) 3 (Europeans)	5	60
United Provinces	133	26	22 (National Agriculturists)	47	228
Total	**707**	**106**	**397**	**385**	**1585**

Open Source Information

Presidency, Assam, NWFP, Bengal, Punjab and Sindh. The Indian National Congress emerged in power in eight of the provinces and as such wanted greater control over these States, on provincial government formation.

Legislative Councils

Table 7.4 Elections and Legislative Councils in British India

Province	Congress	Muslim League	Other parties	Independents	Europeans	Total
Assam			10 (Non-Congress) 6 (Muslim Party)	2	3	21
Bengal	9	7	9 (Krishak Praja Party)	32	6	63
Bihar	8		2 (United)	16	3	29
Bombay	13	2	2 (Democratic Swaraj)	9	4	30
Madras	26	3	5 (Justice Party)	12	8	54
United Provinces	8		4 (National Agriculturists)	40	8	60
Total	**64**	**12**	**38**	**111**	**32**	**257**

Open Source Information

From the very beginning of the introduction of the 1935 Act, the reason for controversy between the Congress party and the Lieutenant-Governors was the 'safeguard' which affected the federal relations between the provinces and the Centre. The working of the responsible government in the provinces was affected as the Lieutenant-Governor used his discretionary power and acted on his special responsibilities as an agent of the Central government, thereby, he exercised control over the provincial government.

More important, however, was the fact that from the outset, Congress ministries in the provinces were under the rigid central party control. It was the party high command that made the choice of Chief Ministers and decided as to who should be included in the ministries. Differences between a Chief Minister and his colleagues were invariably carried to the Centre and settled by the high command. The supreme instance of the unitarian control of the highest party organs over provincial governments, however, came to the fore in October 1939, when elected Congress ministries were taken out of office and the experiment of provincial autonomy brought to an end as a result of a decision taken not by the provincial Congress ministries but by the party High Command.

Eventually, this centralised party control over local governments gave a curious twist to provincial autonomy and created a tradition which spilled over into the post-independent era and has had an important impact on the working of Indian federalism under the new post-independence Constitution.

What, in fact, happened in practice with the Congress party sharing power with the British-India governments in the provinces under the 1935 Act was that constitutional federalism was superseded by political unitarianism. To quote historian R Coupland, 'freed from the control of the legitimate Centre, the provinces were subjected to a far closer and stricter control by the Congress at the Centre'.[13]

The Government of India Act 1935, nevertheless, had a

great impact on the federal system that was envisaged under the present Constitution. The Act and its working laid the foundation on which the founding fathers of the Indian Constitution raised a new federal structure after India's independence. In the Act of 1935, 'we find a plaster cast' for the pattern of Union-State relations set in the Constitution of 1950.[14] It has a significant impact in setting the tradition of a Paramount Federation in the Constitution of free India.

No Congress Role in Act of 1935

The Indian National Congress had no role in shaping the Government of India Act of 1935. The first Round Table Conference (Nov 1930-Jan 1931) which decided the broad outlines of the future federal constitution had no representative of the Indian National Congress. The Second Round Table Conference (Sept 1931), which was attended by Mahatma Gandhi as the sole representative of the Indian National Congress, did find his support to the general principle of federation but could not settle down to the discussion of the details of India's federal set up.

It is to be noted that the Congress did not participate in the Third Round Table Conference (Nov 1932) and discussion on the Government of India Bill, as it had, then launched a civil disobedience campaign. As the Congress party had no share in the framing of the Act and as it differed in several important aspects from the federal scheme recommended by the

Motilal Nehru Committee (1928), it expressed its opposition to the federal part of the Government of India Act 1935.

The Congress party, however, never raised serious objections to many unique or special features not to be found in other federations. These were reservation of bills by the Lieutenant-Governors for the assent of the Governor General/Viceroy, giving of directions regarding the exercise of the executive powers, assigning of functions to provincial government and direction to officers to discharge function of Central government, proclamation of Emergency, federal legislature to legislate for two or more provinces in any matter in the provincial legislative list and many others in the financial field. These features of 1935 Act were in deviation from a normal federal system as they were in favour of a strong Centre and were designed to achieve that particular end. Today, they have become part of the Constitution of India, as the Congress which dominated the Constituent Assembly, was committed to a strong Centre.[15]

Plea for Strong Centre

However, in the decade between 1937-47, the Congress party's commitment to the federation with strong Centre could not be sustained and underwent marked deviation to the other extreme of a minimal Centre and maximum autonomy for constituent units. Unwilling to demand the coercion of territorial units, it was, nevertheless, prepared to pay a considerable price to the federalist forces in order to maintain India as a political entity.[16]

The partition of India, which accompanied the advent of independence on 15 August 1947, inevitably had a catalytic effect on the development of Indian federalism and gave it a new orientation. Two of the major factors – the Hindu-Muslim question and the problem of Indian States had contributed to the development of consensus in favour of a federal polity. However, the partition and the establishment of Pakistan radically altered the attitude of the Indian National Congress towards 'loose federalism as solution to the Hindu-Muslim differences'.

These developments made a profound impact on the federal pattern forged on the anvil of the Constituent Assembly of India. They called for re-examination of the rational of the federal system in the context of a new Indian Constitution. However, they did not completely erode the idea of federalism as an indispensable principle of free India's constitutional system. The natural imperative of federalism in India remained operative.

Pandit Nehru moved a resolution in the Constituent Assembly on 13 December 1946. The resolution envisaged a federal union of India which said, 'The territories shall possess and retain the status of autonomous units, together with residuary powers, and exercise all powers and functions of government and administration except such power and functions as are vested in or assigned to the union, or are inherent or implied in the union or resulting therefrom'.[17]

The need for strong Centre was stressed in the speeches

made by many members of the Constituent Assembly. Sri Krishan Sinha said, India must have a Centralised Republic. S Radhakrishnan was equally emphatic and talked of an urgent need for a strong Centre. BR Ambedkar, a non-Congress member, declared as far as he was personally concerned, he would like to have a strong Centre, stronger than the Centre created under Government of India Act of 1935.[18] Moreover, the members of the Union Constitution Committee in their report were of the unanimous view that it would be injurious to the interests of the country to provide for a week central authority which would be incapable of ensuring peace or coordinating vital matters of common concern and of speaking effectively for the whole country in the international sphere. The soundest framework for Constitution is a federation with strong Centre, they all agreed.[19]

An equally forceful influence towards centralisation was the national pre-occupation with communalism in the years from late 1920s until partition. The exigencies of the present as well as the experience of the past impelled the Constituent Assembly to create a strong Central government since a strong government could survive in the communal frenzy preceding and accompanying partition. The transfer of power, resettlement of refugees and to integrate the princely States in the Indian Union were the immediate factors giving strong support to a powerful Central government. However, on the issue of vital importance like formation of new States and alteration of boundaries or names of existing States (Article 3), which touched upon the very existence of a State, federalism was supported by the members of the Constituent Assembly.

Federal Pattern in Post-independent India

On the whole it was the Congress party which influenced decisively the future pattern of India's federal polity. The Indian National Congress under the leadership of nationalist leaders enjoyed unparralled authority in the Constituent Assembly. The Congress Party, during the national movement, had created a strong party discipline which helped the party and its influential leadership in paving the way for a Centre-oriented Constitution. At the same time, the strong influence of all-India leaders and their parties as a whole favoured a strong federal government. Those provincialists who did not agree with the broad policy framework of the Congress, ultimately had to accept the Congress line.

The Centre-oriented federation, finally designed by the Constitution framers, was the outcome of an effort to provide for regional diversities that characterise India without giving any encouragement to factors likely to endanger the fabric of national unity. The final product of the Constituent Assembly was not only the reflection of the existing unity, but also a devise designed to counter anticipated disunity.[20] Thus, Morris Jones has rightly observed, the facts of informal power structure, Congress dominance in all parts of the country and the concentration of its top leaders at the Centre weighed real relations heavily on the side of New Delhi.[21]

20 years of Centre-State Relations in Free India

The Constitution of India provides for a cooperative federal structure with its slant towards a powerful Centre. The cooperative federal structure of the Constitution was largely determined by the attitude and strategy of the Congress party developed in context of India's freedom struggle. The Constituent Assembly was overwhelmingly dominated by members of the Congress party. The party had clear majority of 63 per cent in the assembly, a majority that increased to 82 per cent after the country was partitioned.[22]

In addition to its numerical strength, the Congress party provided important ideological leadership for the nation under stalwarts like Jawaharlal Nehru, Sardar Patel and Rajendra Prasad. However, in the initial phase of independence, the leadership was not personalised and centralised because of the presence of many other leaders of equal status and eminence in the party. Enough room was left for accommodating the views of rival factions. The presence of statesmen like Sardar Patel acted as a restraint on the authority of Nehru. The leadership was largely the product of the national movement and, therefore, oriented towards consensus politics. It was able to accommodate divergent points of view.

The supremacy of Nehru became unchallenged after the

death of Sardar Patel. Nehru's position in the party became supreme and all major decisions of the party and government emanated from him. Just one man. This is evident from an often quoted remark of Sanjiva Reddy. He said, 'whatever Nehru wanted he did, when Nehru wanted CB Gupta appointed as Chief Minister of UP, we simply had to work to do it'.[23]

Congress enjoyed an unchallenged dominance both at the Centre and in almost all States during the first twenty years following independence. Hence, in the first two decades of independence, the issue of Union-State relation was relatively dormant and generally received little political attention from political parties. If there were some conflicts between States and the Centre, they were usually resolved within the party organisation. The Union-State tensions were more often an intra-party affair which took the shape of a family quarrel and as such, it was comparatively easy to resolve it with the Congress in power in all States.

During the period of early independence to mid-sixties, the Congress evolved a unitary party structure with Nehru enjoying a pivotal position in it. And both went a long way in shaping a unitary form of India's federalism.[24] Nehru's insistence on planning paved the path for the growth of a highly centralised, elaborate planning mechanism having its bearing on Centre-State relations. There were occasional murmurs from the States resenting the vital decisions of the centrally-dominated Planning Commission impinging on State autonomy. But all such resentments vanished before assuming any serious form in the face of the dominant role of the Congress high command, led by Prime Minister Nehru. A certain bargaining process was no doubt in operation, but all this could occur only within the broad framework of Central dominance and in the final stage, decisions adopted were close to the position of the Centre.

During this period, the Centre and the States worked in close collaboration. However, this trend did not continue for long since Nehru, in his last days, could not wield much power. Much of his charisma had faded away owing to the Chinese invasion in 1962. Gradually, it became manifest that power was slowly moving out of the Centre – with the result, the move for greater autonomy gained ground.

The 'Kamaraj Plan' of 1963 had created dissensions within the party. Important changes took place in State politics and in some States like Gujarat and UP, ministerial changes occurred in disregard of Nehru's wishes. This happened after the war with China and a demoralised Prime Minister could not assert himself. The dispersion of power had begun in the last years of Nehru. Nehru himself, despite his enormous power, did not ever override the interests of States.* The Congress high command

* The said 'main objective' of the Kamaraj plan was the rejuvenation of the party. Six union ministers and six Chief Ministers resigned from the government. It not only demonstrated lessening of Nehru's hold over the party but also ascertained the fact that a new power bloc called the 'Syndicate' was emerging within the Congress. At the beginning, who exactly comprised the Syndicate was not clear.

and Nehru were unable to intervene and therefore, failed to bring States into line with the Central polity after 1962.

The Shastri Period

Nehru's death in 1964 brought to the fore forces that accelerated the pace of federalism towards greater autonomy for the States. The Congress parliamentary party's unanimous choice of Lal Bahadur Shastri as Nehru's successor was supported by leaders who were interested in establishing linkage between two levels of Congress politics, State and the Centre. The State leaders provided the main forum for lobbying in favour of Shastri's candidature at the higher echelons of the party. Shastri was a leader from UP. By the time succession happened, the State units of the party had become enormously powerful and the State bosses were strong enough to exercise pressure on the decision-making in the Congress party. All this affected the shape of Centre-State relations. The important role played by the State party machinery and its bosses made the Centre increasingly aware of their key position in the politics of the Congress party and it became more or less clear that they would no longer play ball in Central control and direction.

The Shastri period, however, was marked by a pronounced centrifugal trend. In his brief tenure, Shastri moved slowly and carefully in his relations with the States and evolved a new style of decision-making through consultation and compromise. This is evident from many events.

For example in 1964-65, as the country was passing through an acute food crisis, Shastri attempted in more than one way, to develop an integrated food policy. He convened a number of Chief Ministers' Conferences and put forward proposals like statutory rationing in eight cities with a population of over a million, and a summery trial of traders who sold food grains at higher prices than those fixed by the government. Shastri's suggestions were given a cold shoulder by the State governments and nothing substantial was achieved. The States even resisted the attempts of the Centre to abolish food zones at a time when the country was surviving on food aid. The States would not have treated the Centre with such scant regard, had Nehru been at the helm of affairs. It is not to suggest that the States never resisted Nehru. But in such a case, Nehru could easily have carried his plans through. In contrast, Shastri was mild and perhaps, had no strong base in the party.

So long as Nehru was alive, Shastri was dwarfed by his personality. He never appeared tough. After the 1965 Indo-Pak war, when Shastri really came into his own, he passed away. His brief tenure of prime ministership leaves little ground to predict the direction he could have given to the Centre-State relation. But nevertheless, one thing became clear – that the question of autonomy of the States was gaining momentum and the States were growing as powerful forces and were, thus, going to play an important role in the selection of India's future Prime Ministers.

In Indira's Time

Once again, after sudden death of Shastri, the issue of succession emerged. Political complications arose and the issue was settled in a way that involved fresh accretion of strength to the States. From the very beginning, Kamaraj had supported Indira Gandhi for prime ministership, but what caused concern to the Congress president was the lack of enthusiasm on the part of the Syndicate about Indira Gandhi's candidature.

But that could be dealt with by the powerful support given by the Chief Ministers and Kamaraj was able to mobilise considerable support for Indira from the Chief Ministers. The Chief Ministers jointly issued a statement requesting Kamaraj to sponsor Indira Gandhi as Shastri's successor. The Congress president and State Chief Ministers of Congress-ruled States were the principal actors in the drama of this succession. The choice of Indira Gandhi as the Prime Minister in 1966 illustrated the dominance of the State party leaders. As Breacher points out: In fact, the second game was dominated by an alliance between the head of the all-India organisational wing of the party and the heads of the governmental wing in the federal units; together they overcame the resistance of a pressure group in the organisational wing at the Centre and ensured the victory of Indira Gandhi.[25]

Enthroning of Indira Gandhi revealed in clear terms the magnitude of the regional pressure in federal politics in the late '60s. Placing Indira at the Centre served the States well for a brief while. In the initial years of prime ministership, Indira Gandhi was busy in consolidating her position in Parliament and Cabinet. She had almost no time to interfere in the functioning of State governments. However, this situation prevailed only for a few years after her succession. Soon she began to centralise power in her hands and this became evident in her dealing with the States. By 1968, kingmaker Kamaraj fell out with his protégé and on 12 November 1969, the Prime Minister of India, Indira Gandhi was expelled from the Congress party for violating party discipline. The party finally split, with Indira setting up a rival organisation (which came to be known as Congress-R-Requisitionists, that came to be known later as Cong-I). In the All India Congress Committee, 446 of its 705 members walked over to Indira's side. Now Kamaraj also joined hands with the Syndicate; primarily, Indira opponents and their faction of the party came to be known as the Congress-O (Organisation). The rivalry was between the Syndicate and the Indicate (Indira faction). Kamaraj and Morarji Desai were the leaders of the INC(O).

Tilted to the Centre

Despite all these intra-party strifes, one cannot deny that during the one-party dominance (Congress-1947-67), Centre-State relations were heavily weighed in favour of the Centre. One party rule reduced public conflict, but it was not without a great deal of infighting and dissent.

The concrete difficulties involved in the smooth operation of the relationship between the Central government and the State governments were brought to the forefront for the first time in the wake of formation of the first CPI-led ministry in Kerala (1957-59). The national ruling party regarded it as a grave threat to its monopoly of political power. The Congress party and its local allies devised a situation in which a democratically-elected government found it impossible to function. Taking advantage of this impasse, the Central government summarily dismissed the CPI-led government. The Congress party and the Central government, thus, dealt with this anomaly in the power structure in such a manner as to give wide currency to the belief that coexistence between the Congress party in power at the Centre and an opposition national or regional party at the State level would be unviable.

However, the period from independence to the fourth general election could not ignore the assertiveness of State leaders on different occasions and they did not like to be portrayed as weak and feeble politicians in relation to the Central government. The example of BC Roy, the then Chief Minister of West Bengal, possessing unquestionable qualities of leadership, can be cited. His stand on the Damodar Valley Corporation could not be underestimated. There was no outright confrontation as the leadership both in the Centre and the States were of a conciliatory nature, so that conflict resolution could take place with the help of consultation and consensus technique. This also points out that during this period, the political network connecting the Centre and the State leadership was used amply to postpone consideration of inconvenient issues.

No strong leaders and Chief Ministers like Kamaraj of Madras, YB Chavan in Maharashtra, CB Gupta in UP or BS Kairon in Punjab, were prepared to act merely as a tool of the Congress high command. As a matter of fact, some of the Chief Ministers pursued their own policies in spite of the dictates from the Centre. Even in cases where Centre's direction on matters of policy were generally accepted by the State Congress governments, the acceptance amounted to very little in practice as the State governments were unwilling to implement the legislation enacted in accordance with the Centre's policies. One prominent example of this was land reforms. The need for ceiling on land holdings and tenancy legislation were passed from time to time by the Central government and Congress high command orders to follow through came to the States regularly. In this respect, most of the Congress ruled States differed from West Bengal, which went through with such reforms even before the rise of the Left in these parts of the country. No Central legislation was implemented in other States and the Centre was helpless in the matter of legislation. This shows that, despite the fact that the Congress was ruling both at the Centre and States, the Centre did not always succeed in enforcing its policies against the opposition of State governments.[26]

Therefore, the period between 1947-67 may be characterised as one of effective leadership and accommodative federalism. In the first two decades of federal experiment in India, the leaders at the Centre and States faced two sets of compromises in order to bring national integration.

*There were compromises which could lead to easing centrifugal pressures by allowing the State borders to remain as they were before or after independence, with predominantly linguistic, tribal or racial characteristics.

*And the second compromise was to develop a national language as a means of linking together the diverse people.

Accommodative federalism and effective leadership during this period were also supported by some contextual factors. During this period, the Congress party was the strongest party not only in the Centre but in almost all the States as well, intra-party cleavages did not threaten its hegemony. The charismatic stature and unquestionable leadership of Nehru favoured the climate of the Centre's political dominance over the States. Moreover, during this period, the State governments were able to enjoy a measure of autonomy within the framework of their constitutionally delimited jurisdiction.

The operational constraint for the States could mainly be attributed to the factor of resource inadequacy rather than to any major redefinition or restricting of Centre-State relations. Again, by and large, there was no organised attempts to destabilise the governmental leadership at the State level during the Nehru-Shastri era. There was always a scope of an accommodation and mutual adjustment of Centre-State relation, mainly because the Centre in general did not take unilateral non-negotiable positions.

A part of this explanation lay in the persistence of the consensus system. The Congress, till this time, had not completely abdicated its role as a party of the national freedom movement, the history of which was a continuous process of accommodation and reconciliation of various interests and points of view. This was also possible because of a relatively homogenous elite both at national and regional level. Thus, all this contributed for smooth function of India's delicately balanced federal Constitution during the first two decades of independence.

Stand of Other Political Parties before the '90s

It is a common observation that the actual functioning of the federal system in any country depends not only on the general legal framework but on the nature and impact of the political parties. It will, therefore, be of some importance to examine to what extent and in what way political parties in India have been able to exert influence on the working of the Indian federalism.

As already explained, the Congress Party had been in favour of strong Centre with sufficient powers to control the policies in regard to matters assigned to the States. The economic and social reconstruction for the purpose of creating a socialist society had been on the agenda of the Congress party and for that reason, it favoured a centralised federalism.

Jana Sangh: Among other parties, the erstwhile Jana Sangh (later BJP) also stood for a centralised federation. The party believed that by setting up a strong national government based upon distinctive Hindu orientation, it was possible to maintain national unity and to protect the nation against various fissiparous forces. Equating a strong Centre with a strong nation, it insisted that national interests have primacy over regional interests. It firmly believed in one nation, one culture and one language. In this belief lay the argument for a uniform civil code.

The Left: The Left parties wanted a system of governance which would ensure substantial autonomy to the States. At the initial phase, since 1967, Left parties in West Bengal and Kerala had adopted a policy of confrontation with the Centre for greater autonomy. Both the CPI and CPI (M) were critical of existing Centre-State relations and demanded its restructuring. The communist parties, in spite of their ideological commitment to centralism, had advocated the theory of the States' rights and devolution of powers and resources to the States. This compromise was in the interest of power in the two States. This is the reason that an important part of their ideology is even today directed towards mobilisation of regional demands against Centre's decisions, enabling States to become a viable unit of the federal polity of India.

In 1968, the Communist Party of India stood for 'changes in federal Constitution of the country so as to divest the Union government of its overriding powers to interfere in the affairs of the States and in order to widen the autonomy of the States, especially in the matter of finance and State economy'.[27] It favoured the abolition of the office of the Governor and establishment of autonomous districts and regions within the States.[28] The CPI (M) favoured 'widest autonomy for the various States comprising the Indian federation'.[29]

Socialists: The Socialists basically believed in the policy of decentralisation 'accompanied with coordination to ensure a national unity, harmony and progress'[30] while the national parties stood for reconstructuring the Centre-State relations. The Akali Dal would like the Constitution to be made 'federal in content' and the States to be given 'more autonomy and more power particularly in the field of finance and legislation'.[31] The DMK called for 'States rights without infringement' by the Centre and the transfer of 'unspecified or residuary powers which are vested in the Centre to the States'.[32]

Regional Parties: Of all the regional political parties, DMK and AIADMK, the Akali Dal and later the AGP in Assam demanded more devolution of authority for the regions. The changes brought about since 1967 have created a situation where there have been radical changes in the party positions all over the country. With the emergence of non-Congress governments in several States and reduction in the Congress strength in Parliament after the 1967 general elections, the position of the States vis-à-vis the Union was strengthened. However, the spectacular success achieved by the Congress in the 1971 Lok Sabha elections had once again established the dominance of the Centre.

Centre-State Relations Since 1989

Paradigm Shift in National Perspective

THE MOST IMPORTANT event of the nineties, having a bearing on shifts in federal politics in the country was the advent of coalition government(s) at the Centre and involvement of regional and smaller parties in the governance at the national level. The political ethos of coalition governments possessed the inbuilt element of accommodation. The spirit of co-operation and the direct involvement of regional parties in federal administration gradually shifted in a good measure and their mindset away from confrontation with the Centre and to reach to a sort of conciliation at the national level.

On the other hand, the weakening of the national parties

at the regional and sub-regional level in electoral politics compelled them also to go for conciliation and coordination with their regional counterparts, and to accept sharing of power with them at the Centre. It can be said that the weakening of the national parties and the sagging nature of their influence in achieving the electoral numbers, in State legislatures and in the Parliament, were also caused by the rising importance of local issues in developmental politics and the belief and confidence of the electorate in regional parties to address the same effectively.

In the above context, it needed no reiteration that the coalition system of governance at the Centre with direct representation of regional parties in the decision-making process, inspite of giving rise to some issues pertaining to good and effective governance, led to somewhat easing of tensions between the Centre and the States. There was also the recognition of the regional parties, from the mid-nineties onwards that they, even as a group, could not become a substitute to the national entities but could, at the same time, carve out political space of their own at the Centre, through electoral gains in their region.

There was also realisation from the side of the national parties that the time had come when the federal government had to be more receptive to accommodate regional aspirations. It was this realisation at both ends that provided the much-required stability to coalition politics at the Centre. Equally, it can be safely reasoned that coalition governments in their own way stabilised the federal spirit in the polity. This phenomenon was aptly articulated by the former Prime Minister, Atal Behari Vajpayee, who in his address at the Columbia University on 24 September 2003, noted:'It is also my conviction that the new experience of successful coalition governments in India has been the ideal for democratic governance, balancing divergent views and accommodating regional and sectorial interests more effectively. India is a rare multi-cultural, multi-religions, multi-ethnic and multi-lingual democracy in the world.'[1]

Indian politics is now definitely regionalised, and coalition governments have become an important ingredient of political articulation. The regional parties are reflective of the socio-political and cultural diversities of the country that provide the required numerical strength to hold the balance of power in a political situation where none of the so-called national parties have a magic number of parliamentarians to justify their independent claims. Despite their distinct identities, the national parties have not remained as decisive as earlier in the environment of coalition politics, for they can no longer afford to ignore regional entities. This is suggestive of an unique socio-political processes in which regional issues gain immense importance in governance, both at the central and provincial levels. On occasions, this results in tight-rope walking for both the national and the regional parties, where the support of the regional parties is crucial for the survival of the coalition at the Centre.

A significant development in the 1990s is the central position that the States in the Indian union have come to occupy in national politics.

Although the Constitution established a federal structure, the absence of strong regional forces in the Constituent Assembly, partition and the resulting emphasis upon the unity and integrity of the country, a single written Constitution, the existence of a one-party dominant system and tall leaders at the Centre led the States to play peripheral roles in the early post-independence period.

Today, the States enjoy much greater autonomy from the Centre, due to the rise of strong regional parties.They are now partners in the national governance, they have greater financial freedom, and following economic liberalisation can also independently enter into negotiations with foreign countries for technical collaboration and aid.

New social identities and groups in the States have asserted themselves, changing the established contours of the States' party systems, leading to fresh political alignments in every national election. The changes taking place in the States are of fundamental importance, as this is the arena in which changes in Indian polity have manifested themselves in recent years and these are feeding into national patterns to a much greater extent than ever before.

Federalism occupies an important place in the political discourse of the coalition government. With or without the knowledge of the participant parties, a successful and stable coalition certainly promotes a sort of cooperative federalism in the Centre-State relations, despite the fact that more often ruling parties in the States do not happen to be partners in the Central government. This results in a more favourable consideration of the demands of the people of different States and regions of the country.

Predominantly, parliamentary tenure of Indian politics was sustained through the period of one-party dominance under the Indian National Congress (with occasional breaches in 1967 and 1977), until the 1989 Lok Sabha elections.

The two most notable changes of the 1990s, in India have been the growing federalisation of the polity and the reforms of the economy with emphasis on economic liberalisation and marketisation. India's federal governance has been witnessing significant changes with the emergence of coalition politics, particularly after 1989, at the Centre. It has substantially altered the power balance between the Centre and the States. The old notion of a strong Centre with dependent units has undergone both qualitative and quantative changes. A new equilibrium in the political and administrative process has appeared which has altered not only the party structure but also the bargaining process which is considered to be one of the major tension areas in India's federal system. States began to play a major role in sharing powers through their Chief Ministers in the meetings of the National Development Council (NDC), particularly after 1989.

Their demand was for a total revaluation and restructuring of the Centre-State relations. These developments, since 1989, have drastically altered the nature of the Centre-State relations and for that matter the functioning of the federal system. Both, the National Democratic Alliance (NDA) and the United Progressive Alliance (UPA) governments in recent years have had to depend on the support of the regional parties. The space gained by these regional parties by supporting the alliances have been fully utilised by them to advance their own interests. In view of the changing political situation, due to the various socio-economic and political developments, there is a paradigm shift in the interpretations of constitutional provisions after 1989.

Centre-State Relations Under National Front Government

In 1989, the Congress was replaced by a minority government, called National Front, led by VP Singh. This marked the beginning of a multi-party system in India. Under the leadership of VP Singh, in the federal arena, power deflation in New Delhi freed the State Chief Ministers.

The Congress (I) State Chief Ministers such as Channa Reddy (Andhra Pradesh), Sharad Pawar (Maharashtra) and Veerendra Patil (Karnataka) who earlier listened to party leader Rajiv Gandhi, but to a great extent guarded their views, now found independence from the Centre and the high command. The Janata Dal Chief Ministers – Biju Patnaik (Odisha), Mulayam Singh Yadav (Uttar Pradesh), Lalu Prasad Yadav

(Bihar) and Chimanbhai Patel (Gujarat) – were potent leaders in their own right and neither VP Singh nor Devi Lal could manipulate them from New Delhi. The Chief Ministers of Tamil Nadu (M Karunanidhi) and Assam (PK Mahanta) were protected from Central intervention because their regional parties were partners in the Central government. Jyoti Basu of West Bengal was widely respected and often consulted for advice by the Central leaders because of his long tenure as Chief Minister. The BJP Chief Ministers Sunder Lal Patwa (Madhya Pradesh), Shanta Kumar (Himachal Pradesh), and BS Shekhawat (Rajasthan) had little to fear because the BJP provided a lifeline for the survival of the Central government. Central leadership, in fact, was so fractured that the regional satrap, Om Prakash Chautala almost brought the Central government down in his several disgraceful bids to crown himself as the Chief Minister of Haryana.[2]

Although, State leadership became strong by the late eighties, there was no change in their relationship with the Centre.The States were in the backyard. VP Singh's coalition government could not achieve anything substantial in re-structuring the federal polity because of internal contradictions.

The Chandra Shekhar government dismissed the DMK government in Tamil Nadu, allegedly because of the pressures of the Congress Party, on whose Parliamentary support, from outside, Chandra Shekhar government had to depend for survival of his ministry. On 30 January 1991, the DMK government which had come to power after winning the 1989 assembly election, was dismissed by Prime Minister Chandra Shekhar using Article 356 of the Indian Constitution. President's Rule was imposed on Tamil Nadu. The reason cited for the dismissal was the deterioration of law and order in the State and the DMK's alleged closeness to the LTTE, a Sri Lankan Tamil group that had gained ascendancy since 1976, demanding a separate state for Lankan Tamils. Irrespective of the point of its justifiability, this dismissal of a State government, like many similar dismissals during the previous three decades, amply showed the vulnerability of the federating units in India's existing federal polity.[3]

The National Front's power was, however, short-lived. The Chandra Shekhar government fell on March 1991 after the Congress withdrew its outside support. Fresh elections were called for both, the Indian Parliament and Tamil Nadu Legislative Assembly in May-June 1991. For the first time general elections were held in three phases, on separate dates in different States. The initial democratic idea of elections being held on the same single day, so as not to allow any other political event to influence the polls, was set aside. One phase of polling was already over when Rajiv Gandhi was killed in Tamil Nadu. It was alleged that Rajiv's IPKF intervention had resulted in revenge in Tamil Nadu. The killing gave the Congress party huge sympathy vote in the remaining two phases of the polls. In Tamil Nadu, Congress ally, the AIADMK won the Assembly elections. One State's political sentiments cost the nation dear for the next 15 odd years.

To be noted is also the fact that many small Tamil Nadu parties were born at this time and some of them played national politics, like the MDMK in the repeal of POTA, another anti-terrorist act.

The Prevention of Terrorism Act, 2002 (POTA) was an Act passed by the Parliament of India in 2002, with the objective of strengthening anti-terrorism operations. The Act was enacted due to several terrorist attacks that were being carried out in India and especially in response to the attack on the Parliament. The Act replaced the Prevention of Terrorism Ordinance (POTO) of 2001 and the Terrorist and Disruptive Activities (Prevention) Act (TADA) (1985–95), and was supported by the then governing National Democratic Alliance. The bill was defeated in the Rajya Sabha (the upper house) by a 113-98 vote, but was passed in a joint session (425 Ayes and 296 Nos), as the Lok Sabha (lower house) has more seats. It was only the third time that a bill was passed by a joint session of both Houses of Parliament.

Analogous to the provisions contained in TADA, the law provided that a suspect could be detained for up to 180 days without the filing of chargesheet in court. It also allowed law enforcement agencies to withhold the identities of witnesses, and to treat confessions made to the police admissible in evidence. Once the Act came into force, many reports surfaced of the law being grossly abused. POTA was alleged to have been arbitrarily used to target political opponents. Only four months after its enactment, State law enforcement officers had arrested 250 people nationwide under the Act, and the number was steadily increasing. A mere eight months later, seven States where POTA was in force, had arrested over 940 people, at least 560 of whom were languishing in jail. Several prominent persons like Vaiko of MDMK, a supporter of Sri Lankan Tamils' bid for freedom, and SAS Geelani of J&K were arrested under the Act. Across the country protests sprang up.

The provisions in the Act mentioned the possibility of both State and Central review committees, but offered few details as to their formation or use. As the Act began to be widely misused by the State governments, the Central government finally established a review committee to hear individual cases related to this Act. At first, the committee functioned in a purely advisory capacity. Tamil Nadu's AIADMK government kept Vaiko in jail for 18 months, four without filing charges. It was State politics playing out on national stage. In December 2003, by an overwhelming majority, Parliament amended the Act with an ordinance designed to expand the scope of judicial review. On 7 October 2004, the Union Cabinet under UPA government repealed the Act.

Union-State relations in India have enlarged into an extended network of organisations and agencies. One important feature of this structural growth is that they have mostly developed outside the framework of the Constitution. Government of India had set up the National Development Council, for intergovernmental consultation and decision-making in the area of planned economic development, in 1952. During the phase of the Congress dominance, NDC was eclipsed by the Congress party's parliamentary board overseeing the working of the Congress governments at the Centre and in the States. In 1970s, the NDC continued to meet once a year. But in 1980s, the relations between the Congress and the opposition grew more and more strained. In the 1980s, the NDC met seven times and the meetings were marked by acrimony and tensions. During 37 years of Congress dominance and the Janata phase, the NDC had 40 meetings with an average of one per year.[4]

Since 1989, special attention has been paid to the institutions which have the potential to strengthen the Centre-State relations. In 1989, during the tenure of VP Singh, two meetings of the NDC were held. One was held on 16 June 1989, to endorse the approach to the 8th Five-Year plan. The other was held on 9 October 1989, in which the government asked the members of the Planning Commission to make a presentation to the assembled Chief Ministers, explaining the rationale for the allocations that had been made to each sector of the economy, and how the principal goals of the plan would be met. In addition to the revival of the NDC, the Inter State Council (ISC) was set up by the National Front on 10 August 1992, on a permanent basis. The provision in the Constitution to set up such a council was not exercised earlier.[5]

Congress Union Government and Centre-State Relations

In 1991, Congress (I) came to power under the leadership of PV Narasimha Rao. It was a minority government at the Centre. It was in power for five years. The government held meetings of the NDC to discuss specific thorny problems like urgent need to stop providing electricity virtually free of cost to agriculture. The meetings of NDC was considered to be extremely useful as it not only helped in strengthening co-operative federalism but also to make the States understand the limitations and compulsions of the Centre as well as the limitations of other States.

In the early period, the Central government continued to intrude into spheres reserved for the States. Several States felt aggrieved that they were getting a raw deal from the Centre. By the early 1990s, there was substantial resentment against excessive centralisation of economic and political power. Alienation and disaffection was strengthened by the failure of the States in lessening regional disparities or level of economic inequalities. The basic issue was the balance in the economic equation between the Centre and States.

Rao Introduced New Economic Policy

Indian federal constitutional arrangements were undergoing a sea change under the impact of the New Economic Policies (NEP) of the 1990s. The pillar of the NEP is the rolling back of the State and a Central role for market mechanisms in the national economy. *In the '70s and '80s, due to constitutional provisions, the entire country was mired in a licence raj that hindered entreprise and economic growth. The Centre exercised tight control over export, import, energy, food, industry and trade. India's centralised political system was integral to the system of economic planning in which the State governments were led by the Central government.*

The new economic regime of the 1990s demanded an effective role for the State governments in the process of economic reforms.[6] This new trend, which set the State governments as important economic actors instead of the Central government, soon became an unstoppable phenomenon.

The old system of Centre-State relations had evolved a system of Centrally-sponsored schemes and Central sector schemes which were implemented by the State governments but financed by the Central government. This changed the Central-State partnerships and PPPs in funding projects, especially development projects.

One of the reasons for inequitable development or unequal pattern of flow of Foreign Direct Investment (FDI) to different States in India was that the liberalisation process in India was crisis driven and not strategy driven. When the economic crisis reached its peak between April and July 1991, following unstable governments, assassination of Rajiv Gandhi, low Foreign reserves and deadlocked finances, the Narasimha Rao government introduced a New Economic Policy that aimed at short term economic stabilisation as well as long term structural reforms.

Liberalisation, Privatisation and Globalisation (LPG) became the main morale booster of economic federalism in the country. States successfully gained economic benefits. Sometimes they also supported the national government on economic policies which did not exactly match their party agenda. They supported LPG to get economic benefits for their States from the IMF and World Bank.

Introduction of Panchayati Raj and Urban Local Bodies

Prime Minister Narasimha Rao was able to implement Rajiv Gandhi's agenda for localisation of India's federalism. Consequently, the government passed the 73rd and 74th Amendments of the Constitution, which are milestones in the evolution of a true federal setup in India. While the 73rd Amendment deals broadly with the Panchayati Raj Institutions (PRIs), the 74th Amendment's main concern is with the governance of Urban-Local Bodies (ULBs). These amendments, it was then thought, were likely to have far-reaching implications on the emerging scenario of federalisation in India.

However, decentralisation in a federal set-up is different from the practiced unitary form of government. In a federation, decentralisation is inbuilt and statutory. Different layers of the government (Central, State and Local Bodies) are given independent financial powers to execute the functions assigned to them as per the Constitution. In India, the above mentioned amendments were needed to accord a statutory status to traditional local body systems. While PRIs have been credited with 29 functions, Municipalities or Nagarpalika hold 18 functions. These functions can be divided into 4 or 5 categories viz. socio-economic schemes, beneficiary-oriented schemes and State or Centrally-sponsored schemes.

Thus, these two acts made both, rural local bodies and urban local bodies, compulsory and statutory organs of governing. Further, the State governments were also entrusted with powers and responsibilities to enable them to function as institutions of self-government and formulate such laws that may contain provisions for the devolution of powers and responsibilities. Their main responsibilities are the preparation of plans for economic development and social justice. However, the fact remains that decentralisation in India has often come to be regarded as a way of reducing the strength of governments and as synonymous with privatisation. By enacting the 73rd and 74th amendment, the national government tried to bring democracy at the grassroot level.

Imposition of President's Rule by the Rao Govt

In the case of States, Prime Minister Narasimha Rao had the same attitude which his predecessors had. Like the previous Congress regimes, he was not hesitant to use President's Rule for partisan purposes. Although he was more careful because of the minority status of his government and declining fortunes of his party in State elections, he did not hesitate to use Article 356 as an instrument to control the opposition ruled States. Totally, his tenure saw eleven incidents of President's Rule between 1991 and 1996. In 1991-92, the Central government used Presidential suspensions in both Meghalaya and Manipur to make room for Congress coalition governments. In these States the governments were revived after the Congress was able to form government. After the demolition of Babri Masjid, the Rao government used Article 356 and obtained the resignation of the BJP government in Uttar Pradesh led by Kalyan Singh. Central government dismissed the governments in three other BJP-ruled States: Madhya Pradesh, Himachal Pradesh and Rajasthan on the plea that these governments would not cooperate with the Centre in implementing its ban on some Hindu fundamentalist organisations.

Thus, the Congress government that came to power in 1991, under the prime ministership of Narasimha Rao, continued with the idea of domination of the Centre, its right to intervene in State affairs, misuse of the office of the Governor and power to impose Presidents' Rule. Despite changes in the governments at the Centre, the trend towards centralisation did not weaken. As per old Congress traditions, Rao also continued to appoint pro-Congress Governors in the States who were in some cases quite uncomfortable in the non-Congress governed States. The Governors were expected to intervene whenever the Congress interest warranted their intervention. However, they had limitations to do so in cases where the non-Congress governments were stable and headed by popular leaders such as Lalu Prasad Yadav in Bihar, Biju Patnaik in Odisha and J Jayalalithaa in Tamil Nadu. The Manipur Governor, Chintamani Panigrahi, was asked to resign for his wrongdoing when he invited the Manipur People's Party, and not the Congress, with the required number of seats in the legislature, to form the government in 1990. VK Nayar had to resign the Manipur Governorship in frustration because the Centre wished Rishang Keishing, who had been indicted for his alleged role in the Naga-Kuki feud, to form the government after the President's Rule was revoked in 1994. Governor Tahiliani (later P Shiv Shankar) did not lament the break-up of the Bhandari (SSP) government in Sikkim in 1994; Governor Motilal Vora did not allow Mulayam Singh Yadav to test his strength on the floor of the Uttar Pradesh legislature after the fall of the Mayawati government in 1995; and Governor Romesh Bhandari was a constant trial to the Tripura Left government of Dasarath Deb.[7]

In respect of the Congress State governments, Rao's writ did not run as authoritatively as that of the previous Congress Prime Ministers. Although Congress dissidents continued to seek his blessings before they initiated a revolt against their respective Chief Ministers, Rao rarely made or unmade Chief

Ministers in the style of Indira Gandhi. He gave the required respect to the Chief Ministers and Congress leaders. He never changed the Chief Ministers, local leaders like Digvijaya Singh and Ashok Gehlot and they rose to prominence during his rule only. It was for the first time in the Congress leadership that Rao was elected as Prime Minister and not a member of the Nehru-Gandhi family and who completed his full term as Prime Minister of India. Lal Bahudur Shastri had died too early to leave any impact on Congress methods of ruling.

Centre-State Relations Under United Front Government

In June 1996, a coalition government of 13 parties was formed under the leadership of HD Deve Gowda. The most distinguishing feature of this government was that it was supported by the Congress party. All the constituent parties had come together in opposition to the BJP. Both, the National Front government of 1989 and the United Front governments of 1996-98, were supported by the Left parties who were strong supporters of the federal principles. The participation of many regional parties in the Central coalition governments brought about checks on the centralisation trend initiated by the Central government.

The formation of the United Front government in 1996 had a definite bearing on the nature of the Indian federal structure. Deve Gowda, the Prime Minister of United Front government, and many of his ministerial colleagues were by and large regional leaders. The result of the regionalisation at the Centre was the acknowledgement of the need to re-cast the Centre-State relations. The acceptance of Common Minimum Programme (CMP) by the UF coalition government was a step in this direction. The Common Minimum Programme was based on the principles of political, administrative and economic federalism. It also emphasised the State rights to meet its developmental needs. The CMP intended to go beyond the recommendations of the Sarkaria Commission because there was at the time a new articulation of the State's rights and the need for greater powers to the States to meet the aspirations of their respective State.

According to the programme, the State would have to be awarded greater say in determining their priorities in developmental programmes, greater freedom to draw their plans within the broad framework of the National Five-Year Plans. It also stood for the transfer of most of the centrally-sponsored schemes to the control of the State governments. The document also promised to amend Article 356 to prevent its misuse. It also promised to re-activate and energise institutions like the National Development Council and the Inter State Council. The regional parties also formed a Federal Front to safeguard the interests of their respective States.[8]

The CMP of the UF government was an important document. It was the first statement of its kind bringing together diverse set of political parties, ranging from such regional parties as the DMK and Telugu Desam Party (TDP), broadly centrist political formations like the Tamil Maanila Congress (TMC) and the Janata Dal, left parties – the CPI and CPI(M). The CMP's perspective on economic policy was also so broad that neither the Congress, nor the BJP had any serious disagreement with it on substantial issues. However, on social and political issues, such as secularism and caste-based reservation, there were sharp difference between the United Front and the BJP.

Hence, the UF's Common Minimum Programme, for the first time, was a strategy chalked out by the Central government to evolve a system in which the States were supposed to perform the actual role which their Constitution makers wanted them to perform as federal partners of the union government. In the financial field also, the UF government made some important decisions in the power sector, import policy and there were some decisions that the government took, keeping in mind the global milieu and national conditions.

Centre-State Relations under Prime Minister IK Gujral

Prime Minister IK Gujral particularly highlighted reforms in the power sector. He ordered a review of power projects to be conducted by the Cabinet Secretary. Gujral encouraged the State Electricity Boards (SEBs) to make good of new opportunities offered by economic liberalisation and convince financial institutions that loans advanced to the sector would be serviced. The UF government liberalised import in at least three instalments, gradually shifting more items from the restricted to the special import list and from the latter to the free import category. It also ended state monopoly over coal and lignite mining, 25 years after their nationalisation. This sector was opened to private Indian companies including those having foreign equity.[9]

The UF government also signed a global telecommunications treaty at a World Trade Organisation (WTO) Conference held in Geneva in February 1997. The treaty opened long-protected telecommunications monopolies to domestic as well as foreign firms. Another major landmark move of the UF regimes was the WTO draft declaration signed by India and 127 other countries at its first ministerial conference in Singapore, on 13 December 1997. It endorsed a global Information Technology Agreement to do away with tariffs on expanding the $600 billion world market in computer-related products. The UF was criticised for surrendering India's interests on labour and investment standards and for bypassing the Parliament. The UF government defended itself by pointing out that (a) the Declaration recognised the International Labour Organisation (ILO) rather than the WTO as the competent body to decide labour standards, and (b) a study group was to examine investment standards, which was confined to the existing norms of trade-related investment measures.

The 10th Finance Commission 1996-2000 recommended

alternative schemes of vertical transfer of resource to the States, instead of the earlier shared pool of non-corporate income tax and Union excise duties. It recommended that all Central taxes, except surcharges be made a common shareable pool, out of which 29 per cent was to devolve to the States. It also recommended that the share of the Union Territories would not be on the grounds used for State share, but it would be decided on the basis of each one's population.[10]

The United Front government imposed Article 356 on those States where non-Congress parties tried to form governments because Congress supported the UF government. In September 1996, Congressman Governor Krishan Pal Singh played the Centre's game in Gujarat when the BJP government proved its majority in the assembly, though marked by unruly behaviour and confusion. He remained indifferent to the BJP's claim of majority, used Article 356 and helped to create a situation leading to the formation of a government by another Congressman, Shankar Singh Vaghela, who led the Gujarat Rashtriya Janata Party. In Uttar Pradesh, the Union government allowed Romesh Bhandari to rule rather than let the political process take its own course. Bhandari did not accept the claim of the BJP, the largest party in the State Assembly, to form the government. He dissolved the elected Assembly and with the BJP leading again after fresh elections, the Congressman Governer kept it in suspended animation to prevent BJP from forming the government. He continued to rule the State at the behest of the

United Front government at the Centre and he continued to discourage any effort of the BJP or any alliance partner not liked by the United Front, to form the government. UP was under President's Rule from October 1995 to March 1997. Both in Uttar Pradesh and Gujarat, the Governors acted as agents of the Centre even though most of the United Front constituents nursing anti-BJPism, including the CPI Home Minister, Indrajit Gupta, who had often criticised the use of Article 356 in the past and were committed to its abolition and the party had been against such a distortion of federal norm in practice.

Inter-governmental Forums

It may appear paradoxical that the frequency of meetings of the National Development Council had declined during the UF government despite their best efforts for greater frequency during the later phase, for greater federalisation of the Indian polity as indicated by different set of parties ruling at the Centre and in the States since 1989. This anomaly could, however, be because of two factors. First, Coalition and minority governments were very unstable, resulting in delays in launching of the plans (1996-1999). Second, different sets of parties including the regional ones ruling the States had been partners in this coalition. This allowed them direct access and opportunity for representation of their views in the union cabinet. Therefore, they were not keen on the activation of the NDC as an inter-governmental forum.

There were only seven meetings of the Inter State Council (ISC) over this decade (since 1990 on its creation). It would appear rather surprising because of the fact that this period had been the one in which there was a paradigm shift in Union-State relations. The issues discussed in these meetings under various governments were fairly common: recommendations of the Sarkaria Commission Report covering the entire gamut of Union-State relations; Article 356; Inter-State River Water disputes; greater autonomy to the States; centrally sponsored schemes; devolution of financial powers to the States and panchayats; Governor's role; consideration of State legislation reserved by Governors for the Presidential assent; resource mobilisation etc. However, there has hardly been any constitutional amendment or Parliamentary enactment in pursuance of the recommendations made by the Inter-State Council (ISC). In fact, on most crucial issues, substantial consensus in the council had been conspicuous by its absence. The discussion on Article 356 and the role of the Governor clearly illustrated this point.[11]

NDA I and Centre-State Relations

In 1999, for the first time, the main opposition party led by the National Democratic Alliance (NDA) formed government under the leadership of Atal Behari Vajpayee. Vajpayee government had been watchful but less intervening in the making-unmaking of the Sate governments except where the

BJP's interests had been at stake. As a political party, BJP had entered into a variety of pre-poll and post-poll alliances to make its presence felt in all the States; as a dominant governing party at the Centre. Given the precariousness of the NDA structure, it had been careful in using the resources of the Centre to capture non-BJP territories, particularly if the State governments in these territories had been well-strengthened and stable (eg. most of the southern States). States like Meghalaya, Manipur, Goa and Pondicherry had unstable governments because of the politics of defections but the Vajpayee government allowed the chips to fall where they did. Manipur came under President's Rule in June 2001, as a last resort, failing due consultation with the Congress president Sonia Gandhi. Uttar Pradesh experienced a brief spell of Presidential suspension of its legislative assembly following a divided mandate of the February 2002 polls. The Centre resisted active intervention in West Bengal inspite of constant bashing from Mamata Banerjee of the Trinamool Congress (an alliance partner) to impose President's Rule in the State. Bal Thackeray of Shiv Sena (another alliance partner) had been estranged because the Vajpayee regime let several opportunities pass to topple the NCP-Congress government in Maharashtra.

Role of Governors During NDA I Government

Although the Centre had appointed a few non-partisan Governors in some States, Governors had been less than meticulous in performing their constitutional role either on their own or as apostles of the Centre. Governor Fatima Beevi erred and lost her tenure when she installed J Jayalalithaa (convicted for corruption) as the Chief Minister of Tamil Nadu on 14 May 2001, despite the fact that she was banned from contesting the election. Jayalalithaa stepped down on 21 September 2001 (she found an answer in Bihar's Rabri Devi and nominated the harmless Revenue Minister, O Panneerselvam as her substitute until she returned as Chief Minister in February 2002) while the Centre watched the entire drama in helpless silence.

Bihar Governor Vinod Chandra Pandey appointed Nitish Kumar (of the Samta Party who resigned as Vajpayee's minister of agriculture) as Chief Minister on 3 March 2000, even though his coalition was ten short from majority in the newly-elected 322-member Bihar Assembly. The Lalu-Rabri combine was furious and so was the Congress party. The RJD-sponsored bandh in Bihar turned violent and Parliament was in pandemonium. Seven days later, on 10 March, Rabri Devi (Lalu Prasad's wife) was installed as Chief Minister to lead the RJD coalition government while Nitish Kumar was re-accommodated in the Union Cabinet.

Governor Khurshid Alam Khan's conduct was called into question in Karnataka when he played into the hands of Chief Minister JH Patel (JD) and dissolved the Karnataka Assembly on 23 July 1999. The Governor, wrote constitution expert AG Noorani, 'acted as an accomplice in the foul act'. In

October 2000, Goa Governor Mohammed Fazal wasted no time in asking the leader of the BJP legislature party, Manohar Parrikar, to assume office (as Chief Minister) since his party was the single largest party in the assembly.[12]

BJP's High Command Culture

In the case of the BJP, the practice of making and unmaking of Chief Ministers had come to resemble that of the Congress high command's culture of naming a Chief Minister and then seeking the endorsement of the concerned State legislative party thereafter. Sonia Gandhi might not have the clout that her mother-in-law had in the Congress party, but the old culture continued to persist. She asked Odisha Chief Minister JB Patnaik to quit. 'Madam has made up her mind', said Sonia's emissary, 'you should put in your papers when you meet her' and he did. Nine months later, she asked Patnaik's successor, Giridhar Gamang, to vacate the CM's chair for Hemananda Biswal and he did in December 1999. 'Whatever my leader decides...' Gamang said, 'After all, I was made Chief Minister by her'. And that is how the Congress lost the State of Odisha. In February 2002, the Congress high command foisted party veteran ND Tiwari to lead the government in Uttranchal.[13]

A somewhat similar process was on in the BJP for the selection and removal of its Chief Ministers: Kalyan Singh-1999, Ram Prakash Gupta-2000, Rajnath Singh-2000 in Uttar Pradesh; Keshubhai-2001, Narendra Modi in Gujarat; Nityanand

Swami-2000, Bhagat Singh Koshyari in Uttarakhand; Babulal Marandi-2000, in Jharkhand. The fortunes of the Chief Ministers depended on the high commands in both these parties. The Chief Ministers' security and continuity depended on the quality of their being effective partners in the federal enterprise. Their central leadership, whether in power or out of power at the Centre, got to carry the burden on standing by their State leaders for their failures. It is another matter that Gujarat did not turn out to be the NDA's waterloo. And the Vajpayee government did stand by Chief Minister Narendra Modi at the risk of its fall in Parliament on 30 April 2002. However, in 2004, the electorate did not return the NDA to power at the Centre, though Modi continued his winning streak in Gujarat for the next 12 years.

Vajpayee, as PM, gave real respect to the Chief Ministers which helped the NDA in managing the government, running it well and doing milestone changes which was one of the turning points in the history of India. NDA united all the allies. It united India and made it into two political poles which gave some amount of stability to the country even if some partners differed in their performance. This is not to say that the NDA government had no hiccups.

However, Governor Vishnu Kant Shastri did not agree with the 'single largest party argument' as presented by Mulayam Singh Yadav of the Samajwadi Party, following the 2002 Uttar Pradesh assembly poll. Instead, he recommended

Presidential suspension of the assembly on 7 March 2002. It was revoked when Mayawati (BSP) formed a coalition government with the BJP on 3 May 2002.

The Shift in Centre-State Relations

It is evident that there has been a paradigm shift in Centre-State relations. The State governments have become more active participants in the federal bargain. Some political and constitutional developments under the BJP-led NDA occured in the early years of the 21st century. Government passed the Eighty-Fourth Constitutional Amendment Bill in 2002, which kept the delimitation of Parliamentary Constituencies in abeyance till 2026. The reason advanced for the amendment was that if delimitations were carried out in 2001, this could unfairly punish those States in the South which have succeeded in checking their growth in population. The Hindi-speaking States in the north where a large chunk of the population was concentrated, thus, lost the opportunity to increase their parliamentary strength.

The National Democratic Alliance (NDA), under Prime Minister Atal Behari Vajpayee, created three more States in 2000 to recognise the demands around tribal identities. It is important to note that these three new States emerged very much within the fabric of India which is a Union of States, reinforcing that our federalism is alive and kicking. Indian federalism had also experimented with sub-State regional development councils to satisfy regional, ethnic and tribal aspirations. Inclusion of languages had been another mechanism in cooperative federalism. In 2003, Bodo, Dogri, Maithili and Santhali languages were included in the Eighth Schedule of the Constitution. Such inclusion allows privileges like simultaneous translation facilities in Parliamentary proceedings, allocation of Central government funding for development of the language and its literature and is an effective tool to include the periphery into the mainstream.

National Commission Review Working of the Constitution

Knowing perfectly well that Article 356 had been the most misused article and that various commissions had recommended remedial measures for the prevention of its misuse, but with little success, the coalition NDA government appointed the National Commission (NCRWC) under Justice MN Venkatachaliah to Review the Working of the Constitution. It was established on 22 February 2000. It was appointed on the basis of a joint resolution of the Government of India, Ministry of Law, Justice and Company Affairs (Department of Legal Affairs). Incidentally, Justice Sarkaria, who had chaired the first Centre-State Relations Commission in 1983, was also a member of this Commission. The NDA took bold steps in setting up this Commission.

It submitted its extensive report in two volumes to the government on 31 March 2002. Its recommendations have far-reaching implications for the structure of government at the Centre and the States, and for inter-governmental relations. *In its analysis, the NCRWC stated that at least in twenty out of more than one hundred instances the invocation of Article 356 might be termed as its misuse.*[14]

The Commission called for comprehensive reforms in the committee system which goes a long way in arresting the decline of Parliament and State legislatures. The Commission proposed three new committees (after disbanding some existing committees like, those on Estimates, Public Undertaking and Subordinate Legislation) – a Constitution Committee (dealing with amendments), a Committee on National Economy, and a Committee on Legislation.

In the domain of Union-State relations, the NCRWC recommended the strengthening of the existing Inter-State Council in tune with the spirit of cooperative federalism requiring proper understanding and mutual confidence and resolution of problems of common interest expeditiously. In addition, the Commission also recommended the establishment of a regulatory Inter-State Trade and Commerce Commission (under Article 307 and entry 42 of the Union List). Article 307 refers to the appointment of authority by the Parliament for carrying out trade, commerce and other related activities within the territory of India ie. freedom of trade and commerce, and mitigation of their restrictions within the country and between States. Another welcome proposal was the suggestion that there will be prior consultation with the Inter-State-Council by the Union government before signing any international treaty which affects the interests of the States on matters included in the State list.[15] For example, the matter of export of Rare Earths from coastal States.

Meetings of the Inter-State Council and NDC

In the financial field, the BJP-led NDA, in 2000, passed the Eightieth Amendment of the Indian Constitution, which simplified the tax structure by pooling and sharing all taxes between States and the Centre, based on a recommendation from the Tenth Finance Commission. This was a substantial move towards a uniform tax structure across the country.

Under the NDA, two meetings of the Inter-State Council (ISC) and National Development Council were held in November 2001 and August 2003, in which the States made substantial gains. It was agreed that the residuary powers which rested with the Union government earlier be shifted to the Concurrent List and the legislation of this list be in consultation with the State governments.

Another important recommendation of the ISC accepted was that the Union government must consult the Chief Minister of the State on the appointment of Governor. The Union government promised to amend the Constitution accordingly. The Srinagar meeting of the ISC also discussed the 'Emergency Provision' in Article 356, and took certain decisions in favour of the States, thereby, curbing the arbitrariness of the Union government with regard to defining and declaring an emergency.

In view of the fight against terrorism, the right to deploy Central forces in a State during an emergency situation was accepted as a prerogative of the Union.

But in other cases, prior consultation with States was considered desirable. Introduction of a system of interchange of officers among the Union and State armed police forces were also accepted. The ISC had taken up 230 of the 247 recommendation of the Sarkaria Commission and 170 of them had already been implemented. The last meeting of the Inter-State Council decided that it would, henceforth, become a forum to sort out important issues of cooperative federalism and socio-economic concerns. Thus, the ISC work reflects the increasing space that the States have now gained in the federal system.

In independent India, Congress gave no role willingly to State parties in the ruling of coalition at the Centre until 2004. Vajpayee, as Prime Minister of the country, made best efforts to provide due share of the States in federal India. Centre made less interventions in the State affairs. They made less use of the unitary powers and provided space to the States.

It is also to be mentioned here that one of the latest bodies constituted to review the working of the then 50-year-old Constitution was the National Commission, established on 27 January 2003. It was a positive step in this field.

Centre-State Relation During UPA I Government

After completion of the full term of the NDA government, elections for the Fourteenth Lok Sabha were held in 2004. The election results could not provide absolute majority to any political party, therefore, it was a hung Parliament. However, Congress-led United Progressive Alliance (UPA) formed government at the Centre which had the support of the Left parties. It was for the first time that the Congress was dependent on other parties to form a government at the Centre. UPA formulated its own Common Minimum Programme (CMP) in May 2004 with the approval of fifteen parties to run the government at the Centre. Manmohan Singh was elected by the Congress parliamentary party as the leader of the party and hence he took oath of the Prime Minister.

As per its Common Minimum Programme, the UPA was committed to take steps towards redressing growing regional imbalances, both among States as well as within States through fiscal, administrative, investment and other means. The CMP proposed several measures for arresting these imbalances: the creation of a Backward State Grant Fund (BSGF) for creating productive assets in the States (Proactive measures); rapid industrialisation in the eastern and northeastern States; alleviation of debt burden of the States; provision for non-statutory grants from the Centre to the States to be weighted in favour of poor and backward States; emphasis on social and physical infrastructure development in the States; speedy implementation of special economic packages of previous governments for the States of the northeast, Bihar and Jammu and Kashmir, and so on. These steps were designed to remove the long-felt anti-Centre sentiments among many States, particularly the backward ones in social and economic terms.[16]

According to Chauhan and Vasudeva, the UPA reiterated its abiding commitment to economic reforms with a humane face that stimulated growth, investment and employment. Further reforms were needed and would be carried out in agriculture, industry and services, it said. The UPA reforms were to be oriented primarily to spreading and deepening rural prosperity by improving the quality of public systems and delivery of public services.[17]

The rural local government known as 'Panchayati Raj', in particular, figured in the CMP (2004) of the UPA. Four important aspects, for the UPA, for consideration were: first, the UPA government to ensure that all funds earmarked to States for implementation of poverty alleviation and rural development schemes were neither delayed nor diverted. Second, the UPA government would consider sending funds directly to the panchayats after consultations with the States. Third, panchayats would be elected regularly. Fourth, Gram Sabha would be the foundation of Panchayati Raj. On the performance side, the UPA government took measures: the formation of a group of ministers under the Ministry of Panchayati Raj (MOPR) for strengthening panchayats and financial devolution of the funds for Backward Regions Grant Fund (BRGF – newly instituted for designated 250 such districts) would be implemented through panchayats; panchayats were assigned the central role in monitoring and implementing the National Rural Employment Guarantee Scheme (NREGS) and so on. The NREGS of the Central government was at that point of time committed to provide 100 days work for the rural poor. This programme has been one of the most successful governmental interventions in favour of the rural poor in recent times, though the success rates of the States in implementing it has not been very satisfactory.[18]

The UPA government's commitment to official language had important federal bearing. The CMP declared that the UPA government would set up a committee to examine the question of declaring all languages in the Eighth Schedule of the Constitution as official languages. The recognition of the languages of the 8th schedule as official languages of India would definitely enhance their sense of ethno-regional-linguistic identity. This was a marked departure from earlier Congress government positions, where just Hindi was recognised since 1936 as the national language, providing fuel to anti-Hindi agitations in States like Tamil Nadu in 1937-40, 1946-50 and 1965. It is over language and ethnicity issues that the Congress lost power in the southern States since 1967. With experience, the ramming down of language in the State's throat had been diluted considerably over the years and the UPA was wiser.

Punchhi Commission on Centre-State Relations

On 27 April 2007, a Commission on Centre-State relations was set up with chairperson Justice MM Punchhi to look into the sea change that took place in the polity and economy ever since the Sarkaria Commission looked into the issue of Centre-State relations.

Justice Punchhi, while delivering a speech at a workshop on the same subject in Punjab University on 10 December 2008, opened his mind and defended the case for *stronger States for a strong Centre*. He drew attention to the need for accommodation for regional aspirations. He also stressed on the globalising context of India and the need for managing the transition successfully. He asserted that harmonious Centre-State relations occupy a significant place in this task. The importance of different layers of government, their need for revenues for ensuring good governance etc were recognised by him.[19]

This Commission submitted its report in 2010 to then Home Minister, P Chidambaram. The Punchhi Commission provided 312 recommendations in a seven-volume report comprising:

1. Evolution of Centre-State relations.
2. Constitutional scheme of relations, covering recommendations regarding Article 19, Articles 355 and 356 and Article 263.
3. Economic and financial relations and recommendations include upgrading of the planning model to remove regional imbalances.

4. Recommendations regarding 73rd and 74th Amendments and the Sixth schedule.
5. Internal security, covering issues like terror, Naxalism, insurgency and communal violence.
6. Environment issues and resource-sharing, particularly of rivers and minerals.
7. Social development and good governance.

The Punchhi Commission dealt at length with Emergency provisions under Article 355 and Article 356 and proposed safeguards to prevent their abuse to dismiss elected State governments. The Commission also studied setups like the National Investigation Agency, and recommended procedures to smoothen cooperation of the States in terror investigations entrusted to the NIA.

Major recommendations of the Punchhi Commission:

Concurrent List Subjects

There should be a mechanism whereby the Centre consults States before introducing items on the Concurrent List. This consultation mechanism should be through Inter-State Council.

Centre should occupy only that many subjects in Concurrent List or any other overlapping jurisdiction which is *absolutely needed* to achieve uniformity of policy in national interest.

On President's Pocket Veto

Once a bill is passed in the legislative assembly and then reserved by the Governor for President's consideration, President applies pocket veto in several cases. Earlier, no communication was provided to the concerned State which has been baffling for the States. The Commission recommended that there should be a mechanism so that the President communicates his decision in reasonable time (within 6 months).

Treaty-Making Power of Union

There is need of some kind of legislation to regulate the treaty-making power of the Union executive with respect to treaties which have anything to do with the matters listed in the State list, the Commission said. There should be greater involvement of States in such treaties.

Appointment of Chief Ministers

There should be clear guidelines for the appointment of Chief Ministers; so that there is some sort of regulation on the 'discretionary power' of the Governor, the report said. *A pre-poll alliance should be treated as one political party*, because that lays down the order of precedence that ought to be followed by the Governor, in case of hung House, which is as follows:

- The group with the largest pre-poll alliance commanding the largest number;

- The single largest party with support of others, including outside of pre-poll understanding;
- The post-electoral coalition with all parties joining the government;
- The post-electoral alliance with some parties joining the government and remaining, including Independents, supporting from outside.

Appointment of Governor

The Punchhi Commission recommended that the person who is slated to be a Governor should not have participated in active politics at even local level *for at least a couple of years* before his appointment. It may be mentioned that the Sarkaria Commission had recommended that the Governor be an eminent person and *not belong to the State* where he is to be posted. The State Chief Minister should have a say in the appointment of the Governor. Appointment of Governor should be entrusted to a committee comprising the Prime Minister, Home Minister, Speaker of the Lok Sabha and Chief Minister of the State. The vice President can also be involved in the process. Such a committee recommends names to the President.

Removal of Governor

For the office of Governor, the doctrine of pleasure should end and should be deleted from the Constitution. The Governor should not be removed at whim of the Central government. The report supported the right of the Governor to give sanction for the prosecution of ministers against the advice of the State government. There should be *provisions for impeachment of Governor* by the State legislature, it said.

Governor as Chancellor of Universities

The convention of making the Governors as Chancellors of Universities should be done away with.

Articles 355 and 356

Articles 355 and 356 should be amended, the Centre should be enabled to bring specific troubled areas under its control for a limited period. This means that the commission recommended 'localising emergency provisions' under Articles 355 and 356, contending that localised areas – either a district or parts of a district instead of the entire State – be brought under Governor's rule. The duration of such an emergency provision should, however, not be of duration of more than three months. In the history of President's Rule (Governor's rule), state of emergency has at times been applied at a stretch for nearly two years.

National Integration Council (NIC)

For internal security, the commission recommended creation of an overriding structure on the lines of the US Homeland Security Department, giving more teeth to the National

Integration Council. This council should meet at least once a year, the report said. In case of any communal incident, a delegation of five members of the council, who would be eminent persons, should visit the affected areas within two days. However, it rejected constitutional status to the NIC.

The Communal Violence Bill

The Commission recommended that the Communal Violence Bill should be amended to allow deployment of Central forces without the concerned State's consent for a short period. The State's consent should not become a hurdle in deployment of Central forces in a communal conflagration, as had happened in the 1990s. However, such deployment should only be for a week, and post-facto consent should be taken from the State.

Appointment of Governors by UPA I Govt

The UPA government, after coming to power in 2004, did not hesitate to change Governors and Lieutenant Governors nominated by the previous NDA government, most of whom were elderly leaders of the BJP. Between June and December 2004, as many as 19 States and Union Territories (UTs) saw their Governors and Lieutenant Governors (LGs) replaced one after the other. In June 2004, in Delhi, LG Vijai Kapoor was replaced by BL Joshi. In the same month, in Kerala, Governor TN Chaturvedi (former BJP MP and Governor of Karnataka), who was holding additional charge (after the death of Sikander

Bakht) was replaced by RL Bhatia (a former Congress minister of state for External Affairs). In Madhya Pradesh, KL Seth was replaced by Balram Jakhar (a former Congress Union Minister and Speaker of the Lok Sabha). In the month of July, five Governors/LGs were changed. In Goa, Kedar Nath Sahani (senior BJP leader) was asked to leave and was replaced by SC Jamir (former Congress Chief Minister of Nagaland). In Gujarat, Kailashpati Mishra (a senior BJP leader) was replaced by Balram Jakhar for twenty two days before another former Congress Union Minister Nawal Kishore Sharma took over the charge. In Pondicherry, NN Saha (a former diplomat) was replaced by Mukut Mithi (former Congress Chief Minister of Arunachal). In Uttar Pradesh, Vishnu Kant Shastri (an old BJP member) was replaced by Sudarshan Agarwal (Governor of neighbouring Uttaranchal) for six days before he, in turn, was replaced by T Rajeshwar (a former Director of the Intelligence Bureau). In August, Manipur Governor, Arvind Deve was replaced by SS Sidhu (both former bureaucrats).[20]

In November 2004, the UPA government dismissed the Governors of five other States, namely, Andhra Pradesh, Bihar, Odisha, Punjab and Rajasthan. In December 2004, four other Governors of the States were replaced. In Arunachal Pradesh, VC Pandey was replaced by a former diplomat, SK Singh. In Jharkhand, Ved Marwah was replaced by Congress loyalist Syed Sibtey Razi. In Maharashtra, Mohammad Fazal was replaced by former Chief Minister of Karnataka SM Krishna. In West

Bengal, former BJP MP, Viren J Shah was replaced by Gopal Krishna Gandhi, a former diplomat and the youngest grandson of Mahatma Gandhi.[21] The replacement of Governors by the ruling party (Congress) reflected their attitude towards the institution of Governor, which had not changed in the new millenium. In its first term, the UPA used this institution to its fullest to appease and accommodate party leaders and sympathisers.

Use of Article 356 by UPA I

Like previous governments, in spite of the multi-party character of the UPA government, it also used Article 356 for its political interest. UPA-I used Article 356 in the States in order to prevent the non-Congress parties from forming governments.

In 2005, elections were held for Bihar and Jharkhand Legislative Assemblies. In both the States no single party got absolute majority. The assembly was put under Article 356. The NDA, through its leader Nitish Kumar, made efforts for the formation of government in Bihar. Almost all the 70 NDA MLAs announced support to Nitish Kumar; 21 out 29 MLAs merged their parties with JD(U). This exercise was to be completed on 23 May 2005. All other small parties also supported NDA government. In order to prevent the NDA from forming the government, the Governor of Bihar gave a report to the Central government for the dissolution of the Legislative Assembly on 21 May 2005, which was based on irrelevant and inadequate considerations. Thus, there was a breakdown of constitutional machinery in Bihar, which was not borne out of the facts since Nitish Kumar enjoyed the support of almost 135 MLAs.

Similarly, in Jharkhand, the Governor, Syed Sibtey Razi invited the UPA, led by the JMM's Shibu Soren, to form the government. The Central government actively prevented the BJP from forming the government in the State. Soren remained Chief Minister just for ten days before he lost the vote of confidence in the Assembly. Faced with no choice, the Governor was forced to invite former BJP Chief Minister, Arjun Munda, to once again head the Jharkhand government. After 18 months, in September 2006, Munda's government fell due to the withdrawal of support by independent MLAs belonging to the smaller parties. These MLAs, it was alleged, were bought up by the pro-Congress lobby. Madhu Koda, an independent MLA, became Chief Minister with the support of the entire UPA. Soren, Koda all had huge charges of corruption against them.

Thus, despite the presence of a number of regional parties in the UPA coalition, the Congress did not shy away from first, appointing sympathetic Governors in the States, then using their discretionary powers to install State governments or destablise unfriendly ones. Thus, as a matter of fact, in the last 65 years, the Congress party used or misused Article 356 maximum times for partisan reasons.

Second Administrative Reforms Commission

On 31 August 2005, the UPA set up a review commission, called the Second Administrative Reforms Commission (SARC), to prepare a detailed blueprint for revamping the public administration system under the chairmanship of Veerappa Moily. After Veerappa Moily resigned with effect from 1 April 2009, V Ramachandran was appointed as its chairman. The Commission was given the mandate to suggest measures to achieve a proactive, responsive, accountable, sustainable and efficient administration for the country at all levels of the government. The Commission was asked, among others things, to consider the following: (i) Organisational structure of the Government of India. (ii) Strengthening of financial management system. (iii) Steps to ensure effective administration at the State level. (iv) Steps to ensure effective district administration. (v) Local Self-government/Panchayati Raj institutions. (vi) Citizen-centric Administration. (vii) Promoting E-governance. (viii) Issues of Federal Polity. (ix) Crisis Management. (x) Public Order.[22]

The purpose of constituting such a commission was to make the system effective in the changing conditions at the national and international level. Its basic purpose was to popularise 'good governance' to achieve the developmental goals by democratising the process of governance. The Commission paid special attention to the changing nature of federalism and opined that the last decade (1999-2009) had witnessed significant maturing of our federalism.

It said, the States are being increasingly empowered to determine their own policies and programmes, and the Union is evermore sensitive to local needs. However, the role of the Union is expanding in substantial measures, in recent years, in new ways, it noted. It pointed out that Education, Healthcare, Rural and Urban development and Social Security are either State subjects, or largely under State jurisdiction. However, the services are increasingly driven by Union policies and funds. Paucity of resources at the State level – need for standardisation of services, compulsions of reducing regional disparities, and the imperatives of meeting the challenges of a growing economy in the modern world – have necessarily enlarged the Union's role in these sectors.

Developments during UPA-I clearly indicated that there were pulls and pushes in federal polity. Though the various commissions set up by the government recommended the need for strong States, to strengthen the Centre and for harmony between the States and the Centre, the UPA-I did not drift from the polity of favourable attitude towards those States which were ruled either by the Congress or its coalition partners.

Centre-State Relations During UPA II Government

In the 2009 elections, the Congress-led UPA II government, under Manmohan Singh, again came to power at the Centre. It completed its two years and stepped into the third year on

23 May 2011. However, the celebration was overshadowed by taints of scams, rising prices and decision-making paralysis. In the next three years, governance quickly spun out of control and the government was struggling to come out of the shackles of the 2G telecom spectrum allocation scam (where its Tamil ally, the DMK, was severely implicated), the Commonwealth games scandal, the Adarsh housing scam and several other such mind-blowing economic twists. On 23 May 2011, the UPA II government released a 218-page report card or white paper. Report emphasised that the terms of reference on corruption included fast tackling of all cases of public servants accused of corruption. The report also covered many specific sectors like agriculture, rural development, education, external and internal challenges, railways and environmental issues etc. Food inflation was a major concern in the last financial years. The Prime Minister said that his government had taken several measures to address the problems and he continued his efforts in 2010-11 and intended to do more in the future.

UPA II's Failed Attempt to Dismiss Karnataka Government

In Karnataka, the BJP's BS Yeddyurappa's government took office first in November 2007 but President's Rule was imposed here within a week. It then again took office in May 2008. In early October 2010 it was made to face a trust vote which it won. After this, the Speaker illegally disqualified sixteen MLAs, eleven from the BJP and five independents. All these MLAs were ministers in the Karnataka government before they submitted a memorandum to Governor HR Bhardwaj expressing lack of confidence in Yeddyurappa. The High Court also upheld the Speaker's decision on 29 October 2010. But the Yeddyurappa government tided over the political crisis, also by disqualifying sixteen MLAs.

By May 2011, after six months of political horse-trading, the Governor sent a special report to the Centre, recommending President's Rule and keeping the assembly in suspended animation, citing breakdown in Constitutional mechanism. The Opposition BJP, on 22 May 2011, set a 24-hour deadline for the UPA government to reject the Governor's recommendation to impose President's Rule in the State. A senior BJP leader, M Venkaiah Naidu said, if the Centre did not act within 24 hours, the BJP would be compelled to launch a nationwide agitation both against the Central government as well as the Governor. Naidu alleged that in the last six days, the State government had not been allowed to function by the Governor and the inordinate delay in decision by the Centre was also affecting the interest of the State and the people. He said that any further delay would be a negation of the people's mandate which went against the spirit of federal structure. Naidu alleged that the Congress-led UPA at the Centre was the real director and the Governor was only an actor in this shameful drama. It was alleged that the script was written by Congress leaders in Delhi and executed by Raj Bhawan in Bangalore.

Moreover, in the light of political development in Karnataka, the Governors' recommendation of President's Rule in Karnataka appeared blatantly partisan. His action went against democratic system and deserved to be condemned. The Karnataka power tussle was evidence of the changing nature of Indian federalism. Prior to 1989, in such situations, most of the time, the will of the Centre had prevailed and States were subdued. In 2011, the situation had dramatically changed and the State government proved its constitutional obligations. Centre was not able to dismiss the elected State government. The BJP government in Karnataka continued in power till May 2013, until the next assembly elections. The party, of course, changed the CM from Yeddyurappa to Sadananda Gowda to Jagadish Shettar. Nevertheless, it was a landmark event in the federal history of India.

Continuity of Policies and Programmes between NDA and UPA

UPA government made the National Development Council a more effective instrument of cooperative federalism. The NDC started meeting at least twice a year and in different States and it took up the issue of the financial health of the States and steps to be taken in this regard. The Inter State Council (ISC) also activated all Centrally-sponsored schemes except in national priority areas like family planning which was to be transferred to the States. On 6 January 2009, a Chief Ministers' Conference was held in Delhi where the multi-dimensional challenges including terrorism, left-wing extremism and insurgency in the northeast were highlighted. Again, on 29 June 2009, a second Chief Ministers' Conference was held in Delhi, on the issue of rural development, drinking water and sanitation.

There have been, to some extent, continuity of policies and programmes between the NDA and UPA governments. The UPA's (2004-14) approach to Indian federalism, and to the States, did not represent a complete break with that of the NDA (1999-2004), its predecessor. In some fundamental respects, concepts such as the understanding of Indian nationhood had significant bearing on Indian federalism. The UPA and the NDA are set apart politically but in the ongoing and practical aspects of governance, there has been continuity. This is so because, first, all the policies are long term, and second, a sudden withdrawal of policies with the change of government is not cost-effective, and could be counter-productive, giving the nation periods of no governance, every five years.

The Backward States Grant Fund (BSGG) programme of the UPA was one instance of continuity as well as a break with the NDA. The programme had begun during the NDA government during the Tenth Plan as Rashtriya Sam Vikas Yojna (RSVY) in 2003-2004. Its purpose was to ensure development of the backward States by helping to create productive assets. The RSVY was not discontinued but was subsumed under the UPA as the Backward Region States Grant Fund (BRGF) policy with a wider coverage of districts, and far greater amount of funds. There were very little terms of difference. The programme aimed to catalyse development in backward areas by providing infrastructure, promoting good governance and agrarian reforms, covering through supplementary infrastructure and capacity building. In terms of coverage, while the RSVY had 147 districts in 27 States, the Backward Region Grant Fund covered 250 districts in 27 States. Interestingly, both the NDA and UPA had included 27 of India's 29 States under the above programme. The BRGF, placed under the Ministry of Rural Development, had two funding windows: a Capability Building Fund (CBF) and a United Grant Fund, that took the factor of population into account.

The programme was launched as late as 29 February 2007, that is after about two years in office of the UPA. While launching the programme from Barpeta district in Assam, a backward district in a backward State, Prime Minister Manmohan Singh (who was a Rajya Sabha member from Assam) said that a sum of Rs 3,750 crore was available for 250 backward districts of India (each district getting about Rs 10-15 crore) for developing their infrastructure and for filling up gaps in development. He also pointed out that the entire programme would be implemented through the Panchayati Raj Institutions and other local self-governing bodies.

Operation Sadbhavana (operation good will) was another area of continuity, in policies and programmes, between the

NDA and the UPA. This programme of extending welfare and development activities to the border areas was a post-Kargil initiative of the Indian army, and a brainchild of Lt General Arjun Roy, who was the leader of the 14th Corps of Northern Command of the Indian Army. He initiated it as a part of the service that the military could deliver to the border areas, a service which would pave the way for the ideal military of the future.[23] It was a goodwill gesture of the army, started with funds from the Central Government Border Area Development Funds (CGBADF) and the Ministry of Defence in which the army engaged itself in various welfare and developmental activities in the border areas of J&K, more particularly Ladakh, in order to redress the credibility of the government and its institutions as an aid to civil government, so that people's trust is restored, and in the process violence is disarmed. The funds received for the programme since 2001, from various sources, were very satisfactory and amounted to around, Rs 603 million.[24] Operation Sadbhavna had many limitations but on the whole, social scientific assessment of the programme identified many positive achievement.

Incidence of Imposition of Article 356 Declined Since 1989

On analysis of the Centre-State political developments since 1989 and particularly during NDA I and UPA I & II coalitions, it has become clear, on the basis of the approaches of the governments and their policies and programmes, that there has been a paradigm shift in the nature of Indian federalism. Development of the party system in favour of coalition governments at the Centre, also led to the growth of cooperative federalism. Growth of cooperative and bargaining federalism has been gaining momentum with the passage of time.

Although all Central governments imposed Article 356 in the States but the occasions of Central interventions in the States under Article 356 perceptibly declined after 1989 and in the 1990s. Between 1950-89 there were 79 Presidential/Central interventions in the States, which work out an average of two per year. The bulk of these emergencies were declared during the Congress rule under Indira Gandhi, ie. forty-eight times and during the regime of the Janata Party, sixteen times. In the first four years, even after the 1989 Lok Sabha elections which practically ended one-party dominance, the high incidence of President's Rule in the States prevailed. This was partly because the rules of the game of coalition and/or minority governments had not been learnt yet and partly due to the turbulence of the Hindutva movement. During this interlude, there were eight proclamations between 1990 and 1991 and seven between 1992 and 1993.

Thereafter, the decline was noticeably sharp: Only four proclamations in the seven years between 1994 and 2000. It was because of the coalition governments at the Centre that the BJP and the Congress had to manage with the support of regional parties and governments who also had regions of power in the States. Therefore, the Centre could not dare to dismiss any State government by the use of Article 356 because there was the question of the Centre's own survival. So, the Centre-State relations were managed in the spirit of give and take. The process of imposing Article 356 had also become difficult because a greater awareness had arisen among regional parties and the general public. For example, the Bihar crisis, wherein the BJP had to face stiff opposition for imposing Article 356. The NDA government, after witnessing the declining financial condition and deteriorating law and order situation, had decided to impose President's Rule in Bihar, which was strongly supported by Bihar's Governor. But the President returned back the cabinet recommendation on the ground that the Rabri Devi government (RJD) commanded absolute majority in the assembly. Thus, the Bihar experience of 1998 shows that in the 1990s, the Indian federal system is marked by greater awareness and greater coordination between the Centre and the States.

Deployment of Armed Forces

The issues of law and order also proved to be a complex one. As provided in the Constitution, the Centre can use its directive power to deploy its armed forces including Central Reserve Police Force (CRPF) and Border Security Force (BSF) at its discretion and the States are constitutionally obliged to obey such Central directives. Normally, these forces could be deployed on the request and consent of the State concerned. The basic problem arises from the role of the Centre in the period of strife, like strikes, bandhs, gherao and general lawlessness. In some of the States, like Kerala and West Bengal, the situation assumed alarming proportions during Left rule. For example, on 17 September 1968, the Kerala government turned down the Center's request that necessary measures, including arrests, under prosecutions, should be taken under the provision of the Central ordinance, promulgated as a sequel to the Central employees' strike. In another instance, when the Central government had deployed CRPF in West Bengal, it was opposed by the then Chief Minister, Jyoti Basu, of West Bengal. He held the view that this was an unwarranted intervention of the Centre in the affairs of the States.

The issue of deployment of Central armed forces in the States does not become a controversial issue in a uni-party system. But in multi-party system of diverse hues and complexion, the stress is much more on tension management due to the inherent conflict, mutual distrust and above all, political motivation. So, deployment of CRPF/BSF has been a serious issue of Centre-State tensions.

But later on, from the developments of 1990s, it has been observed that the attitude of the Centre towards the States has changed, due to the coalition governments at the Centre and also due the participation of regional parties in forming these governments. In such changed political environment, it has not been possible for the Central governments to behave in the old dictatorial style. Now the Centre has become more tolerant and coordinating. It has had to adopt a pragmatic outlook while facing strong constrains from the States.

The central problem today is not of Union-State relations, but of greater decentralisation of economic and political powers to lower levels. The only way to strengthen the Union and the States is to make both the levels to lose their extra weight, to shed monopoly of power in all areas and concentrate on essentials, following a principle of rules concerning what the people are owed. The economic liberalisation has to and must come along with decentralisation of political power and management. To preserve India as a 'Union of States' it is necessary to work for building it as a federal union of autonomies with sharing of powers from the grassroots levels to the Parliament.

Impact of Economic Reforms on Centre-State Relations

In the financial relations, the 1990s witnessed a logical rupture in the Indian political economy: forty years of stated, Centralised and planned economic development was replaced by a market-led, liberalised and globalised model of political economy. The new framework in which the World Trade Organisation (WTO) is the sole arbiter is based on the ideology of viewing the state as the real focus of power and the market as the sole platform for economic growth. Not only this, the globalisers and foreign investors have defined a new agenda for governance.

Decentralisation of governmental power and refederalisation of the polity are the two interrelated programmes suggested by the globalisers for achieving the goals of economic growth in the new market-led economic regimes.

It needs to be emphasised that the India of 1990s was witnessing a new journey, based on the ideology of 'roll back the state' and the federalism of the 1990s had been greatly influenced by the emergence of coalition politics and there was a shift in the philosophy of achieving economic goals through market mechanisms. Further, the State governments had become the real focus of power and decision-making under the new economic policy regime of the 1990s, because foreign investors had to deal with local levels of decision-making for establishing their projects. For example, Bengaluru emerging as an IT hub, Chennai as an automobile hub, new economic power centres emerging in Gurugram, Noida etc.[25]

While analysing the impact of economic reforms on federalism, one must take into account the Seventh Schedule of the Constitution which deals with the division of powers and revenue resources between the Centre and States, eg. industries figure in Union, State as well as in the Concurrent lists. Entries 7 and 52 of the Union list include industries declared by the Parliamentary law as necessary for the purpose of defence or for the prosecution of war and for any such thing which is beneficial in public interest to be in Centre's control. Subject to the limitations, industries are a subject in the State list by entry 24. However, factories are in the Concurrent list by entry 36. Likewise, the economic and social planning is also in the Concurrent list by entry 20. In the era of Centralised development, industry planning was heavily under the control of the Government of India.

Gradual deregulation of industrial licensing provided a new opening to the State governments, which now compete with each other to invite industrialists, both Indian and foreigners, to invest in their own States. The capitals of more developed States are now frequent destinations for visiting foreign dignitaries including former US President Bill Clinton and former World Bank President JD Wolfensohn, and industrialists. Deregulation in this area has nationally increased the autonomy of States and reduced the Centre's powers. But, the Competitive Disadvantage suffered in this area by backward States is likely to worsen regional economic disparities even more than at present.

Due to globalisation and liberalisation, Centre's dominance over financial resources are declining and there is a trend towards decentralisation and devolution of power and resources. In most of the States, regional parties are in power and at the Centre the coalition government comprising representation of different parties. Consequently, local aspiration is well represented and, in fact, have found expression over the years. Due to changing political and economic systems, the States have mounted joint attacks against the Centre's dominant fiscal position. Moreover, the Centre also feels incapacitated to set its fiscal house in order without the States' cooperation.

Due to economic liberalisation, there is perceptible retreat by the Central government. There is decline in fiscal transfers from Centre to the States. The budgetary support by the Central government for Central plan has declined and this has serious repercussion on the State budgets and has accentuated the fragile economic conditions of already weak States. Consequently, in economically fragile States, the State governments have had to withdraw as 'a promotor of socially-desirable production activities' by withdrawing their fiscal and monetary incentives. The Central government has also had to withdraw as a regulator by prescribing and describing certain rules and regulations in order to achieve the macro-economic and other social economic objectives.[26]

The Centre's declining capacity to reduce regional economic disparities is likely to further widen the gap between States in the years ahead. The economic policies and liberalisation process is likely to create greater economic disparities among the States as the Centre's responsibility and capacity to support depressed and extremely poor areas decline and the demand for more fiscal sharing by economically developed States increase.

After 1990s, Indian States had been categorised into three categories on the basis of their capacities to implement and take advantage of the new regime of economic reforms. In the first category of successful developing States – reformer States – were Andhra Pradesh, Maharashtra, Gujarat, Tamil Nadu and Karnataka. The intermediate category of States included Odisha and West Bengal. The States which were demarcated as lagging behind were all the other States including large States like UP and Bihar. Every State, developed or underdeveloped, was left to take care of its own interest in the economic regime of globalisation, liberalisation and privatisation.

In the post-liberalisation and economic reforms period, it was noticed that there was decline in urban poverty rates, but rural poverty remained unredressed. Inter-State disparities have not only tended to increase over the years but have shown a qualitative deterioration in many ways. In the post-reform period, poor States like Rajasthan, Uttar Pradesh, Bihar, Odisha have not shown any reduction in poverty, whereas rich States like Andhra Pradesh, Gujarat, Karnataka, Tamil Nadu, Maharashtra, Punjab recorded decline in poverty. This trend towards increasing disparity among States is likely to make Centre-State relations more complex and might pose serious threat to national unity and integrity.

The *Economic and Political Weekly* published three articles by eminent economists in early 2000, and all the three argued that the post-reforms period saw the growth of regional imbalances and Inter-State disparities. Further, the backward States have the largest share of Below Poverty Line (BPL) population and the quantities of social groups have increased, depending on the levels of development achieved by the State government, the experts said. 'If the above findings and inferences are valid, then the gains of faster growth, since 1980-81, have been unequally shared by different sections of the Indian society. Growth has favoured urban India, organised sector, richer States and property owners against rural India. It has been a period of growth with inequality', R Nagaraj concluded.[27]

The political power has shifted from the Centre to the regions in the decade of globalisation. Montek Singh Ahluwalia concluded that, 'some States have done exceptionally well, several others show a strong performance, while some are doing very poorly'.[28] NJ Kurian divided fifteen States of India into two groups: a forward group and a backward group. The forward group consists of Andhra Pradesh, Gujarat, Haryana, Karnataka, Kerala, Maharashtra, Punjab and Tamil Nadu. The backward group comprises Assam, Bihar, Madhya Pradesh, Odisha, Rajasthan, Uttar Pradesh and West Bengal.[29]

Kurian wrote: '...there are considerable disparities in socio-economic developments across the Indian States. Efforts through the planning process during the first three decades of the Indian republic had only partially succeeded in reducing regional disparities. The accelerated economic growth since the early 1980s, with increased participation of the private sector, appears to have aggravated regional disparities. The ongoing economic reforms since 1991 with stabilisation and deregulation policies as the prime instruments and playing a very significant role for the private sector seem to have further aggravated the inter-State disparities.'[30]

The retreat of the state and neo-classical economic ideology of market-led growth has increased economic inequalities and regional disparities and new tension areas have emerged between the Centre and the States and also between more prosperous States and the backward ones. The growing inter-State and regional disparities are a real threat to the authority of the Central government because of its own commitment to private investment-led growth. This is not an imaginary fear. In 2000, when the Eleventh Finance Commission recommendations were in the process of implementation, the Chief Minister of Andhra Pradesh led a delegation of a few Chief Ministers of performing States to plead that they should not pay the price for non-performing States.

To sum up, the political economy approach to the understanding of Indian federalism provides us with a key to open new areas of conflict among the States of India. On the basis of this approach, it is inferred that India has created a dangerous decade in the twenty-first century, because the Central government will soon lose control over the States, which will refuse to share their benefits with their poor cousins.

Thus, we see the Indian Central government is under siege from regional barons of India. The Vajpayee-led government was hostage to the pressures of the States that were partners in the coalition. As Rob Jenkins observed in the 1980s, '...New Delhi began dancing to the tune of the State governments. This is a very significant departure from the past twenty-five years, if not longer... the new clout of the regional parties in central coalitions, which is likely to remain for the forceable future, changed all that. Chief Ministers from United Front parties called many of the shots, as did those allied with the subsequent BJP-led coalition'.[31]

The approach was favourable to the developed States and eventually lead to a situation when backward States will not be able to compete with the developed States. Present development data clearly indicates the rising disparities in different States. These observations prove that the Indian-economic-social setup needs positive approaches and radical interventions by the national government to bring uniformity in the developmental activities all across the country.

In the rapidly changing economic situation in the second decade of the millenium, a serious review of federal finance practice is required. Measures are also required for Centre-State coordination. Since independence, federal financial relations were never favourable for the development of cooperative federalism. For the first forty years, protective elderly bias in favour of Congress-ruled States and a big brother attitude of the Centre was responsible for the regional disparities.

After 1991, extreme openness, non-protective attitude of the Centre towards the backward States and self-centred approach of the richer States made the situation grimmer.

Cooperative federalism is perceived to be the best device to meet the complexities of the fiscal federal relations in India. It is likely to help in bringing prosperity to the nation as different levels of government share the national resources and markets. It is hoped that cooperative federalism will develop harmonious relations between the Centre and States and among States themselves while encouraging healthy competition among them. Thus, a new federal arrangement to increase the autonomy of the States and the activation of grassroots inter-governmental institutions can transform India into a cooperative and constructive federal polity.

Role of President/Governor & SC in Indian Federalism

President/Governor

The 1990s witnessed a new federal fervour in the Indian political system. The whole matrix of constitutional heads of State – the President and Governors and the heads of governments – the Prime Minister and Chief Ministers – were now compelled by the changed circumstances to function differently.

The President and Governors have come to be elected or appointed from diverse parties due to a multicoloured pattern of inter-party composition of the Presidential Electoral College (consisting of elected members of the Parliament and State legislative assemblies). Different sets of parties or coalitions in power at the Centre and States have shown greater autonomy and discretion. This has increased the autonomy of the State governments.

It was in 1997 that for the first time, the President (KR Narayanan) openly asked the Prime Minister (IK Gujral) and his cabinet, to reconsider the proposal for the dismissal of a State government (UP) before signing the proclamation. The United Front Cabinet at the Centre subsequently dropped the idea. This action of President Narayanan stands out in sharp contrast to President Fakhruddin Ali Ahmed, who did not even meekly confront the Prime Minister (Indira) and signed the proclamation of national emergency. Ahmed did not even suggest to Indira Gandhi to consult her cabinet on the matter. In contrast, President Narayanan, a widely respected statesman, elected to the office with a non-BJP majority in the electoral college, had often obliquely expressed his views on issues related to secularism and the review of the Constitution.

In the changed political scenario, President Narayanan also sought clarification (February 2000) from the NDA government, in a communication to Prime Minister Atal Behari Vajpayee, about the Centre's role in the decision of the BJP government in Gujarat to lift the fourteen-year-old ban on government employees joining the Rashtriya Swayamsevak Sangh (RSS). Under pressure from DMK Chief Minister, M Karunanidhi, of Tamil Nadu and Samta Party (allies of the ruling NDA), the Centre advised the Gujarat government to retract, and the latter complied. A similar move to remove the ban on civil servants joining the RSS, in Uttar Pradesh and Himachal Pradesh, was dropped. Moreover, President Narayanan also sought legal opinion about Uttar Pradesh (Regulation of the Public Religious Buildings and Places) Bill, 2000, passed by the legislature led by the BJP.[32]

APJ Abdul Kalam served as the 11th President of India from 2002-2007. He was always full of ideas aimed at the development of the country. People loved and respected Kalam so much during his tenure as President that he was popularly called the People's President. During his tenure as President, Kalam took interest in the sphere of India's science and technology. He firmly believed that India needs to play a more assertive role in international relations.

The 1990s also witnessed the display of greater autonomy exercised by Governors. There was Governor Surjit Singh Barnala of Tamil Nadu resigning, in the early 1990s, in protest against the dismissal of the DMK government and his transfer to Bihar. The Centre removed Nagaland Governor MM Thomas in 1992, when he dissolved the assembly on the advice of Chief Minister Vamuzo Phesao, without consulting the Centre. Uttar Pradesh Governor, Romesh Bhandari, went to the extreme of dismissing a BJP government faced with the drop of legislative majority due to internal defection in the ruling party and appointed a defector as Chief Minister, ignoring President Narayanan's plea for discretion. The United Front Prime Minister, IK Gujral and his cabinet, maintained a tactical silence. Bhandari was stopped in the task by the Supreme Court restoring the dismissed Chief Minister.

Thus, the role and position of President and Governor has undergone qualitative changes. Under one-party dominant system of the Congress, the Presidents and Governors were mere tools in the hands of the Centre. Prestigious institutions gained their constitutional role due to change in the polity. Due to increased participation of the regional parties in Central government, the State governments are now commanding greater influence over who is appointed the Governor. The Governor has now become more active.

The Supreme Court

Another factor that has significantly contributed to the federalisation process is the changing contour of judicial behaviour. Appointed by the federal executive, under the Constitution, the judiciary in India enjoys considerable autonomy, which has been further strengthened by case law, whereby in appointing Judges of the Supreme Court and the High Courts, the President is bound to act on the advice of the Chief Justice of India and his colleagues. The judiciary has by now come into its own. Not that the judges functioned as partisan instruments under one-party dominance. The point is that of judicial activism on constitutionalism, civil rights, poverty and ecology as well as the courts' federally-oriented role is positively associated with changes in the party system in the late 1960s, 1980s, and mid-1990s.[33]

There was a long history of misuse of the amending power of the Parliament and the executive power to takeover a State government under the pretext of constitutional emergency before the Supreme Court indicated a shift in prevailing patterns of judicial behaviour in the Golaknath case (1967) and the SR Bommai vs Union of India (1994) judgements.

Additionally, the Golaknath* judgement was delivered on 27 February 1967, and the process of the Fourth General elections began on 15 February 1967. It ended one day after the verdict in which the Congress Party secured a bare majority in Parliament and lost in nearly half of the States. This was probably an opportune time to immunise at least the fundamental rights from the virus of mending the constituent power. The court intervened to ensure that the second-generation politicians – Jawaharlal Nehru was no more – would not be tempted to make fundamental rights of the Indian people into a play-thing of manuplated legislative majorities.[34]

The most federally oriented judgement of the Supreme Court in the Bommai case on misuse of Article 356 is associated with the onset of the multi-party system, after the decline of the Congress and the Janata Party on the heels of the 1989 Lok Sabha elections. There had also been numerous individual instances of questionable dissolution of assembly and/or dismissal of State governments by the Centre, of which the court took cognisance.

The Supreme Court of India finally put its foot down in the SR Bommai and others Vs Union of India case (1994),

---

* Golaknath v. State of Punjab (1967 AIR 1643, 1967 SCR (2) 762), or simply the Golaknath case, was a 1967 Indian Supreme Court case, in which the Court ruled that Parliament could not curtail any of the Fundamental Rights in the Constitution.

ruling that, 'while the satisfaction of the President regarding the breakdown of the constitutional machinery in a State is subjective in nature and exercised on cabinet's advice, it was a conditional rather than an absolute power exercisable on the basis of some relevant material'. The court went on the say:

> The proclamation under Article 356 (I) is not immune from judicial review. The court will not go into the correctness of the material or its adequacy. Its enquiry is limited to see whether the material was relevant to action…if the court strikes down the proclamations, it has the power to restore the dismissed government in office and revive and reactivate the legislative assembly wherever it may have been dissolved or kept under suspension.[35]

The court added that though clause (I) of Article 356 implies that the Centre has power to dismiss a State government and dissolve its Assembly, it must be held having regard to the overall constitutional scheme that the President shall exercise it only after the proclamation is approved by both Houses of the Parliament under clause (3) and not before.[36] The Bommai judgement, unless reversed by the Supreme Court itself, has become the new Constitution for federal takeover in a constitutional emergency. It is a great leap forward in the direction of federalisation of Centre-State relations.

In 1998, Romesh Bhandari, Governor of Uttar Pradesh was of the view that Chief Minister Kalyan Singh's ministry had lost majority in the assembly. His ministry was dismissed without giving him the opportunity to prove his majority on the floor of the House and Jagdambika Pal was appointed as the Chief Minister. This was challenged by Kalyan Singh before the High Court. The High Court stayed the Governor's decision by passing an interim order. The interim order of the High Court was challenged by Jagdambika Pal before the Supreme Court. The Supreme Court directed a composite floor test to be held between the contending parties, which resulted in Kalayan Singh securing majority. Accordingly, the interim order of the High Court was made absolute.

In 2005, the Governor of Jharkhand was ordered by the Supreme Court to hold a floor test to determine which party's political alliance commanded a majority in the State. The court made it clear that the discretionary power, under Article 164 (I), of the Governor is subject to judicial review. Exercise of such power came constitutionally but to be ensured by conducting floor test, thus, the democratic principle propounded in the SR Bommai case was again sounded in this case. So was the procedure in the case of Arjun Munda vs the Governor of Jharkhand.

The Supreme Court took up the case of Karnataka on 13 May 2011. In October 2010, the Speaker of the Karnataka Assembly had illegally disqualified sixteen MLAs, eleven from the BJP and five Independents. A bench of Justice Altamas Kabir and Cyriac Joseph said that the Speaker's action, on the Chief Minister's complaint, failed to adhere to the principles of natural justice and constitutional provisions. The bench set aside the Speaker's order as well as the Karnataka High Court's order which had upheld disqualification of the MLAs. The bench said that a Speaker must rise above party affiliation while adjudicating applications seeking disqualification of MLAs.

Not long ago, Supreme Court took action in the case of the 2G spectrum allocation scam. The court asked the UPA government, why no action was taken against the then Telecom Minister A Raja, despite several indicators poining to a looming scam ahead. Thus, the SC tried to pressurise the Central government.

The Supreme Court, on 4 July 2011, also appointed a special investigation team (SIT), headed by former apex court Judge BP Jeevan Reddy, to look into the issue of black money (ie. the country's parallel and illegal economy). It was charged to monitor the investigations to find black money and steps taken to bring back the money stashed away in foreign banks. Besides Justice Reddy, the Court also appointed its former judge MB Shah as the vice-chairman of the panel. A bench comprising Justice B Sudarshan Reddy and SS Nijjar directed that a high-level committee should be constituted by the government to look into the issue of black money. The committee would forthwith be a part of the SIT. The bench also directed the Central government to disclose the names of all persons who had been issued show cause notice by the authorities in connection with the probe into the black money issue. The SIT is supposed to keep the Supreme Court informed of all major developments by submitting periodic status reports. The Supreme Court directed the Central and State governments to extend all cooperation to the SIT.[37]

Judicial activism has played an important role in disciplining the political parties in the country. Developments of the '90s clearly indicate that judiciary has so far proved its worth in the judicial reviews. By reviewing the government's decisions, Supreme Court has helped to strengthen the federal practices in India.

Thus, in view of the rising aspirations of the people, it can be clearly stated that the political scenario in the country has drastically changed. There has been persistent demand for reorienting and restructuring of the Centre-State relationship. The emphasis is on less intervention by the Centre and to give the States a large share of power and authority.

The demand for a shift in the federal set-up of India, which began with the 1967 elections, progressed to some extent with installation of the Janata Government in 1977. But mature and concrete shape took place with the emergence of coalition governments in rapid succession after 1996. It is an accepted principle that the Centre can be strong only if States are healthy and prosperous.

With the rise of regional parties and emergence of coalition governments at the Centre and in most of the States, the dynamics of Indian polity moved towards cooperative federalism. One can hope that imbalances and over-centralism in federal polity of India will be rectified through appropriate constitutional measures and by allowing healthy conventions to grow in this context. The demand for more autonomy cannot be brushed aside easily. Some combination of regional parties seems to be indispensable for any future government, as well as for the present one. A compromise on the issue of regional autonomy, more powers to the States and non-interference by the Centre in the affairs of the State have to be made because coalition governments have, of late, become an indispensable and inevitable part of Indian politics.

The need of the hour, thus, is the devolution of power in tune with the logic of democracy from the Union to the States and from the States downwards to the panchayats and the villages.

Centre-State relations of the NDA II government in New Delhi, led by Narendra Modi, will need to be watched carefully. In the last four years, the BJP has had a contentious relationship with the government of Delhi, led by AAP and Arvind Kejriwal, Puducherry, Tamil Nadu and elsewhere. At the time of going to press, the nation is on the brink of general elections. If the BJP returns to power at the Centre, the relations will have to be assessed after 2023, if not, just for five years. India will have to wait and see how the wind blows.

Centre-State Relations and National Security

Federalism Weakening India's Counter-Terrorism Measures?

SINCE INDEPENDENCE, INDIA has achieved considerable progress on varied fronts but it still has significant illiteracy and unemployment and a near one-fifth of its population subsists below poverty line. India is a large country with about 1,200 islands, an EZZ of several million square kilometres and land and sea borders which span nearly 23,000 kms. Besides this daunting geographical factor, it has a large and growing population of about 1.3 billion which comprises varying socio-cultural and religious communities who speak 179 languages and 550 dialects. The vastly varying socio-cultural and religious traditions of its communities are embedded in thousands of years of its past. Needless to say, the governance of India poses enormous challenge and safeguarding the country's security is truly a colossal task.

India's past experiences have been of internal disturbances, as also incidents involving communal conflicts, which have led to large-scale human and economic losses in various parts of the country. However, it would be relevant to point out that the States have the constitutional responsibility for the maintenance of police and public order and are vested with powers to make all required laws and to take all necessary executive decisions for ensuring internal security within their jurisdiction. In so far as the Union is concerned, it has the much larger responsibility of protecting the State against war, external aggression and internal disturbances.

The founding fathers of the Indian Constitution offered a justification for a strong Centre, as reflected in the debates of the Constituent Assembly. While speaking in the Constituent Assembly, Pt Nehru said, 'Now that the partition is a settled fact, we are unanimously of the view that it would be injurious to the interests of the country to provide for a weak central authority which would be incapable of ensuring peace, of coordinating vital matters of common concern and effectively for the whole country in the international sphere'.[1]

The drafters of the Indian Constitution have introduced provisions like Article 352, Articles 355 and 356. Article 352 and 356 deal with extraordinary situations where total constitutional machinery fail or there is a threat to the unity and integrity of India. Article 355 was incorporated in the Constitution with a view to assign role to the Union in case of internal imbalance. Article 356 confers extraordinary powers on the Union to deal with the constitutional breakdown in a State whereupon all functions of the State government may be assumed by the Union government.

Cumulative effect of these provisions is that there is unmarked division of power between the Union and the State with respect to National Security and Internal Security.

Often, the Union government carries the responsibility of National Security and State governments are responsible for maintaining internal security. If we go by the Constitution, Public Order and Police are included in the State List (List II Seventh schedule). Hence for maintaining internal security, State governments are responsible. Article 246 (3) confers power to make laws and to take all necessary executive actions. Thus, in normal circumstances, State governments are responsible for maintaining internal security. As regards to the Union's responsibility, Constitution provides Article 355.

Article 355 of the Indian Constitution states, 'It Shall be duty of Union to protect every State against external aggression and internal disturbance and to ensure that the government of every State is carried on in accordance with the provision of this Constitution'. Up till now, the Union Government has helped by providing the necessary legal framework – and also by providing armed and paramilitary forces of the Union whenever required for the maintenance of Internal Security.

However, problems like terrorism, naxalism and violence have shackled the Indian security system. Such activities need to be prevented and controlled in a civilised state. Now, the security problems have gone beyond the reach of the individual State governments. At present, security problems need to be addressed in coordination by the Union and State as the entire country is a congruent land mass which makes the movement of terrorists and criminals easy. One can commit a crime in one part of the nation and take shelter in another distant part. One State police needs permission to operate in another State even in respect of just arrest. Unfortunately, constitutional division of power creates barriers also between the Union and the State for addressing issues of internal security jointly.

Relationship between National Security and Internal Security

While our Constitution makes reference to *security* and not to *national security*, it would be incorrect to arrive at the conclusion that the Union and the State have distinct and separate duties for safeguarding the country and providing safety and security to the people of India. It can perhaps be postulated that the lack of reference to national security in our Constitution, if such a specific mention was at all required, may be for better reason than the immediate concerns of the founding fathers of our Constitution. They were, at that juncture of our history, deeply concerned about the challenges of nation-building and how the gigantic problems of resettling millions of refugees, large scale poverty, illiteracy, hunger, unemployment and wide-spread under development would need to be tackled. It was not envisioned that within days of our gaining independence, India would have to face Pakistan-sponsored invasion of Kashmir. The external threat was not limited to this just one post-independence event. Within a few years of independence India had to face major security challenges due to Pakistan-sponsored proxy war, violent activities of the Left-Wing extremist groups and insurgencies in the northeast region, also supported by China.

The Pak ISI has been launching unceasing campaigns to spread radicalism and provides training, weapons, communication systems, funds and a variety of logistical support to enable its terror groups to infiltrate into Jammu and Kashmir and spread violence and chaos. It has also been continuing its attempts to revive Sikh militancy in Punjab and, besides, pressuring various Sikh militant groups to join hands with the Kashmir-Centric terrorist outfits. Side by side, the Indian Mujahdeen and other terrorist groups, based in Pakistan and several other neighbouring countries, have been continuing their endeavours to perpetrate terrorist violence in the country.

The armed struggle being carried out by the Left extremist groups, which aim at securing political power through barrels of the gun, continues to pose serious security problems in several parts of the country. Various insurgent groups in the northeast are still active. Ever since the advent of terrorism in India, issues relating to the effective management of national security have emerged as perhaps the most crucial challenge faced by the Union.

The broad understanding of the term 'national security' has been that it comprises all facts of external security, which relates to protecting the country's territories against war and external aggression and internal security includes all matters relating to the maintenance of peace and public order across the length and breadth of country.

With the passage of time, such a sectoral approach has become erroneous and untenable. Any scope for segregating the management of issues relating to internal and external was obliterated when Pakistan launched its proxy war in Jammu and Kashmir. Furthermore, *over the past nearly four decades, issues relating to the management of internal and external security have got deeply and inextricably intertwined.* It would be relevant to also point out that over time, the sources of security threats have got geographically spread far beyond our immediate neighbourhood to countries in Southeast Asia, Middle East and in the Western hemisphere (like the Khalistan movement funded in Canada and Pakistan). In view of these complexities it needs to be recognised that our security concerns relate to innumerable targets and activities within our country.

Mumbai Attack: A Wake-up Call

On 26 November 2008, as India painfully watched real-life terror on TV and waited for nearly a day for commandos to land in Mumbai after terrorists had captured leading hotels and attacked several landmark buildings, killing scores of Indians and tourists, millions of citizens were angered by what appeared to be an inexplicable delay in providing security. Observers were seized by a puzzle: what could possibly have prevented police counter-action for so long?

Security experts were of opinion that India's Centre-State laws and practices were the principal culprit, although Congress governments ruled the Centre and the State. It is also clear that if it is not addressed urgently, Mumbai-type responses to attacks cannot be ruled out in future. The wake-up call in Mumbai should force the parliamentarians to think about bringing some suitable amendments in the Constitution with regard to the provisions dealing with the country's security.

As per laws and practices, public order is entirely on Indian Constitution's 'State List', not on the 'Central List' or 'Concurrent List'. Unlike the US, *federal crime is not a concept in Indian law, and it cannot be introduced unless the Constitution is amended.* Its relevance has been debated within government circles since the late 1960s, but the idea of the federal crime remains legally elusive. Even when the Indian Airlines flight from Kathmandu was diverted to Kandahar, in December 1999, leading to the release of terrorists from Indian jails in return for the safety of the passengers, the case could not be registered as a federal crime. The Indian Airlines reported to Delhi police that its plane, due to arrive at Delhi airport, was missing. It was registered as a Delhi-based – in other words, State-based crime.[2] The attack on the Indian Parliament building is yet another case in point. Whose job is it to protect the building and the people inside? Delhi Police's or a Central security force's? Terrorist targets cannot be imagined, but protective measures can as attacks can be anticipated. Such targets are not only in Delhi but across the country.

Central agencies – including the National Security Guards (NSG), who are especially trained for urban terrorism – simply cannot function without cooperation of the State government and State police. Protocol demands that often, they cannot enter a State without the State's request and/or permission. India's commandos were all in Delhi when Mumbai was terrorised. After the Mumbai attack, hubs have been created in Hyderabad, Chennai and Kolkata. As a consequence, they can be deployed more quickly, but for operations, they still need the cooperation of the State police. They have no knowledge of ground-level specificities and need geographical-topographical and logistical support at ground zero.

Similar is the case of the Central Bureau of Investigation (CBI), the leading investigating agency of India. The CBI was established under Delhi Special Police Establishment Act, 1946. Its direct jurisdiction covers Delhi and the centrally administered Union Territories. To investigate, it must receive consent, or be ordered to do so by the Supreme Court or High Court. State governments have the constitutional right to deny permission for CBI investigations.

So long as the Congress party ruled both in Delhi and the States, there was no such resistance. Such matters were handled as internal negotiations within the party. The rise of coalition era has made Indian politics much more democratic and competitive, but it has consequently led to the suffering of national security.

National Investigation Agency (NIA)

Immediately after the terrorist attack on Mumbai, the Central government (UPA-I) set up the National Investigation Agency by passing the National Investigation Agency Act 2008 in December 2008. This agency was constituted with the objective of an investigation agency at the national level to investigate and prosecute offences affecting the sovereignty, security of India and security of the State.

NIA is a special agency constituted under the Act for investigation and prosecution of offences which are mentioned in the Schedules of the Constitution. The officers appointed under this Act by the Central government shall have power throughout India in relation to the investigation of scheduled offences. Further, all the power, duties, privileges and liability which the police officers have in connection with the investigation of offences are conferred therein.

The Bombay High Court, in the case of Pragya Singh, Chandrapal Singh Thakur vs State of Maharashtra (the Malegaon blast case) observed: the primary objective to establish the NIA is to better tackle cross-border crimes with inter-state and international organisation and ramifications like terrorism to ensure that the sovereign duties owed by the Union to the citizenry of the protection of life, liberty and property are more properly complied with. The NIA deals with cross-border terrorism-related cases having national and international ramifications. Any investigation done by the NIA involves collection of sensitive intelligence and information, which includes designs, plan and preparation to commit terrorist acts and disclosures of which is likely to affect the security of the informants as well as investigators of the case besides affecting the investigation adversely and may even lead to disastrous consequences affecting public order/national security.[3]

The Act has the following features:

1. This legislation is applicable to the whole of India, citizens of India outside India, in service of the government wherever they may be and persons on ships and aircrafts registered in India.
2. The Constitution of the National Investigation Agency for the investigation and prosecution of offences are specified in the schedule under the Act. The officers of the agency are to have all the powers, privileges and

liabilities which police officers have in connection with the investigation of any offences.

3. The superintendence of the NIA shall vest in the Central government and the administration to vest in the officers designated on this behalf by it.
4. The police officers in charge of the police station on receipt of the report of the offence shall forward it to the State government which in turn to the Central government. If the Central government is of the opinion that the offences are scheduled offence, it shall direct the agency for investigation of such offence.
5. The transfer of investigation and trial of the offence to the State government with the previous approval of the Central government.
6. Agency may investigate other offences connected with the scheduled offence.
7. The State government shall extend all assistance to the agency for investigation of the scheduled offences.
8. The provision of this act with regard to investigation shall not affect the power of the State government to investigate and prosecute any scheduled offence or any other offences.
9. The Central government shall constitute special courts for the trial of the scheduled offences. The special court is to be presided by a judge of the level of sessions judge or additional sessions judge, to be appointed by the

Central government on the recommendation of the Chief Justice of the High Court.

10. The public prosecutor and additional public prosecutor shall be appointed by the Central government. The special public prosecutor may also be appointed for any case or class or group of case.
11. The act also provides for procedure to be adopted and powers to be exercised by the special courts for trial of the scheduled offences. It seeks to provide that offences punishable with imprisonment for a term not exceeding three years or with five or with both may be tried summarily. The special court will have all the powers of the court of sessions under the code of criminal procedure for the purpose of trial of any offence under this act.
12. The proceedings of this act shall be held in camera if the special court deems it necessary or on application made by witness or public prosecutor.
13. If the special court is of opinion that it has no jurisdiction to try any offence, the cognisance of which has already been taken by it, such cases are to be transferred by the special court to any other court having jurisdiction under the court.
14. Moreover, if the Central government is of opinion that a scheduled offence has been committed and which is required to be investigated then Central government

can take *suo motu* action and can direct the agency to investigate the offence.[4]

National Investigation Agency has an important role to perform. However, the Act should be strengthened through requisite amendment. For example, all the crime related to terrorism, such as, production and distribution of fake currency notes, espionage, smuggling of arms and ammunition, money laundering, drugs, organised crime, hijacking and many other crimes should be brought under the preview of NIA. NIA should have jurisdiction in all types of crimes on presumption that they are related to terrorism, unless proved otherwise. Unfortunately, National Investigation Agency is a pure investigation agency. *Function of intelligence gathering, and counter intelligence does not come under its jurisdiction.* Mere Investigation Agency at Central level does not fulfill the requirement of present security demands.

NN Vohra, a security expert and former Governor of Jammu and Kashmir, is of the view: As of now, we have only the NIA which was enacted in a rush after 8/11 terror attack. This statute requires considerable strengthening to ensure immediate cognisance of offences committed anywhere in the country to be followed by prompt investigation. Also, the list of offences covered by this law needs to be dynamically reviewed and enlarged and, side by side, attention given to upgrade and enhance the powers and modalities for special investigations. Further, the obtaining procedures for the establishment of special courts and the completion of trials within given time frame also need to be urgently reviewed and rationalised. If NIA is to function as the nodal agency to counter terrorism, cyber crimes and other major threats, it shall need to be provided very strong and prompt support by the Central and State intelligence agencies and by the law enforcement machinery all over the country.[5]

National Counter-Terrorism Centre (NCTC)

The guideline of the US National Counter-Terrorism Centre is, 'Lead our nation's effort to combat terrorism at home and abroad by analysing the threat, sharing information with our partners, and integrating all instruments of national power to ensure unity of efforts'.[6]

This comment is useful – needs to be made effective for every nation. For countering-terrorism policy, of the foremost importance is to develop counter-intelligence which is related to counter-terrorism.

Intelligence system is an important factor to fight against terrorism. Effective intelligence systems involves:

1. Gathering information about the hideouts of the terrorists.
2. Studying *modus operandi* of terrorists.
3. Scanning of information.
4. Using source of information on the basis of criminal-terrorist nexus.

5. Surveillance with the use of modern technologies.
6. Share and exchange of information on priority basis.
7. Identifying the methods, propaganda and instruments used by terrorists.
8. Identifying the possible targets of terrorists and to take measures thereon.
9. Setting data base.
10. Improving inter-service cooperation.

In USA, the National Counter-Terrorism Centre was established with goals to provide terrorism-related information to the intelligence community; provide detailed lists of terrorists, terrorist groups, and worldwide terrorist incidents; support the response to terrorist incidents in the US and worldwide; write assessments and briefing for policy makers.[7]

It is believed that the number of terrorist incidents in this new millennium which have caused a large number of causalities, could have been avoided and it occurred due to intelligence failure, eg. the Madrid train bombings in 2004, London Subway bombings 2005 and the Mumbai attacks in 2008.[8] Those examples are only indicative of the general intelligence failure, and subsequent investigations suggest that there are many such incidents of intelligence failure world over.

India has a large number of intelligence agencies and security agencies, such as the Research and Analysis Wing (R&AW), Aviation Research Centre (ARC), Intelligence Bureau (IB), National Technical Research Organisation (NTRO) and

Defence Intelligence Agency (DIA) etc. In India, the lead anti-terrorism organisation is the Research and Analysis Wing (R&AW), which reports to the Prime Minister. Domestically, the Intelligence Bureau is the domestic intelligence service situated in every State. India's lead police agency is the Central Bureau of Investigation (CBI).

However, the structure governing all these agencies is such that they operate in a decentralised manner. A systemic, uniform flow of information/intelligence countrywide, to all sister organisations, agencies and government (both States and Central) does not happen.

There is no centralised authority or Ministry that can coordinate or collaborate between different intelligence and security agencies. For example, Indian intelligence intercepted a telephone call on 18 November 2008, indicating an attack on Mumbai, the commercial capital, but the military and civil security services failed to act on the warnings. Mumbai Police Chief Hassan Gafoor told a news conference that security authorities 'had an alert that hotels like Taj could be exposed to such danger'. A US intelligence official* also revealed that India had received two warnings, even listed specific targets, including

* A vital letter, which was filed in one of the Jundal case litigations, was from Daniel Clegg, the then legal attache in the US embassy in Delhi. He had offficially assured India of the 'total cooperation of the US government' in access to David Hadley and had noted that India had received warnings from the USA. A senior US official had also said this to Home Minister Chidambaram, during his official US visit following the Mumbai attacks.

Taj Hotel.[9] It can be identified as a case of intelligence failure because of lack of cooperation and coordination amongst various agencies.

A number of terrorist incidents are found to have complex inter-State and international linkages, and possible connection with other activities like smuggling of arms and drugs, pushing in and circulation of fake Indian currency, infiltration from across the borders etc.

Keeping all these in view, it was felt that there was a need for setting up of an agency at the Central level for investigation of offences related to terrorism and certain other acts which have national ramifications. Several experts and committees, including the Administrative Reforms Commission in its Report, had made recommendations for establishing an umbrella agency having ability to investigate terrorist incidents.[10] On the basis of such recommendations National Investigation Agency was established in 2008.

Mumbai attacks of 2008 shows intelligence and coordination failures. In this context, the concept of a National Counter-Terrorism Center (NCTC) was mooted. The agency was modelled on the National Counter-Terrorism Center of the USA and the Joint Terrorism Analysis Centre of Britain.[11] The NCTC had been envisaged as an umbrella organisation, which would examine the positioning of agencies like the National Investigation Agency (NIA), the National Technical Research Organisation (NTRO), the Joint Intelligence Committee

(JIC), the National Crime Records Bureau (NCRB) and the National Security Guard (NSG). NCTC was planned to be put under Intelligence Bureau.

During his Intelligence Bureau Centenary Endowment Lecture in December 2009, the then Home Minister detailed his proposal to set up the NCTC. He said that the NCTC would have broad mandate to respond to acts of terrorism committed by any group. This would require it to perform intelligence, investigation and operations services, with representation from all intelligence agencies. During the lecture, the Minister also mentioned that the then existing MAC (Multi-Agency Centre) would be subsumed in the NCTC. Other agencies such as NATGRID, NIA, NTRO, JIC, NSG and the NCRB would also come under the NCTC. The intelligence agencies of the Ministry of Defence and the Ministry of Finance would continue to remain under the respective Ministry, but their representatives would have to be deputed mandatorily to the NCTC.[12] It took three years to even get an order.

NCTC Order, 2012

In early 2012, the Manmohan Singh government issued the National Counter-Terrorism Centre (Organisation, Function, Powers and Duties) order 2012. It set up the NCTC under the provisions of the Unlawful Activities (Prevention) Act, 1967. The preamble to the order stated that a need has been felt to have a 'Single and effective point' of control and coordination of all counter-terrorism measures. It also stated that it is desirable that the body be equipped to 1. integrate all intelligence; 2. analyse it; and 3. effectively respond to it.

Following are the provisions of the order:

1. The National Counter Terrorism Centre will be located in the Intelligence Bureau (IB).
2. Besides its core staff, NCTC will have officers on deputation/secondment from other agencies such as R&AW, JIC, NTRO, DIA etc.
3. NCTC shall have three divisions: Intelligence, Analysis, and Operations.
4. The officers of the operation division of NCTC shall have the power to arrest and search under Section 43A of the Unlawful Activities (Prevention) Act, 1967 (ie. if the officer is aware of a design to commit any offence under the Act).
5. NCTC shall have the power to set up Inter-State Intelligence Support Team.
6. NCTC shall have the power to requisition the services of the NSG or other special forces.
7. NCTC shall have power to seek information from any agency that provides such information.
8. The Multi-Agency Centre shall be subsumed in and be a part of the NCTC.
9. All civil authorities in the territory of India and all authorities of the GOI (Government of India) located

outside India shall act in aid of the NCTC.

10. There shall be a Standing Council consisting of the Director and three Joint Directors of NCTC, and the heads of the Anti-Terrorist Organisation in each State.
11. The duties of NCTC shall be to:
    - Plan and coordinate actions of counter-terrorism.
    - Integrate intelligence, analyse it and persue the leads; coordinate with existing agencies for an effective response.
    - Maintain a comprehensive database of terrorists and all information pertaining to terrorists.
    - Coordinate with investigation and intelligence agencies to ensure that terrorist cases are solved, and perpetrators are brought to justice.
    - Prepare daily threat assessment reviews and disseminate them to Central and State governments.[13]

NCTC Trapped in Deadlock of Centre-State Relations

The proposed NCTC – whose aims included preventing, containing and responding to terrorist attacks – found itself trapped in the political quagmire of Centre-State relations during the UPA regime. In particular, the non-Congress ruling States of Gujarat (BJP), Tamil Nadu (AIADMK), Odisha (BJD), Himachal Pradesh (BJP), Madhya Pradesh (BJP), Punjab (SAD), Karnataka (BJP), Bihar (JDU), Tripura (Left) and West Bengal (Left) were bitterly opposed to the proposal. Their main objection revolved around the potential violation of the principle of federalism as they argued that the NCTC would encroach upon the powers of the State. Opposition parties also expressed fears that if NCTC was made part of the IB, the powers given to it under Unlawful Activities (Prevention) Act could be misused. The States said that it went against the constitutional provisions which place law and order under the States. It may also be noted that it was all the non-Congress parties, including the BJP, who were most vocal in their opposition to the NCTC.

Some specific concerns of the States include the following:

1. NCTC is 'controlling and unilateral' in nature. Many States prefer joint operations instead of 'unilateral' operations by the proposed counter-terrorism agency.
2. NCTC will infringe upon the duties of the State police forces. The officials of NCTC would have the right to enter States and search/arrest people without informing the State machinery.
3. There could be arbitrary exercise of power. This would undermine the rights and privileges of the States.
4. NCTC has been formed within the IB which has no accountability to Parliament.
5. NCTC is empowered to seek information from any State agency.
6. Though the US NCTC coordinates counter-terrorism

> effort, it does not have any power to act on its own in matters such as arrest, detention, interrogation, searches etc. It works through authorised organisations such as the Federal Bureau of Investigation (FBI).[14]

The Centre (the Congress-led UPA government, in other words) argued that it has the power to establish NCTC under Article 355 of the Constitution. It also pointed out that the power to seek information is already available with the Multi-Agency Centre, so no new power was given to NCTC. Also, it was of the view that a counter-terrorism agency had to have some operational capability to be effective.

It may be noted that during the parliamentary debates on the NIA Bill 2008 and the Unlawful Activities (Prevention) Act (UAPA) Bill, there were also several dissenting voices. These Bills had received the full support of the BJP which even alleged that the Congress was being apologetic about tabling these two legislations in the Parliament. The BJP claimed that the Unlawful Activities (Prevention) Act (UAPA 2011) was modelled on the Prevention of Terrorism Act, 2002, enacted by the National Democratic Alliance government, led by their party. Among the few MPs who raised objections on the issue of federalism were K Francis George (Kerala Congress-Joseph) and MP Veerendra Kumar (Janata Dal-S) in the Lok Sabha. Also, CPI's Gurudas Dasgupta was in favour of sending both Bills to the Parliamentary Standing Committee for scrutiny.[15] In the Rajya Sabha, Sitaram Yechury (CPI-M) suggested an amendment to make the association of the State governments mandatory in the investigation and trial of offences. He also suggested amendment to the UAPA on the detention clause. D Raja (CPI) suggested the deletion of the entire clause enabling presumption of guilt of the accused. However, the Rajya Sabha had rejected all these proposed amendments.[16]

Although similar issues were raised during the debate on the NIA Bill in 2008, the government could push through the legislation due to the favourable domestic environment. Since the memories of 26/11 were still fresh, no political party dared to oppose it in fear of being seen as soft on terror.

However, since NCTC was a much larger institution that was envisaged to subsume the existing intelligence organisations within itself, the goal of the NCTC also got mired in departmental wranglings. Also, Secretary R&AW, KC Verma sent a dissent note to the government on the creation of the NCTC; he was supported by the then National Security Advisor MK Narayanan. In a detailed note, Narayanan pointed out that even in the USA, the NCTC does not have an Operations wing. It merely collects, collates and analyses information and then feeds the CIA, FBI and other intelligence organisations.[17]

The revised draft, however, altered the original position by keeping the NCTC out of IB and stipulated that it work directly under the Ministry of Home Affairs. It was also clarified that upon identification of a terrorist or terror groups, operations would be carried out in conjunction with the State police. It was also clarified that the arrested suspects would be handed over to the State police. But all these clarifications did not satisfy the States and as a result, the all-important terrorism fighting organisation remained hanging in limbo for the next five years. It is thus a very pertinent and recent example of the impact of narrow domestic politics on counter-terrorism policy and action.

In 2017, with a majority BJP-led coalition in power for three years at the Centre, the government once again made a feeble attempt to revive the NCTC project. On 20 May 2017, Union home secretary Rajiv Mehrishi met Intelligence Bureau chief Rajiv Jain and National Investigation Agency head Sharad Kumar to discuss the structure and legal framework of the NCTC. Yet, a year later, the media reports, NCTC will not happen any time soon, especially with the country going into parliamentary polls in 2019.

Security expert NN Vohra suggests that the 'the Union should take urgent steps, in close consultation with States, to evolve and promulgate the National Security Policy and thereafter, draw up and implement a time-bound action plan to fill all existing gaps and establish a country-wide institutional framework for safeguarding the country on every front'. He further suggests: I would again stress that if the sovereignty, unity, and territorial integrity of our country is to be effectively protected, then it is of foremost importance that the Union and States act in very close concert to ensure an efficient implementation of the National Security Policy. It is equally necessary that all matters relating to national security are viewed with utmost concern and prompt decisions are taken to ensure that not the slightest chink is left to subvert the national interest.[18]

The seriousness and urgency to strengthen the security apparatus, particularly intelligence gathering machinery, was highlighted in most clear terms by the then Home Minister, while addressing the Lok Sabha on the Mumbai terror attacks. He categorically stated that 'South Asia is in the eye of the storm of terror. Several terrorist organisations operating from territories beyond India's borders have been identified as the source of the terrorist attacks in India' that have occurred over the last several years.

Here below is the text of Home Minister P Chidambaram's address to the Lok Sabha on the Mumbai terror attacks in December 2008:

> I wish to make a statement on the terrorist attacks that took place in Mumbai between November 26, 2008 and November 29, 2008. With deep regret, I have to report to this House that 164 persons (civilians and security personnel) lost their lives and 308 persons were injured. Among the civilians killed were 26 foreigners belonging to many nationalities. Besides, nine terrorists were killed in the operations by the security forces. One terrorist was overpowered and captured.
>
> At the outset, I wish to pay homage to the innocent

civilians who were killed and the brave security personnel who laid down their lives in order to save the lives of many others. I offer my heartfelt condolences to the bereaved families. The Government of India and the Government of Maharashtra have announced a set of measures as compensation for the terrible loss suffered by the families. Monetary compensation and free treatment have been offered to the injured. While words of sympathy and money can never adequately recompense the loss, I sincerely hope that our gesture will bring some comfort to the affected families.

The broad facts of the horrific tragedy are, by now, known to the Honourable Members and the people of India. According to information gathered during the course of the investigations, it appears that 10 Pakistani nationals belonging to the Lashkar-e-Taiba, a proscribed terrorist outfit, had left Karachi on November 23, 2008; boarded a launch by the name of Al Hussaini; accosted and hijacked an Indian fishing vessel, MV Kuber, off the coast of Gujarat; killed its occupants; and a few miles short of the coast of Mumbai abandoned the fishing vessel, got into an inflatable rubber dinghy, and landed near Budhwar Park, Colaba, Mumbai between 8.00 p.m. and 8.30 p.m. on Nov 26, 2008.

The terrorists split into four groups and the main targets of the four groups were (i) Chhatrapati Shivaji Terminus (CST); (ii) the Leopold Cafe and Taj Hotel; (iii) the Oberoi-Trident Hotel and;(iv) the Nariman House. These attacks involved indiscriminate firing, throwing of grenades and bomb blasts at 13 locations. Considering the extensive publicity that the whole episode has already received in the media and through official statements, it may not be necessary for me to go into the details of what happened at each of these locations.

I shall now give you a brief account of the response of the authorities to the terrorist attack. At the CST, security personnel belonging to the Mumbai police and the RPF confronted two heavily armed terrorists. After causing mayhem at CST, the two terrorists escaped via a lane opposite the station. Meanwhile, as soon as news of the firing at the CST and near Cama Hospital was received, police officers rushed to the sites.

There was an unexpected – and fortuitous – confrontation between the two terrorists and the police personnel in which three officers were killed. Subsequently, the two terrorists were challenged by a police party and, in an exchange of fire, one terrorist was killed and one was captured alive. The name of the apprehended terrorist is Mohammed Ajmal Amir. Interrogation and investigation have revealed that he belongs to Village Faridkot, in District Ukada, in the province of Punjab in Pakistan.

As information about the terrorist attacks poured in from the Nariman House, Taj Hotel and the Oberoi-Trident Hotel, police parties were rushed to the places.

Shortly before 11 p.m. on November 26, 2008, information was received by the Central Government that there were incidents of firing in several places in Mumbai. Immediately, the Central Government authorities got in touch with the authorities of the Government of Maharashtra.

At the request of the Government of Maharashtra, the local Army and Navy authorities were asked to provide assistance. Accordingly, the Army deployed five columns to cordon off the affected areas and the Navy deployed their commandos to deal with the terrorists. Meanwhile, at about

11.30 p.m., the Government of Maharashtra asked for the National Security Guards.

The Central Government immediately alerted the NSG and mobilised their counter terrorist units, based at Manesar in Haryana. A group of around 200 men (which was reinforced the next day) was airlifted to Mumbai late that night. They were deployed at the various sites of the operation in the early hours of November 27, 2008.

The operations were conducted under very difficult circumstances: the terrorists were heavily armed, there was a hostage situation, and the terrorists had the advantage of shield and height afforded by the tall buildings that they had entered. Nevertheless, through their patience, skill and bravery the security forces were able to neutralise the terrorists and rescued hundreds of persons who had been trapped in the buildings. The operations came to an end at about 8.20 a.m. on Nov 29, 2008.

Cases have been registered and the investigations have been entrusted to the Crime Branch of the Mumbai Police. The authorities of the Maharashtra Police and the Central agencies have extended their full support to the Mumbai Police in the conduct of the investigations. Honourable Members will appreciate that it would not be appropriate to disclose any details of the investigations except to draw attention to the official briefings given by the Mumbai Police. Nor would I be able to comment on the many reports that have appeared in the media from time to time. I would respectfully urge patience until the investigations are completed and the reports are filed before the court of law.

I am, however, able to say that the finger of suspicion unmistakably points to the territory of our neighbour,

Pakistan. The interrogation of the captured terrorist has yielded valuable material evidence. The origins of the ten terrorists who entered India have been established conclusively. There is also abundant evidence gathered from the inflatable rubber dinghy, the fishing vessel and the bodies of the terrorists that has enabled the investigators to reconstruct the sequence of events from the origin to the targets.

I know that Honourable Members – as well as the people of the country – would wish to ask a number of questions concerning the nature and extent of the terrorist threat to India, the intelligence gathering machinery, the preparedness of our security forces, the effectiveness of the operations, and on the path forward. There are genuine concerns on each of these matters. I share these concerns. In the last ten days, even while familiarising myself with the security situation and the working of the Ministry of Home Affairs, the intelligence agencies, the Central Paramilitary Forces and the State Police forces, I have initiated a number of steps that will, I believe, enhance security and restore the confidence of the people.

Honourable Members, in my assessment, South Asia is in the eye of the storm of terror. Several terrorist organisations operating from territories beyond India's borders have been identified as the source of the terrorist attacks in India that have occurred over the last several years.

India told the United Nations Security Council yesterday, 'India will act to safeguard and protect its people from such heinous attacks; however long and difficult that task may be. We have acted with restraint in the face of terrorist attacks. We must do our duty by our people and take all actions as we deem fit to defend and protect them.'

That is our policy. My colleague, Shri Pranab Mukherjee, Minister for External Affairs will intervene in the discussion and deal with the external and diplomatic aspects of the situation arising out of the terrorist attacks in Mumbai.

We have a number of intelligence gathering agencies. Intelligence is shared, evaluated and acted upon. However, I have found that there is a tendency to treat some intelligence inputs that are not specific or precise as not actionable intelligence. Further, the responsibility for acting upon intelligence inputs is quite diffused. In the case of the Mumbai attacks, intelligence regarding a suspected LeT vessel attempting to infiltrate through the sea route was shared with the Director General, Coast Guard and the Principal Director, Naval Intelligence.

The Coast Guard made a serious effort, including deploying vessels and aircraft, to locate the suspect vessel, but was not successful. The Navy found that the coordinates of the vessel, as reported, placed it well within the territorial waters of Pakistan. Nevertheless, the Navy had committed several surface units and aircraft in the zone during the period on November 19-20, 2008. In the absence of further inputs or information from the agencies concerned, the Navy concluded that no further action could be taken on the basis of the available information.

I wish to inform Honourable Members that all aspects concerning intelligence are under my examination. While the basic structure seems sound, there is a need to make intelligence gathering and intelligence sharing more effective and result oriented. Some changes have already been made and more are underway.

The NSG is our best trained and best equipped force to

counter a terrorist attack. On many occasions in the past – and in Mumbai too – they have displayed exceptional courage and skill. They are hampered by the distance between their headquarters and the airport; the absence of a dedicated aircraft; and the poor logistics in the theatre of operations.

Nevertheless, once deployed, the NSG is a very effective counter-terrorist force. I have initiated a number of steps to remove the logistical weaknesses in mobilising and deploying the NSG. A decision has been taken to locate NSG units in a few regional hubs. A decision has also been taken to draw upon the commando units of the Armed Forces to create more regional hubs until a decision is taken to locate NSG units in those hubs too. These decisions will be implemented as expeditiously as possible.

The Mumbai terrorist attacks have brought into sharp focus the vulnerability of our coastline that extends to 7,500 km and the imperative need to enhance maritime and coastal security. A coastal security scheme was approved in January 2005 for implementation over a period of five years with an outlay of Rs 400 crore for capital expenditure and Rs 151 crore for recurring expenditure during the first five years.

We have reviewed the scheme and we have concluded that there is a need to strengthen it and integrate it into a larger security system. A decision has been taken in-principle to create a Coastal Command for overall supervision and coordination of maritime and coastal security. The mandate of the Coastal Command will be to secure India's coastline.

I may also report to this House a number of other decisions that have been taken in order to enhance security:

Intelligence gathering requires human resources and technical resources. We have identified the gaps. Steps are being taken to fill the vacancies in the intelligence organisations expeditiously and to provide them with advanced technical equipment.

India Reserve Battalions are being raised in a number of States with financial assistance from the Central Government. Government has already authorised that two companies of each battalion may be raised as special commando units for which additional assistance will be provided for training, equipment, etc.

It has been decided to set up 20 counter-insurgency and anti-terrorism schools in different parts of the country for training the commando units of the State police forces.

A separate exercise is underway to strengthen the laws relating to terrorist acts. We are in the process of consulting different political parties and I hope to introduce in this session, with the leave of this House, a set of Bills to strengthen the legal provisions relating to the prevention, investigation, prosecution and punishment of terrorist acts. One of the Bills is for setting up a National Investigation Agency. I would urge this House to consider and pass these Bills in this session. I would also urge this House to pass the Amendment Bill to the Prevention of Money Laundering Act, 2002.

The Prime Minister, in his address to the Nation on November 27, 2008 declared the resolve of the Government to take the strongest possible measures to ensure the security of the Nation and the people. I promise, on behalf of the Government, that we will strain every nerve to carry this resolve into determined action. There is one thing that I wish to make clear: given the nature of the threat, we cannot go back to 'business as usual'. In the next few weeks and months, it will be my endeavour to take certain hard decisions and prepare the country and the people to face the challenge of terrorism.

I appeal to all sections of this Honourable House and to the people of India to stand united and brave in the face of the challenge of terrorism. I ask you to remember the extraordinary courage of Assistant Sub-Inspector Tukaram Omble who grabbed the barrel of the gun and took all the bullets in his chest to enable his fellow policemen to overpower Mohammed Ajmal Amir Kasab.

I ask you to remember the supreme sacrifice made by Major Sandeep Unnikrishnan who ordered his men to stay back while he confronted the terrorists. Ordinary men and women like us cannot match their bravery, but we can stay united in our resolve and in our actions. Nothing should divide us – not religion, not language, not caste. In our fight against terror, there will be need for self-restraint, discipline and even some sacrifice. I seek your support; and I have no doubt that, with your support and the support of the people, we shall overcome and vanquish the forces of terror.[19]

Conclusion

Lack of Emergence of One Dominant Alternative Party

Federalism in India has been evolving over the past six decades and has entered a dynamic state, which has seen the emergence of coalition governments at the national and State levels. With democracy taking root in the past century, the 21st century is expected to be known as that of federalism.

The federal idea in India does not, however, follow the orthodox pattern of federalism represented by the American Constitution or the Australian Constitution. For a vast country like India having different languages, dialects and cultures, federalism is the only road. The federal idea in India tries to strike a balance between centripetal idea of unity and integrity of the nation and the centrifugal idea of linguistic and cultural diversity of regions.

The era of dominance by the Indian National Congress has ended. Congress remains a major party, but it must now operate with a multi-party system. The influence of the Congress got reduced to a great extent after the 2014 elections and the BJP, which has increased significant influence at national as well as State level, has overtaken the Congress in representational politics.

The dominant party system of the Nehru-Gandhi era that led to the formation of Congress majority governments was replaced after the ninth parliamentary election in 1989 by a regionalised multi-party system and coalition governments. The people of different parts had begun stridently vocalising their actual or perceived neglect by the Central government. This created an ideal ground for the formation of many regional parties in different States of India and this trend has been continuing. As a result, regional parties can be found in all States of India. Some of them are so powerful that not only have they formed State governments on their own but also, they have reduced national parties to a secondary position. A pertinent example is the Aam Aadmi Party in Delhi, the Center's seat of power, where both the ruling BJP dominating Parliament and the grand old party Congress are in the shadow. In a vast India, a small party rules this tiny Union Territory, India's power hotspot.

At present, the national parties are forced to make compromises with the regional parties to have a foothold in State politics. Thus, the TDP in Andhra Pradesh, NC and PDP in Jammu and Kashmir, RJD and JD (U) in Bihar, NCP and Shiv Sena in Maharashtra, DMK and AIADMK in Tamil

Nadu, the SAD in Punjab, the AGP in Assam, and SP and BSP in Uttar Pradesh have so much clout in their respective States that the national parties have to align with them to share power at the State as well as at the national levels.

The decline of the Congress party did not result in the emergence of any dominant alternative party; instead, a heterogeneous set of political parties captured the votebank of the Congress. Broadly speaking, mainly three or four types of parties filled the vacuum created by the Congress. These were the Left parties, Janata Party, Janata Dal and Socialist Party. But after the 1990s fragmentation of the Congress party, the votebank of the Congress was significantly eroded, providing the BJP and some other caste and region-based parties with opportunity to rule The issues of Mandal, liberalisation, privatisation and globalisation since the 1990s changed the votebank of the Congress. These issues increased regional, State and caste-based political parties in Indian democracy.

The Turning Point: 1989 General Elections

The shift from dominant party to multi-party politics and the rise of State parties, at the expense of the national parties, have undone the centralising thrust of the 1950s' Constitution. One telling sign of this is the reduced use of Article 356, the 'President's Rule' clause that was used – some would say misused – by majority governments at the Centre to remove irksome State governments. With State-based parties now holding the balance of power in New Delhi, freewheeling invocations of Article 356 are a thing of the past.

Since 1989, different kinds of coalitions and minority governments in New Delhi have reflected the paradigm shift in the nature of India's political system. From a state-controlled, socialist leaning model to economic liberalisation of the 1990s, the dismantling of the permit-licence raj and an increasing reliance on markets has fostered the emergence of a 'federal market economy' and a political dispensation that allows it. Economic liberalisation has been marked by a decline in public investment and a rise in the private investment, the displacement of the federal Planning Commission by the market, and the emergence of the States as critical actors in economic reforms growth.

The result has contributed to a transformation of India's federal system. The process of liberalisation indicates that the States have become more significant players in India's federal market economy. The new economic policy saw the gradual emergence of the federal market economy with decision-making powers shared between the Centre and the States. At the same time, measures of economic sovereignty and decentralisation has now placed the onus on the State Chief Ministers to accelerate the economic growth in their respective areas. However, fiscal federalism in India still continues to be more dominated by the Centre, despite gradually increasing economic liberalisation since 1991.

Era of Coalition Politics

Indian politics is now regionalised and coalition governments have become an important ingredient of political articulation reflecting the socio-political and cultural diversities of the country. What appeared to be a mere trend in 1967, when several Indian States saw the formation of opposition (specifically anti-Congress) coalition governments, now seems to have become a pattern. So, the formation of stable coalition governments in New Delhi is the culmination of a process. Although the two major pan-Indian parties, namely the BJP and Congress, have failed to capture a majority in the national legislature, their critical importance makes them nodal in the formation of any coalition government. This will perhaps lead to the rise of a 'bi-nodal' party system in the near future whereas the regional parties, despite their inevitable role in government formation, will have to remain politically insignificant, independent of these two major parties.

Nonetheless, the regional parties that provide the required numerical legislative strength seem to hold the balance of power in a political situation in which none of the national parties has the magic number of parliamentarians to justify their independent claim. So, despite their distinct identities, the national parties are no longer as decisive and dictatorial as before in the environment of coalition politics; they cannot afford to ignore the regional parties entirely. On occasions, these result in a tightrope walk for both the regional and national parties where the support of the regional parties is absolutely crucial for the survival of the coalition. Under such circumstances, political blackmailing by the coalition partners cannot be ruled out to squeeze advantages when the coalitions are most vulnerable. An example here is the case of the BJP on the eve of the 2019 elections.

The BJP today has a wafer thin majority with its effective strength standing at 273 in the 539-member House. In 2014 it had 282 seats and could have formed a government without allies. With allies, it had a strength that crossed the 300 mark and the party was in a position in 2015 and 2016 to conduct a massive demonitisation and GST roll-out exercise across the nation without prior opposition consultation. The situation has, however, changed for it in 2017-18. Four seats in Parliament are unrepresented, so effectively it is a House of 539 seats. The ruling party has lost bypolls in Uttar Pradesh, Rajasthan and Chhattisgarh, and at the time of writing it has just 273 seats. The majority mark is 270. So, carving out a pre-poll alliance has become absolutely important for it. It has also lost three crucial States it ruled for more than a decade – Rajasthan, Madhya Pradesh and Chhattisgarh. Although, so long, people have voted differently for State and Central elections, democracy can be a bit of a gamble – one can actually never say how the voter will vote, when elections are fair. So, the BJP has to live with guesswork about whether voters in MP, Rajasthan and Chhattisgarh will vote BJP in the summer of 2019. The era of coalition politics has signified a break with the past.

A coalition situation arises when an election fails to throw up a party with a majority of seats in Parliament, and for this reason, the Parliament is unable to form a government according to the majority decision-rule for government formation and maintenance in conformity with the *confidence convention* of parliamentary government, with confidence vote tied to the popularly elected House of the Parliament. In such an eventuality, either a minority government or a coalition government may be formed.

Strictly speaking, the only minority government since 1989 formed in India was that of the Congress party led by PV Narasimha Rao (1991-96). A minority government is an executive coalition which is typically formed by the largest or one of the largest parties short of majority, with one or more smaller parties extending support to it from the parliamentary floor without joining the government. Such a government is an executive as well as legislative coalition.

The idea of a coalition has struck roots in two different ways: on the one hand, the consistent failure of the national parties, including the Congress and BJP, to win even a simple majority in Parliament (except in 2014 when BJP crossed half the mark), creates a clear possibility for a coalition with willing partners to constitute a government; the remarkable success of the parties with regional roots is also, on the other hand, illustrative of a decline of the national parties for their inability to articulate the 'regional voices'. The increasing viability of the coalition is the outcome of a complex socio-political churning, indicative of a new model of governance ruling out the single-party domination completely.

The Centre is now restrained by the regions or States to such an extent that there is hardly a national party on the political horizon who can form government independently. The national parties, be it the Congress or BJP, has become increasingly regionalised, the Centre is now completely dependent upon the regional parties for its very survival. The political career of the 'region' has thus, swung from a State of dependence on the Centre to one of being in a position to bring influence on it.

Coalition and minority governments at the Centre appeared after long spells of Congress dominance until 1989. The coalition governments at the Centre formally began in 1989 and have continued since then. However, the first informal coalition government at the Centre ever was formed in 1977. This coalition was popularly known as the Janata Party government. The decade (1989-99) featured a series of unstable coalition and minority governments, following each other like a game of musical chairs. In 1996, 1998 and 1999 general elections the BJP had the largest number of MPs in the Lok Sabha. It was able to increase its core votes to one in five votes. The emergence of smaller parties tends to exercise more power and authority in deciding the fate of bigger parties like the Congress and the BJP to govern India, and federal system also tends to be more federal and real when coalition system operates at the national and State level.

Election results of 1999, 2004, 2009 and 2014 have revealed that India has firmly entered into the phase of coalition politics. A closer scrutiny of the pattern of results indicate that the parties which understood the grammar of coalition politics effectively could benefit more than those parties which failed to do so. In 1996, for instance, when the then Prime Minister, Atal Behari Vajpayee, sought a Confidence vote in the Lok Sabha, the entire Indian political spectrum opposed the BJP government. But, within the next two years, with the right kind of political maneuvering, the BJP, which had begun as a predominantly north Indian party dedicated to Hindutva, had to shelve that agenda in order to accommodate key coalition partners, especially secular State parties from south India that cared less for anti-Muslim communalism.

The Congress, at its Pachmarhi conclave (1998), took a stand against coalition politics and maintained that it can come to power on its own. This helped the BJP-led NDA to come to power in 1998 and 1999. But, soon the Congress learnt lessons from its debacle. The party revised its stand at its Shimla conclave in 2003. The Congress declared its readiness for coalition. However, Pranab Mukherjee was the lone voice stating contrarian view as he believed that sharing a platform and/or power with other parties would undermine the Congress party's identity. He maintained that the party should not forsake that identity for the sake of forming a government; there was no harm in sitting in opposition, should that happen. His voice fell on deaf ears.[1] In fact, the Congress high command took personal initiative to implement this changed stand in 2004 elections. The Congress could chalk up a formidable alliance in many States after it had revised its stand on coalition politics. For instance, the Congress could arrive at winning alliances with the RJD in Bihar, the NCP in Maharashtra, the DMK-led front in Tamil Nadu, the JMM in Jharkhand, TRS in Andhra Pradesh and PDP in Jammu and Kashmir. The only exception, perhaps, was Uttar Pradesh where despite its earnest efforts, the Congress could not reach an agreement with either the Samajwadi Party or the BSP.

Ideological Incompatibility and Politics of Opportunism

Coalitions in India have largely been non-ideological or office-seeking where partners are united for electoral gain, irrespective of their ideological compatibility. Even the Left Front, which is ideologically well knit, appeared to have ignored programmatic differences with the Congress while supporting the UPA government in opposition to the BJP-led coalition. Besides the Left parties, the other UPA allies came together with specific political goal to fulfill under the UPA regime. The Andhra Pradesh based TRS support for the Congress was largely due to the latter's assurance for a Telangana State. Similarly, the Maharashtra based NCP – despite its reservation about the leader of the Congress, Sonia Gandh because of her foreign origin – was part of the UPA government, presumably because of a strategic calculation for electoral gain and had joined as an ally of the Congress in the State assembly elections that followed the 2004 Lok Sabha polls and had continued with UPA-II .

There are today many leaders who are playing an important role in the State and national politics but have criminal background. Coalition politics has helped in spreading the malady of political corruption much more comprehensively throughout the Indian political system. Regional political parties do not give up their parochial approach and, therefore, are narrow in their outlook. In this system, power shifts from the Centre to the States. All the regional partners of the Central coalition government have their regional agendas. As a result, the States tend to become stronger and the Centre too weak. Under the influence of self-seeking politicians, coalition politics has become vulnerable to opportunism, inefficiency and deprivation. *The most significant drawback of the coalition system is that it is the worst manipulator of the popular mandate.* And UPA-II was an extreme evidence of how bad it can get.

Consolidation of Coalition Governments

The argument that coalition governments cause political instability is partly true, thereby resulting in uncertainty in governance. In the early phase of coalition politics, there were frequent changes in government. But, over the period of time, coalition governments have consolidated. Different political parties are clearly identified with one or the other coalition formulation. Even at the Centre, coalition governments are running full term. Therefore, it seems that the political instability created by coalition politics was a transient phenomenon. Coalition politics has also transformed over a period of time. In the initial stage, political parties came together to form coalitions either to come to power or keep their common enemy out of power. The coalition partners differed on many aspects but shared power.

In the second stage, political parties, despite differences, formed coalition after arriving at a Common Minimum Programme (CMP) before or after elections. Such a CMP was a negotiated document striking a balance between the positions held by various coalition partners. Such arrangements cannot be considered as completely opportunistic because this displays a certain degree of pragmatism in the era of coalitions. This was, in fact, a strange characteristic of India's coalition phase. It is evident from the arrangement at the Centre in 2004 that opportunism was to a certain extent voluntarily leashed by the awareness that the frying pan was better than the fire. A case in point is the Left parties, bitter enemies of the Congress in two States, ideologically entrenched against the ambivalent Congress. The CPI (M) won 41 out of the 44 seats by defeating the Congress in 2004 elections in its State parliamentary constituencies. However, still it had to support the Congress-led government at least from the outside to keep the Congress-led government in power against the BJP. Such a kind of peculiar arrangement is bound to create some strains and problems within coalitions.

UPA II Government and Scams

The UPA II government stepped into the third year of its second term on 23 May 2011 and celebrated. Dogged by scams and unable to move ahead on economic reforms in a big way, the UPA II government was struggling to come out of its shackles. From the 2G scam, the Commonwealth Games scandals and the Adarsh Housing row, the Prime Minister might not have had such a harrowing time in the last months even when his government was surviving on the support of the Left parties during the first term. In the 2G spectrum allocation scam case even the Supreme Court was prompted to pull up the Prime Minister, asking him why no action was taken against the then Telecom Minister A Raja despite several indicators pointing to a looming scam ahead. Apart from A Raja landing himself in Tihar Jail, the other bigwigs to give him company were Congress MP Suresh Kalmadi, charged with irregularities in the conduct of the Commonwealth Games, and DMK MP Kanimozhi, not a good advertisement for the government at celebration time. The winter session of Parliament in 2011 was washed out entirely amid a strident demand for a JPC into the 2G scam, being dubbed by the opposition as 'the biggest scandal in independent India with a national loss of Rs 1.76 lakh crore to the exchequer'.

However, the Prime Minister kept on asserting that the guilty in scams would be punished through due process of law and steps would be taken to prevent them in the future. Faced with problems, the UPA government failed to project a cohesive picture with the Prime Minister himself pleading that he was not as big a culprit as was being made out to be and he had to work under coalition compulsions.

The government had not taken a clear decision on the Lokpal Bill and there was also a controversy between the government and Anna Hazare. Civil Society members, led by the Gandhian crusader Anna Hazare, wanted to have the Prime Minister under the Lokpal's ambit but the government representatives overruled the demand. Following Anna Hazare's initial, much publicised protest action, a second major protest saw controversial events taking place at Ramlila Maidan, New Delhi, on 4 June 2011. The figurehead for this protest was Baba Ramdev and his aim was to highlight the need for strong legislation to bring back to the country what has been called 'black money' deposited abroad. Ramdev demanded that untaxed money invested should be declared as the wealth of the nation. In the controversy on the Comptroller and Auditor General's Report on Commonwealth Games expenditure, in which the Chief Minister of Delhi,

Sheila Dikshit, was indicted, the BJP demanded her resignation on the ground of the CAG report.

Manmohan Singh had to complete two years of his second term with a stigma of being a weak Prime Minister. His inability to take action against Ministers, accused of corruption or sheer inefficiency, was an obvious indicator of his lack of power within the government. The disharmony on various crucial policy matters was another sign of his deficiency. However, these symptoms were more a reflection of structural weaknesses in the prevailing ruling system than of individual failing on the Prime Minister's part. There were, in fact, two sources of weakness in the UPA arrangement. The first was induced by the compulsions of coalition government, the second by the nature of the ruling party itself. Though the Congress won many more seats in 2009 than it did in 2004, it was still dependent on smaller parties whose agendas were inconsistent and unpredictable.

Effective Mechanisms Required for Coalition Governments

Both the NDA and UPA are, as such, illustrative of coalitions that are not ideology inspired, but formed by parties clustered around two pan-Indian parties for specific gains for constituencies they represent. On the other hand, by forming alliance with well-entrenched regional or State-based parties, both the BJP and Congress are guided by calculations for electoral victory for the coalitions under their stewardship.

Coalitions in India appear to be *quid pro quo* arrangements. The smaller regional parties form alliance with the leading national parties for a national presence, while national parties agree to join hands with them to capture office.

On the eve of the 2019 general elections, the Congress has decided not to ditch its burden-allies like the DMK and JMM, although it is acutely aware that it was alliance with these parties that had cost it its credibility in the 2014 elections. The Congress is in a Catch-22 situation: it knows that it cannot ditch the DMK as the BJP, weakened itself, is just waiting with gates open for anyone who is not with the Congress. The Congress has not been able to woo the SP, BSP or the AIADMK who are likely to sit on the fence till the last minute. If these parties do not ally with either of the national parties, there is a likelihood of vote-splitting that will not allow either the BJP or the Congress to form a stable government, even a coalition government in keeping with the pre-poll spirit. Post-poll adjustments have to be then made, which does not augur well for either the BJP or the Congress. A hung parliament is no good for any country, it gives out the signal that the nation is weak. The call of this political generation is a stable country.

Strong leadership, effective mechanisms for ensuring ministerial accountability and discipline, mechanisms for coordination between ministries, and intolerance for misuse and abuse of power are essential for effective coalition governments. There has to be coalition *dharma*. Members of a coalition government may retain their party identities, but they must, in public, represent their governments. They have one leader in the government, that is the Prime Minister, and they must be obedient to him in public. Their corruption should not be blatant and should not embarrass the government. Indian politicians have to quickly learn this dharma. Just a month ahead of the 17th Lok Sabha elections, the prediction, even from media houses like the *Organiser*, has been 'hung' parliament and this can only generate greater pressure from regional allies on both the national parties for pre-poll commitments. At the time of writing, indications are, India's next general elections for a new decade can only entrench coalition politics further. The age of coalition is not transitory and will last for long. The writing on the wall is clear: no single party on its own is capable of ruling a diverse country such as India. Hence, this is a phase of politics of *samanvay* (coordination).

Coalitions to date

Constituent Assembly president and President of India, Dr Rajendra Prasad, and the staff of the Constituent Assembly photographed at the Council House on 24 January 1950.

First Congress Ministry and the Nehru Cabinet taken in August 1950. Seated (left to right): Sri Prakasa (Commerce), Hare Krishna Mahatab (Industry & Supply), NV Gadgil (Works, Mines & Power), Rafi Ahmad Kidwai (Communication), Sardar Baldev Singh (Defence), Sardar Vallabhbhai Patel, Deputy Prime Minister (Home & States), Pandit Jawaharlal Nehru, Prime Minister (& External Affaris), C Rajagopalachari, Minister without Portfolio, Jagjivan Ram (Labour), BR Ambedkar (Law), Gopalaswami Ayyangar (Transport & Railways), KM Munshi (Food & Agriculture), CD Deshmukh, (Finance). Standing (left to right): Khurshed Lal, Deputy Minister, Commincations, Satya Narain Sinha, Minister of State for Parliament Affaris, K Santhanam, Minister of State for Railways and Transport, CC Biswas, Minister of State for Minorities, RR Diwakar, Minister of State for Information and Broadcasting, AP Jain, Minister of State for Rehabilitation and BV Keskar, Deputy Minister, Foreign Affairs.

The last meeting of the first Parliament's standing Committee on working of schemes of the Ministry of Production at Parliament House New Delhi, on 27 March 1957. KC Reddy, Minister of Production, (Top left) presided.

President N Sanjiva Reddy administering the oath of the office of Ministers of State to Jagbir Singh, Janeshwar Mishra, Ram Kinkar and Nar Singh at the ceremony held at Rashtrapati Bhavan in New Delhi on 1 January 1979. The photo also shows President Reddy, the Prime Minister, Morarji Desai, Deputy Prime Minister Charan Singh and Deputy Prime Minister Jagjivan Ram.

President N Sanjiva Reddy administering the oath of the office of the Prime Minister to Charan Singh at Rashtrapati Bhavan in New Delhi on 28 July 1979.

President R Venkataraman, Prime Minister VP Singh (from 1989-1990) and others in group photo in Rashtrapati Bhavan.

President R Venkataraman, Prime Minister Chandra Shekhar (from 1990-1991) and others in New Delhi.

President Shankar Dayal Sharma with Prime Minister PV Narasimha Rao and others in New Delhi on 13 September 1995.

President Shankar Dayal Sharma administering the oath of office to Prime Minister HD Deve Gowda (from 1996-1997) at Rashtrapati Bhavan in New Delhi.

President KR Narayanan administering the oath of office of Prime Minister to Atal Behari Vajpayee at a swearing-in-ceremony at the forecourt of Rashtrapati Bhavan in New Delhi on 19 March 1998.

Swearing-in-ceremony of Prime Minister Manmohan Singh (2004). President APJ Abdul Kalam is also seen in the picture.

The newly inducted Cabinet Ministers with President Pratibha Devisingh Patil and Prime Minister Manmohan Singh (19 January 2011).

President Pranab Mukherjee administering the oath of office of the Prime Minister to Narendra Modi, at a swearing-in-ceremony, at Rashtrapati Bhavan on 26 May 2014.

The first NDA coalition led by Atal Behari Vajpayee. (Open source photo in Indian media).

President Johnson with Indira Gandhi, discussing the US food aid to India. The Union government was at that time under intense pressure from the States to get food aid from Russia. (28 March, 1966. White House Photo Office).

Prime Ministers who headed Coalition Governments

Jawaharlal Nehru

Morarji Desai

Charan Singh

VP Singh

Chandra Shekhar

Atal Behari Vajpayee

HD Deve Gowda

IK Gujral

Manmohan Singh

Narendra Modi

Leaders of Political Parties (1940s-1950s)

Subhas Bose

Shyama Prasad Mookherjee

BR Ambedkar

C Rajagopalachari

Leaders who opposed Congress

Liaquat Ali

Pattom Thanu Pillai

JB Kripalani

CN Annadurai

Ram Manohar Lohia

Madhu Limaye

Jayaprakash Narayan

George Fernandes

Leaders who Supported Coalition Politics after Independence

Devi Lal

PV Narasimha Rao

Chandrababu Naidu

M Karunanidhi

Rajiv Gandhi

J Jayalalithaa

Mamata Banerjee

Farooq Abdullah

Bibliography

Regional Political Parties in India

1. Prakash Chander, *Indian Government and Politics*, Cosmos Bookhives Pvt Ltd, New Delhi, 2001-p-29-30.
2. Ram Reddy G and Sharma BAV, *Regionalism in India – A Study of Telangna,* Concept Publishers, New Delhi, 1979, p-87-88.
3. KC Markandan, *Aspects of Indian Polity*, ABS Publication, Amritsar, 1990, p-782.
4. Ibid.
5. Maurice Duverger, *Political Parties: Their Organisation and Activity in the Modern States*, Methuen, London, 1955, p-289.
6. Ibid, p-283.
7. Ibid, p-286.
8. Ibid, p-284.
9. Ibid, p-110.
10. Sita Ramayya P, *The History of Indian National Congress*, 1968, vol-II, p-8.
11. CAD Constituent Assembly Debate, vol-XI, p-993.
12. KC Markandan, *Aspects of Indian Polity*, ABS Publication, Amritsar, 1990, p-785.

13. SK Jain, *Party Politics and Center State Relations in India*, Abhinav Publication, New Delhi, 1994, p-157.
14. Wallace Paul, General Elections 1996 : Regional Parties Dominant in Punjab and Haryana, *Economic and Political Weekly*, Vol XLIII, 15 November, 1997, p-19.
15. Mohapatra Bishnu, Politics in Post-Cyclone Odisha, *Economic and Political Weekly*, Vol XXXIII, No 6, 15 April, 2000, p-1354.
16. Mohapatra Bishnu, Elections and Everyday Politics, *Economic and Political Weekly*, Vol XIX, No 54, 22 Jan, 2000, p-173.
17. Verinder Grover, *Sociological Aspects of Indian Political System*, Deep and Deep Publication, New Delhi, 1990, p-85.
18. Ibid.
19. M Dhruva Kumar, *Community and Purpose in America*, McGram Hill, New York, 1971, p-5.
20. KK Ghai, *Indian Government and Politics*, Kalyani Publishers, Ludhiana, 2002, p-530.
21. Ibid, p-529-30.
22. VB Singh, Support Bases of Political Parties : A Study of Bihar Elections, 1995, Paper presented at a seminar on State Assembly Elections, Indian Council of Social Science Research, New Delhi, 1995 – Unpublished.
23. K Srinivasulu and Prakash Sarangi, Political Realignments in Post-NTR Andhra Pradesh, *Economic and Political Weekly*, vol-XXIX, No 45, 21-28 August, 1999, p-2457.
24. Mayers James, Transformation of Opposition Politics in West Bengal, *Economic and Political Weekly*, vol – LIX, No 11, 15-22 August, 1998, p-2254.
25. Sudha Pai, The Indian Party System Under Transformation : Lok Sabha Elections 1998, *Asian Survey*, vol 44, Nos 5 and 6, Sept 1998, p-845.

26. Gould Harold, *The 12th General Election in Karnataka : The BJP Achieves its Southern Beachhead*, Viking Publishers, New Delhi, 2005, p-183-209.

27. Palishikar Suhas and Nitin Birmal, Fragmented Marathas Retain Formal Power, in Wallace Paul and Ramashray Roy (eds), *Lok Sabha Election : 1999,* forthcoming, Sage Publishers, New Delhi, 2002, p-102-103.

28. KK Ghai, *Indian Government and Politics*, Kalyani Publishers, Ludhiana, 2002, p-529.

* The party tables are from Wikipedia, party websites and the Election Commision of India.

** Contribution of Shodhganga essays on the subject are acknowledged.

Dominance and Decline of Indian National Congress

1. Kandadai Sheshadri, *Studies in Indian Polity*, Uppal Publishing House, New Delhi, 1986, p-1.

2. Mushirul Hasan, *Nationalism and Communal Politics in India 1916-1928*, Manohar Publications, New Delhi, 1979, p-28-29.

3. Hari Hara Dass, *The History of Freedom Movement in India* (1857-1947) National Publishing House, New Delhi, 1998, p-26-39.

4. Ibid, p-86-105.

5. SR Bakshi, *Swaraj Party and the Indian National Congress*, Vikas Publishing House Pvt Ltd, New Delhi, 1985, p-1.

6. Basudev Chatterji (ed), *Towards, Freedom – Documents on the Movement for Independence in India* 1938, Part-I, Oxford University Press, New Delhi, 1999, p-1.

7. Judith M Brown, *Modern India*, Oxford University Press, New Delhi, 1984, p-286-88.

8. Ramashray Roy, *Perspective of Indian Politics*, Discovery Publishing House, Delhi, 1987, p-378-380.
9. Paul Wallace, Introduction: The New National Party System and State Politics, in Paul Wallace and Ramashray Roy (eds), *India's 1999 Elections and 20th Century Politics*, Sage Publication India Pvt Ltd, New Delhi, 2003, p-2-3.
10. Madhu Limaye, *Birth of Non-Congressism*, BB Publishing Corporation, Delhi, 1988, p-251.
11. Ibid, p-251-252.
12. Ibid, p-263-264.
13. Madhu Limaye, *Cabinet Government in India*, Radiant Publishers, New Delhi, 1989, p-118-119.
14. Bidyut Chakrabarty, *Forging Power, Coalition Politics in India*, Oxford University Press, New Delhi, 2006, p-93-94.
15. Granville Austin, *Working a Democratic Constitution: The Indian Experience,* Oxford University Press, New Delhi, 2000, p-309.
16. Paul Wallace, Introduction: The New Party System and State Politics, in Paul Wallace and Ramashray Roy (eds), *India's 1999 Elections and 20th Century Politics*, Sage Publication India Pvt Ltd, New Delhi, p-3-4.
17. Nicholas Nugent, Rajiv Gandhi and the Congress Party: The Road to Defeat) in Subrata Kumar Mitra and James Chiriyankandth (eds), *Electoral Politics in India, A Changing Landscape*, Sigment Books, New Delhi, 1992, p-33.
18. MP Singh and Rekha Saxena, *India at the Polls, Parliamentary Elections in the Federal Phase,* Orient Longman Pvt Ltd, New Delhi, 2003, p-252-53.
19. Francine R Frankel, The Failure to Rebuild Consensus, in Marshall M Bouton (ed), *India Briefing 1987*, Oxford University Press, New Delhi, 1987, p-25.

20. WH Morris Jones, *The Government and Politics of India*, 2nd ed, Hutchinson University Press, London, 1967, p-66.

21. WH Morris Jones, *The Government and Politics of India*, BI Publications, New Delhi, 1971, p-11.

22. Alaxander Chicherov, *Jawaharlal Nehru and the Indian National Congress,* Allied Publishers Pvt Ltd, New Delhi, 1985, p-105.

23. Karli Srinivasulu, Regime change and shifting social bases: The Telugu Desam Party in the 12th General Election, in Ramashray Roy and Paul Wallace (eds), *Indian Politics and the 1998 Election, Regionalism, Hindutva and State Politics*, Sage Publication India Pvt Ltd, New Delhi, 1999, p-212.

24. CP Bhambri, Indian Politics 2001-2004, *Political Process and Change of Government*, Shipra Publication, Delhi, 2005, p-51.

25. Mahesh Rangarajan, Polity in Transition India After the 2004 General Election, *Economic and Political Weekly*, vol. XL, No. 32, August 6, 2005.

26. Amit Prakash, Coalition Politics in Indian Reality, *Mainstream*, Vol XXXIX, No. 19, April 28, 2001, p-29.

27. Lamrence Saez and Rekha Saxena, The 2004 General Election in India, *Mainstream,* Annual December 25, 2004, p-96-97.

28. Vanikant Barooah, Incumbency and Parliamentary Elections in India, An Analysis of the Congress Party's Electoral Performance 1962-1999, *Economic and Political Weekly*, vol XLI, No. 8, February 25, 2006, p-739-40.

* Information available in Open Source platforms, newspapers, Shodhganga and other websites are all acknowledged.

Dawn of the Coalition Era in Indian Politics

1. D Devanathan, Strengthening Coalition Experiment of Centre: A Few Suggestions, *Coalition Government in India: Emerging Trends, Third Concept*, vol. 12, No 143, January 1999, p-26.
2. Shrawan K Singh, *Coalition Government in India, Emerging Trends, Third Concept*, Vol. 20, No. 229, March 2006, p-52.
3. Susheela Kaushik and NS Sankara Raman, Politics in Tamil Nadu: Rise and Fall of the Giant, in SK Chaube and Susheela Kaushik (eds), *Indian Democracy at the turn of the Century*, Kanishka Publishers & Distributors, New Delhi, 1999, p-211.
4. Rekha Saxena, Coalition Experiments: Problems and Prospects, *Mainstream*, vol XXXVI, No. 18, April 25, 1988, p-11-12.
5. Shrawan K Singh, *Coalition Government in India: Emerging Trends, Third Concept,* vol 20, No. 229, March, 2006, p-53.
6. E Sudhakar, *Coalition Era in Indian Democracy, Emerging Trends, Third Concept*, vol-18, No. 212, October 2004, p-11-12.
7. Parvathy AA, *Emergence of Coalition System in India:Problems and Prospects, Emerging Trends, Third Concept*, vol. 19, No. 217, March 2005, p-9.
8. E Sudhakar, *Coalition Era in Indian Democracy, Emerging Trends, Third Concept,* vol 18, No. 212, October 2004, p-12.
9. Kamala Prasad, Political Verdict of the Lok Sabha Poll, *Mainstream*, vol. XXXVI, No. 14, March 28, 1998, p-10.
10. UN Gupta, *Indian Parliamentary Democracy*, vol. I, Atlantic Publishers and Distributors, 2003, p-23-24.
11. Lawrence C Dodd, *Coalitions in Parliamentary Government*, Princeton University Press, UK, 1976, p-127.

12. Sukumar Muralidharan, Back to Polls, *Frontline*, 21 May, 1999, p-4.
13. Rekha Saxena, Coalition Experiment: Problems and Prospects, *Mainstream*, vol. XXXVI, No. 18, April 25, 1998, p-12.
14. Lawerence C Dodd, *Coalition in Parliamentary Government*, Princeton University Press, UK, 1976, p-229.
15. Rekha Saxena, Coalition Experiment: Problems and Prospects, *Mainstream*, vol XXXVI, No. 18, April 25, 1998, p-22.
16. V Krishna Ananth, Brahmanisation of the Dravida Legacy, *Seminar*, No. 480, August 1999, p-42-45.
17. Subrata K Mitra and VB Singh, *Democracy and Social Change in India: A Cross-sectional Analysis of the National Electorate*, Sage Publications India Pvt Ltd, New Delhi, 1999, p-134.
18. Amit Prakash, Coalition Politics in Indian Reality, *Mainstream*, vol-XXXIX, No. 19, April 28, 2001, p-29.
19. Vidya Stokes, Coalition Governments Fault lines in Indian Polity, in Ajay Bhandery (ed), *Sanga Sarkar Visasyank*, Vidhan Sabha Secretariat, January-June 2000, p-10.
20. Akhtar Majeed, *Coalition Politics and Power Sharing*, Manak Publications Pvt Ltd, New Delhi, 2000, p-2.
21. Rekha Saxena, Coalition Experiment: Problems and Prospects, *Mainstream*, vol XXXVI, No. 18, April 25, 1998, p-12.
22. SK Khanna, *Coalition Politics in India*, Commonwealth Publishers, New Delhi, 1999, p-1.
23. E Sudhakar, *Coalition Era in Indian Democracy, Emerging Trends, Third Concept*, vol 18, No. 212, October 2004, p-12.
24. Sandeep Shashtri, Making Coalition Governments More Effective, *Mainstream*, vol XXXV, No. 10, February 15, 1997, p-10.

25. Shivraj Patil, on National Government, *The Statesman*, New Delhi, April 1995, p-1.

* Contribution of Shodhganga essays on the subject are acknowledged.

Prominent Features of Coalition Politics

1. Nikhil Chakarvarty, Future of Coalition Politics, *Mainstream*, vol. XXXV, No. 19, April 19, 1997, p-21.
2. Madhavan Kutty, Where is the Mandate Mr Kesri? *The Indian Express*, April 10, 1997, p-6.
3. Shekhar Gupta, Way Paved for new Government, *The Indian Express*, April 19, 1997, p-1.
4. *The Indian Express*, November 30, 1997.
5. http://www.cnn.com/world/9704/19indianprimeminister.
6. S R Bommai v. Union of India ([1994] 2 SCR 644 : AIR 1994 SC 1918 : (1994)3 SCC1).
7. Sukumar Murlidharan, The Oil Shock, *Frontline*, Vol 17, No. 21, October 27, 2000, p-27.
8. *The Tribune*, October 7, 2000, p-1.
9. Right leaning political parties and ideological groupings have all been clubbed together as the Sangh Parivar under the agies of the RSS. Not all of these groupings and factions contest in electoral politics but in general they occupy similar political positions as the BJP and form vocal support groups.
10. *The Indian Express*, February 7, 2002.
11. Swapan Dasgupta, NDA Under Siege, *India Today*, Vol XXVI, No. 13, March 26, 2001, p-29.
12. *The Tribune*, May 15, 2001.
13. Swapan Dasgupta, NDA Under Seige, *India Today*, Vol

XXVI, No. 13, March 26, 2001, p-26.

14. *The Tribune,* March 21, 2001.

15. http:/www.nerve.in/tags: Telangana+rashtra+samite.

16. *The Tribune*, July 16, 2006.

17. Prakash Karat, Voices, *India Today*, Vol XXX, No. 4, January 24, 2005, p-10.

18. https://www.brookings.edu/on-the-record/the-indo-u-s-nuclear-deal/

    https://www.mea.gov.in/in-focus-topic.htm?24/Civil+Nuclear+Cooperation

    https://en.wikipedia.org/wiki/India%E2%80%93United_States_Civil_Nuclear_Agreement

19. Lakshmi Iyer, Co-ordination Panel: Left in Centre, *India Today*, Vol XXXIX, No. . August 16, 2004, p-18.

20. *The Tribunes* July 7, 2006.

21. Anita Katyal, LS Altercation: Failure of UPA Floor Managers, *The Tribune,* March 2007, p-2.

22. Sitaram Yechury, Left Hand Drive: Careful at the Crossing, *The Hindustan Times,* May 24, 2007, p-10.

Coalition Politics during Pre-NDA Period

1. Bidyut Chakrabarty, *Forging Power: Coalition Politics in India*, Oxford University Press, New Delhi, 2006, p-52.

2. Rajni Kothari, The Congress System in India, *Asian Survey*, Vol. IV, No. 12, Dec. 1964, p-35.

3. SL Mahashwari, Politics of Coalition, *Economic and Political Weekly*, No. VII, 1970, p-118.

4. Rekha Saxena, Party Transition and the Electoral Turning Points in India, Trends in Social Science Research, Delhi, vol. 5, No. 1, p-276.

5. Arshi Khan, Coalition Politics in India Since 1967, in: Akhtar Majeed (ed), *Politics and Power Sharing*, Manak Publication, 2000, p-155.
6. George Fernandes, Rules of Coalition Politics, An Interview with S Berthier, *Asian Affairs*, No. 10—ISSN 1029-1903, Hong Kong, Winter, 1999-2000, p-27.
7. Minoo Masani and Girilal Jain, Is Party System Dying? Sunday Review, *Times of India,* New Delhi, 25 May, 1989.
8. AS Narang, *Indian Government and Politics*, Jawahar Publications, New Delhi, 1997, p-509.
9. Arshi Khan, Coalition Politics in India since 1967, in: Akhtar Majeed (ed), *Politics and Power Sharing*, Manak Publication, New Delhi, 2000, p-158.
10. VP Singh, Interview N Ram and Sukumar Muralidharan in *Frontline,* 13(12) 15-28 June 1996, p-16.
11. Ibid.
12. VP Singh, Interview to Prabhu Chawla in *India Today*, 15 December, 1989, p-30.
13. *India Today*, New Delhi, 31 December, 1989, *The Hindu*, 8 December, 1989.
14. George Fernandes, Rules of Coalition Politics, An Interview with S Berthier, *Asian Affairs*, No. 10-ISSN 1029, Hong Kong, Winter, 1999-2000, p-29.
15. *India Today*, 26 May, 1996.
16. Rajni Kothari, as quoted by Nadia Mustaq Abasi, Indian Elections, Emerging Trends, *Strategic Studies*, vol. XX, No. 2-3, spring summer, Islamabad, 2000, p-30.
17. Sudha Pai, Transformation of Indian Party System: The 1996 Lok Sabha Elections, *Asian Survey*, vol. XXXVI, No. 12, December 1996, p-1174-1180.
18. Arun Kumar, *The Turning Point: 1996 Poll Story*, Konark Publishers, Delhi, 2007, p-27.

19. Sudha Pai, Transformation of Indian Party System: The 1996 Lok Sabha Elections, *Asian Survey*, vol. XXXVI, No. 12, December 1996, p-1182.

Coalition under BJP-led National Democratic Alliance

1. Paul Wallace, Introduction: Indian's 1998 Elections – Hindutva, The Tail Wags the Elephant and Pokhran, in Ramashray Roy and Paul Wallace (eds), *Indian Politics and the 1998 Elections: Regionalism Hindutva and State Politics*, Sage Publications, New Delhi, 1999, p-17.
2. Meenu Roy, *Elections 1998: A Continuity in Coalition*, National Publishing House, Jaipur, 1999, p-69-70.
3. Shaila Seshia, Divide and Rule in Indian Party Politics: The Rise of Bhartiya Janata Party, *Asian Survey*, vol. XXXVIII, No. 11, November 1998, p. 1048.
4. Anthony Heath and Yogendra Yadav, The United Colours of Congress: Social Profile of Congress voters, 1996 and 1998, in Zoya Hasan (ed) *Parties and Party Politics in India*, Oxford University Press, New Delhi, 2008, p-128.
5. Nagindas Sanghavi and Usha Thakkar, Regionalisation of Indian Politics, *Economic and Political Weekly*, vol. 35, No. 7, February 2000, p-516.
6. Eswaran Sridharan, Coalition and Party Strategies in India's Parliamentary Federation, *Publications,* vol 33, No. 4, Autumn 2003, p-141. Publication is an open source journal.
7. Partha S Ghosh, Wither Indian Polity, *Economic and Political Weekly*, vol. 34, No 48, November-December, 1999, p-341.

Constitutional Provisions for Centre-State Relations

1. PB Rathod, *Indian Administration: Dynamics and Dimensions*, Common Wealth Publishers, Delhi, 2005, p-102.

2. Jeevan Nair and UC Jain, *Centre-State Relations*, Pointer Publisher, 2000, p-42.
3. JN Pandey, *The Constitutional Law of India*, Central Law Agency, Allahabad, p-296-297.
4. CAD (Constituent Assembly Debate), Vol VII, No 1, 1948-49, p-353.
5. Ibid, p-353.
6. Constitutional Article 256 and 257.
7. Constitutional Article 249.
8. Ravi P Bhatia, Evolution and Strengthening of Union-State Relations in India, *Vidhan Mala*, Vol. II, No. 1-2, January-December 2004, p-14.
9. Durga Das Basu, *Introduction to the Constitution of India*, Prentice Hall of India, Private Limited, New Delhi, 1998, p-311.
   a. https://www.hindustantimes.com/real-estate/does-rera-have-an-overriding-effect-on-state-laws/story-gflTANpWZd6hpa1cWIQj8K.html
   b. https://www.thehindu.com/opinion/lead/should-water-be-moved-to-concurrent-list/article2113384.ece
   c. https://www.downtoearth.org.in/news/water-may-shift-from-state-to-concurrent-list-33406
10. Hari Har Das and S Mohapatra, *Centre-State Relations in India*, Ashish Publishing House, New Delhi, 1986, p-93.
11. Ibid, p-93-94.
12. BL Fadia, *Indian Government and Politics*, Sahitya Bhavan Publications, Agra, 2005, p-235.
   a. https://www.legalcrystal.com/cases/search/name:constitution-of-india-article-252-power-of-parliament-to-legislate-for-two-or-more-states-by-consent-andadoption-of-such-legislation-by-any-other-state

b. https://www.legalcrystal.com/cases/search/name:constitution-of-india-article-252

13. Babulal Fadia, *State Politics in India*, Radiant Publishers, New Delhi, 1984, p-97.
14. PB Rathod, *Indian Administration: Dynamic and Dimensions*, Common Wealth Publishers, Delhi, 2005, p-108.
15. SS Tiwana, Centre-State Relations in India: A Plea for State Autonomy, *Punjab Journal of Politics*, Vol XXVI, No. 1, 2002, p-2.
16. Sharada Rath, *Federalism Today*, Sterling Publishers Private Limited, New Delhi, 1984, p-38.
17. Hari Har Das and S Mohapatra, *Centre-State Relations in India*, Ashish Publishing House, New Delhi, 1986, p-115.
18. Subh N Singh, *Centre-State Relations in India*, HK Publishers and Distributors, New Delhi, 1990, p-111.
19. Hari Har Das and S Mohapatra, *Centre-State Relations in India*, Ashish Publishing House, New Delhi, 1986, p-116.
20. UN Gupta, *Indian Federalism and Unity of Nation*, Vohra Publications & Distributors, Allahabad, 1998, p-134.
21. DD Basu, *Commentary on the Constitution of India*, Kamal Law House, Calcutta, p-14-15.
22. KM Munshi, The Super Cabinet, *Radical Humanist*, December 6, 1959, p-571.
23. SS Tiwana, Centre-State Relations in India: A Plea for State Autonomy, *Punjab Journal of Politics*, Vol XXVI, No. 1, 2002, p-2.
24. Administrative Reform Commission, Interim Report on the Machinery of Planning, New Delhi, 1967, p-15.
25. Lok Sabha Debates, Third Series, Vol XXIII, No. 18, 11 December, 1963, Column 4208.
26. Sarita, *Federalism in India: A Quest for New Identity*, Regal Publications, New Delhi, 2009 p-81.

27. AT Philip and KH Shivaji, *Indian Government and Politics*, Sterling Publishers, New Delhi, 1981, p-86.
28. Babulal Fadia, *State Politics in India*, Vol (1), Radiant Publishers, New Delhi, 1984, p-104-105.
29. Constituent Assembly Debate (CAD), Vol VII, p-927.
30. Ian Copland and John Rickard, *Federalism, Comparative Perspectives from India and Australia*, Manohar Publishers and Distributors, New Delhi, 1999, p-272.
31. K Santhanam, *Centre-State Relations in India*, Asia Publishing House, New Delhi, 1960, pp-34-35.
32. KR Bombwall, Federalism and National Unity of India, the *Journal of Constitutional and Parliamentary Studies*, Vol 1, No. 1, 1967, p-68.
33. Granville Austin, *Working a Democratic Constitution: The Indian Experience,* Oxford University Press, New Delhi, 1999, p-566.
34. Ibid, p-566.
35. Sampurnanand, *Memoris and Reflection*, Asia Publishing House, Bombay, 1962, p-155.
36. Partha Chatterjee (ed), *State Politics in India*, Oxford University Press, New Delhi, 1999, p-243.
37. Granville Austin, *Working a Democratic Constitution: The Indian Experience,* Oxford University Press, New Delhi, 1999, p-569-570.
38. Lawrence Saez, *Federalism Without Centre: The Impact of Political and Economic Reform on India's Federal System*, Sage Publications, Delhi, 2002, p-37.
39. Prabhat Dutta, *India's Democracy: New Challenges*, Kanishka Publishers, Distributors, New Delhi, 1997, p-86.
40. Lawrence Saez, *Federalism without Centre: The Impact of Political and Economic Reform on India's Federal System*, Sage Publications, Delhi, p-38.

41. Hari Har Das and S Mohapatra, *Centre-State Relations in India*, Ashish Publishing House, New Delhi, 1986, p-189.

42. Ian Copland and John Rickard, *Federalism, Comparative Perspectives from India and Australia*, Manohar Publishers and Distributors, New Delhi, 1999, p-170.

43. RS Sarkaria Commission on Centre-State Relations, Questionnaire, New Delhi, 1983, p-1.

44. Lawrence Saez, *Federalism without Centre: The Impact of Political and Economic Reform on India's Federal System*, Sage Publications, New Delhi, 2002, p-84-85.

45. Ibid.

46. Granville Austin, *Working a Democratic Constitution: The Indian Experience*, Oxford University Press, New Delhi, 1999, p-611-612.

47. Lawrence Seaz, *Federalism without Centre: The impact of Political and Economic Reform on India's Federal System*, Sage Publications, New Delhi, 2002, p-83.

48. Anil Kumar Jana, *Indian Politics at the Crossroads*, Commonwealth Publishers, 1998, p-85.

Growth of Federal Polity in India and Centre-State Relations

1. KR Bombwall, *The Foundation of Indian Federalism*, Asia Publishing House, Bombay, 1967, p-56.

2. Ibid, p-57.

3. Asok Chanda, *Federalism in India*, George Allen Unwin Ltd, London, 1965, p-15.

4. Ibid.

5. AB Keith, Speeches and Documents on Indian Policy, 1750-1921, London 1922, vol. 3, p-133.

6. BG Spare, The Growth of Indian Constitution and Administration, Bombay edition, 1925, p-276.

7. CN Vakil and HM Patel, Finance Under Provincial Autonomy, quoted in KR. Bombwall, *The Foundation of Indian Federalism*, Asia Publishing House, Bombay, 1967.

8. KR Bombwall, *The Foundation of Indian Federalism*, Asia Publishing House, Bombay, 1967, p-211.

9. Report of the Joint Committee on Indian Constitutional Reforms, 1933-35, para-56, p-33.

10. Speeches & Documents on the Indian Constitution, Vol-I London, 1945, p-145.

11. The INC resolution 1934-36, Allahabad, p-77.

12. Jinnah's Speech, Speeches & Documents on the Indian Constitution, vol-I, London, 1945.

13. R Coupland, *India Resettlement*, OUP, London, 1945, No. 5, p-56.

14. KR Bombwall, *The Foundation of Indian Federalism*, Asia Publishing House, Bombay, 1967, p-222.

15. Ram Joshi and RK Hebsur (Ed), Congress and the Federal Balance of Congress in Indian Politics: A Centenary Prospective, Bombay, 1987, p-94.

16. KR Bombwall, *The Foundation of Indian Federalism*, Asia Publishing House, Bombay, 1967, p-242.

17. Constituent Assembly Resolution, para-3, p-59.

18. Constituent Assembly Resolution, p-101.

19. The Second report of the Union Power Committee, 5th July, 1947, p-70-71.

20. LM Singhvi, Cooperative Federalism : A Case for Establishment of an Inter-State Council, in the, *Journal of Constitutional Parliamentary Studies*, New Delhi, Vol. III, No. 4, Oct-Dec 1969, p-211.

21. Morris Jones, Parliament in India, London, 1957, p-81.

22. Morris Jones, From Monopoly to Competition in India's Politics, *Asian Review*, Vol-I, No 1, November 1968, p-5.

23. Austin G, *The Indian Constitution, Corner Stone of a Nation*, Oxford, 1966.

24. Breacher Michael, *Succession in India*, Oxford, London, 1966, p-31.

25. Ibid, p-238.

26. Report of the Study Team on Centre-State Relations ARC, Vol-I, Delhi, 1968, p-1-2.

27. CPI : Six Point Programme, 8th Party Congress, 1968.

28. CPI Election Manifesto, 1971.

29. EMS Namboodripad, *India Under the Congress Rule*, National Book Agency, New Delhi, 1967, p-2004.

30. Policy Statement adopted by the Second National Conference of the Praja Socialist Party, held at Gaya, 26-30 December, 1955.

31. Akali Dal Election Manifesto, 1971.

32. Ibid.

Centre-State Relations Since 1989

1. Commission on Centre-State Relations Report, Vol-I, Evaluation of Centre-State Relations in India, March 2010. http://interstatecouncil.nic.in/volumI.pdf

2. BD Dua, *Indian Federalism in the New Millennium*, Manohar Publishers, New Delhi, 2003, p-147-148.

3. Ashok Mukhopadayhay, India's Federal Polity: Emerging Trends in the Nineties, in Anil Kumar Jana (ed), *Indian Politics at the Crossroads*, Commonwealth Publishers, New Delhi, 1998, p 85-86.

4. CP Bhambhari, Central Government in the Age of Globalisation: New Directions of Indian Federalism, in BD Dua and MP Singh ed, *Indian Federalism in the New Millennium*, Manohar Publishers, New Delhi, 2003, p-391.

5. Ibid, p-392.
6. Ibid, p-325.
7. Ibid, p-152.
8. Ravinder Nath Pal, Constitutional Foundations of Indian Federalism: Theory and Practice, in Rameshwar Roy (ed). *The Federal Experience in India and Russia*, Shipra Publications, New Delhi, 2003, p-55.
9. Manoj Mitta and Smruti Koppikar, Centre-State Relations: Changing Equations, *India Today,* Vol XXI, No. 12, 16th-30th June 1996.
10. Report of Tenth Finance Commission (1995-2000).
11. Balveer Arora, Political Parties and the Party System: The Emergence of New Coalition, in Zoya Hasan (ed), *Parties and Party Politics in India,* Oxford University Press, New Delhi, 2002, p-522.
12. CP Bhambhari, Central Government in the Age of Globalisation: New Directions of Indian Federalism, in BD Dua and MP Singh ed, *Indian Federalism in the New Millennium,* Manohar Publishers, New Delhi, 2003, p-167.
13. Ibid, p-168.
14. Sunder Ram, ed, *Federal System and Coalition Government in India: Conflict and Causes in Centre-State Relations,* Kanishka Publishers and Distributors, New Delhi, 2007, p-113.
15. Subhash C Kashyap, *Union-State Relations in India,* in *Indian Journal of Federal Studies,* Manak Publications Pvt Ltd, Meerut, 2003, p-39.
16. Rajinder Chouhan and Shailja Vasudeva, *Coalition Government in India: Problems and Prospects,* Deep and Deep Publications Pvt Ltd, New Delhi, 2011, p-221.
17. Ibid, p-226-27.

18. D Bandopadhyaya, Guiding Role of Central Finance Commission Regarding States Counterparts, in *Economic and Political Weekly*, Vol XLIII, No. 22, 31st May-6th June, 2008, p-27.

19. RK Kundu and SH Kundu, Centre-State Relations and Local Bodies: Perspective of the Second Commission on Centre-State Relations in India, in *Vidhanmala*, Vol. VI, No. 2, Shimla, Himachal Pradesh Vidhan Sabha Secretariat, 2010.

20. Rajinder Chauhan and Shailja Vasudeva, *Coalition Government in India: Problems and Prospects*, Deep and Deep Publications, 2011, p-96-97.

21. Ibid, p-99.

22. Report of Second Administrative Reforms Commission-2005.

23. R Aggarwal and M Bhan, Disarming violence: Development, Democracy and Security on the Borders of India, in *Journal of Asian Studies*, Vol 68, No. 2, May 2009).

24. Ibid, p 520-527.

25. CP Bhambhri, Central Government in the age of Globalisation: New Directions of Indian Federalism, in BD Dua and MP Singh, (ed), *Indian Federalism in the New Millennum*, Manohar Publisher, New Delhi, 2003, p-320-321.

26. Nirmal Jindal, Economic Liberalisation and Fiscal Distribution in Indian Federation, in *Indian Journal of Federal Studies*, Manak Publications Pvt Ltd, Meerut, 2005, p-123.

27. R Nagraj, Indian Economy Since 1980: Virtuous Growth or Polarisation, in *Economic and Political Weekly*, Vol XXXV, No. 32, August 5-11, 2000.

28. Montek Singh Ahluwalia, Economic Performance of States in Post-Reforms Periods, *in Economic and Political Weekly*, Vol XXXV, No. 90, May 6-12, 2000, p-28-38.

29. NJ Kurian, Widening Regional Disparities in India: Some Indicators, *Economic and Political Weekly*, Vol LLXV, No. 7, February 12-18, 2000, p-539.

30. Ibid, p-548-49.

31. CP Bhambhri, Central Government in the Age of Globalisation: New Directions of Indian Federalism, in BD Dua and MP Singh, (ed), *Indian Federalism in the New Millennium*, Manohar Publisher, New Delhi, 2003, p-331.

32. Chakrabarthy, Bidyut, *Forging Power: Coalition Politics in India*, Oxford University Press, New Delhi, 2006, p-190.

33. Akhtar Majeed, Grey Areas of Indian Federalism, *Indian Journal of Federal Studies,* Manak Publications Pvt Ltd, Meerut, 2005, p-152.

34. MP Singh, India's National Front and United Front Coalition governments: A Phase in Federalised Government, *Asian Survey*, Vol XLI, No. 2, March-April 2001, p-200.

35. All India Report (AIR) Supreme Court 1994, p-212-13.

36. Ibid, p-212.

37. *Tribune,* 4th July, 2011.

Centre-State Relations and National Security

1. Debate in the Constituent Assembly. This part was presented by Pt Nehru, http//parliamentofindia.nic.in/ls/debate/vol5p3.htm

2. Ashutosh Varshney, *How Has Indian Federalism Done*, Sage, New Delhi, 2013, p-59.

3. Editorial, National Investigation Agency, *Sakal Time*, November 2013.

4. National Investigation Agency Act, 2008.

5. NN Vohra, Governor of Jammu and Kashmir, at RN Kao Memorial Lecture on National Security Management – Some Concerns, on January 21, 2018.

6. US National Counter terrorism Center) (http://www.nctc.gov/

7. National Counter Terrorism Centre, Wikipedia, http// en.wikipedia.org/wiki/National-Counterterrorism-Center.

8. A Law Enforcement Perspective to Intelligence Failure in Mass Casualty. Terrorist Attacks by Global Jihadist Movement: A Comparative Study of Terrorist Attacks of September 11, 2001 and November 15-20, 2003, Ozcan, New Jersy 2013.http://dga.rutgers.edu/wp-content/uploads2012/10/A-Law-Enforcement-Perspective-to-Intelligence-Failure-in-Mass-Casualty-Terrorist-Attacks-by-Global-Jihadist-Movement-A-Comparative-Study-of-Terrorist-Attacks. Pdf.

9. Mumbai Attacks: India Calls in Foreign Intelligence to Fight Terrorists, *The Telegraph*, December 6, 2008.

10. National Investigation Agency, at http://www.nia.gov.in/aboutus.aspx

11. Anand Mishra, Indian Counter Terrorism, *Governance Today*, June 3, 2015, http://governancetoday.co.in/indian-counterterrorism-policy/

12. P Chidambram, A New Architecture for India's Security, Intelligence Bureau Endowment Lecture, New Delhi, 23 December, 2009.

13. National Counter Terrorism Centre Organisation, Function, Powers and Duties) order, 2012.

http://www.satp.org/satporgtp/countries/india/document/papers/2012/NCTC_2012.pdf.

14. FAQ: What's NCTC & Why are Centre and States Fighting? 23 February, 2012. http://www.rediff.com/news/slide-show/slide-show-1-faq-whats-nctc-why-centre-and-states-are-fighting/20120223.htm.

15. Lok Sabha Text of Debates (17th Dec, 2008) and Rajya Sabha Text of Debates (18th December, 2008).
16. Bhibhu Prasad Routray, A Countery-Terror Architecture for India, RSIS Monograph, No. 37, 2013.
17. Ibid.
18. NN Vohra, Governor of Jammu and Kashmir, at RN Kao Memorial Lecture on National Security Management—Some Concerns, on January 21, 2018.
19. *The Coalition years: 1996-2012*, by Pranab Mukherjee, former President, Rupa, New Delhi, 2017, Appendix 5, p-255-261.

Conclusion

1. Pranab Mukherjee (former President), *The Coalition Years*: 1996-2012, Rupa, New Delhi, 2017, p-63.